QUALITATIVE RESEARCH:
Analysis Types and Software Tools

QUALITATIVE RESEARCH:
Analysis Types and Software Tools

Renata Tesch

UK   RoutledgeFalmer, 11 New Fetter Lane,
      London EC4P 4EE
USA   RoutledgeFalmer, Taylor & Francis Inc.,
      325 Chestnut Street, 8th Floor,
      Philadelphia, PA 19106

First published 1990

Transferred to Digital Printing 2002

RoutledgeFalmer is an imprint of the Taylor & Francis Group

British Library Cataloguing in Publication Data

Tesch, Renata
  Qualitative research: analysis types and software tools.
  1. Social sciences. Research. Qualitative methods
  I. Title
  300′.723
  ISBN 1-85000-608-3
  ISBN 1-85000-609-1 (pbk.)

Library of Congress Cataloging-in-Publication Data

Tesch, Renata.
  Qualitative research: analysis types and software tools / by Renata Tesch.
  Includes bibliographical references
  ISBN 1-85000-608-3 : ISBN 1-85000-609-1 (pbk.)
  1. Social sciences—Research—Methodology. 2. Social sciences—Research—Data processing. I. Title. II. Title: Qualitative research.
  H62.T37 1990
  300′.28′553—dc20   89-26059
                                                            CIP

Jacket design by Caroline Archer

Printed in Great Britain by LSL Press Ltd, Bedford

Contents

Schematic Table of Contents

Introduction:

What this book is about

How to read this book

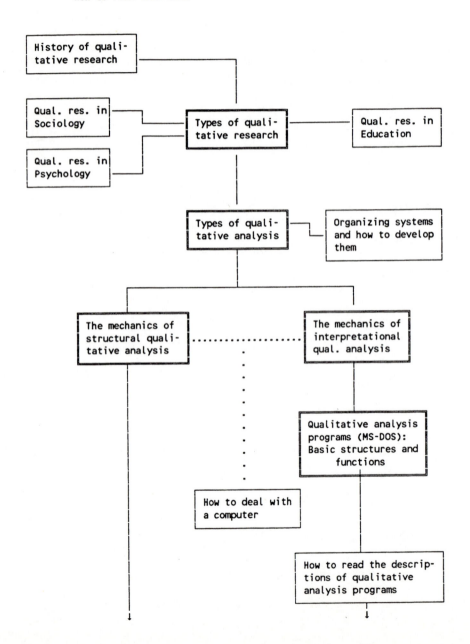

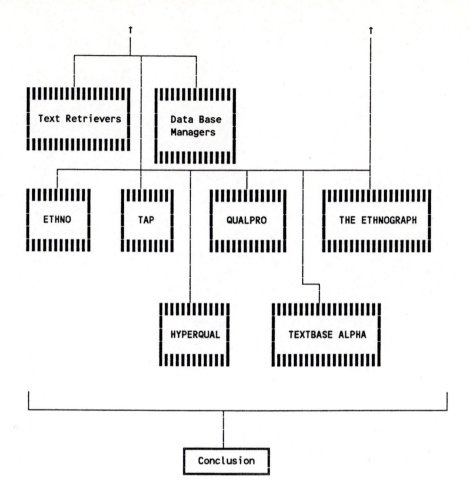

What This Book Is About

Quantitative and Qualitative Research

There was a time when most researchers believed that the only phenomena that counted in the social sciences were those that could be measured. To make that perfectly clear, they called any phenomenon they intended to study a 'variable', indicating that the phenomenon could vary in size, length, amount, or any other quantity. Unfortunately, not many phenomena in the human world come naturally in quantities. How many people tune in to a certain television show, how long they watch it, and what their average age is, for instance, are variables of interest to a person curious about human affairs, but such observable behaviors and statistics merely scratch the surface.

Why did people choose this show? What do they get out of it? What does it make them feel like? Why do people watch television in the first place? To understand more about human phenomena of this kind, two ingenious sleights of mind were needed: first, one had to create concepts or 'psychological constructs' such as 'motivation', 'conformity', etc., and second, one had to invent a way of measuring a concept, i.e., a way of making assertions about its quantity or intensity. Developing measuring 'instruments' and comparing groups of people on how they scored on these instruments (on a self-concept scale, for instance, or an achievement test) consumed a major portion of the social scientist's time. Even things as tenuous as opinions and attitudes were converted into numbers (dislike very much = -3, dislike = -2, dislike a little = -1, no opinion = 0, like a little = 1, like = 2, like very much = 3), which in turn were plugged into statistical formulas that yielded other numbers. Of course, even hard-headed quantitative researchers concede that a person scoring 3 probably does not like the matter in question precisely three times as much as a person scoring 1. Nor would anyone claim that a confidence level of .05 is definitely more acceptable than one of .06 when considering whether the size of differences between score results obtained from comparable groups could have occurred by chance or not. Yet at least the procedure is objective and, besides, it is the only accepted method for testing hypotheses about the way the social world functions that has been invented so far.

Then again, Sigmund Freud discovered plenty about the way human beings function, and so did Jean Piaget. Neither of them tested hypotheses, or used large and representative enough samples of people to satisfy the rules of statistics. Yet they both made important assertions about human beings and created many psychological constructs for use in the description of their theories. Freud employed a perplexingly simple way of finding out why people acted and thought or felt the way they did. He asked them. Sometimes they didn't know. Or they were ashamed to tell, or they were afraid even to acknowledge the matter to themselves. So Freud observed. Both Freud and Piaget were master observers. They tried to make sense of what they saw, or, as you could also say, they tried to find out what it means (Wertz, 1987).

Which of these two ways of doing research is the best, measuring and testing, or observing/listening and interpreting? That depends on what you believe. Obviously, researchers invent a lot of things: concepts, instruments, interpretations, statistical confidence levels, theories, and so forth. They try to convince themselves and others that they have good reasons for concocting these intellectual tools, and the more systematic, truth-loving, and skeptical of their own processes and presuppositions they are, the more they are trustworthy. Ultimately, the process of research is a process of persuasion. You must believe what you find most convincing.

The philosophers among researchers will tell you that it is a ridiculous simplification to boil down research to mere methods, as we have done here. Conducting scientific investigations is not a matter of following recipes. Research does not take place in a neutral environment. It is guided by assumptions about the nature of knowledge, and it has political antecedents and consequences. Is the human/social world, just like the physical nature, governed by natural 'laws'? Or is human behavior something we can't predict, something onto whose inner workings we can only shed more or less light in our effort to understand? Once we believe we can predict, to what extent do we therewith enable people in power positions to take advantage of such knowledge? Do researchers have an ethical obligation to use research for the sake of empowerment of the very people they examine? The debate about these important issues goes on in respectable journals and at mighty conferences. You are left with taking your own stance.

Whatever you decide, a historical fact is that since the 1970's more and more researchers have become interested in a 'new paradigm' that moves us away from numbers and back to asking people questions and to observing. When we ask questions about human affairs, the responses come in sentences, not numbers. We collect as 'data' narratives, or, as I like to call them, stories. Likewise, observations result in notes that take the form of a description of events; again, we deal with stories.

In the wake of the new paradigm, these data have come to be called 'qualitative'. Although technically not incorrect, I don't like the term. It will not let us forget that when we work with these data, we are in opposition to something, namely the quantitative research tradition. Furthermore, the word is stilted. It is not one commonly used by people in the English-speaking world; when they hear it, they assume it must have something to do with 'being excellent', as in 'high quality'. Freud and Piaget would have been mildly surprised to find their work thus labelled, although they probably would not have objected to having their research considered outstanding. It might be more proper to call these data 'textual', and of the type of research that is based on them 'descriptive' or 'interpretive/critical'. However, once a term has caught on in a community, trying to change it is about as fruitful as trying to unteach a parrot.

Qualitative data, for better or worse, now means any data that are not quantitative, i.e., qualitative data are all data that cannot be expressed in numbers.

The Analysis of Qualitative Data

Books that describe ways in which quantitative data can be analyzed are called statistics books. They are remarkable in the sense that they all say pretty much the same thing. The authors of the books mostly differ in the way they introduce and explain the various statistical procedures. (I suspect the reason why so many books on the same subject exist is that statistics are considered difficult to learn, and authors feel challenged to find ways of making the process clearer and easier to understand.) Of course, new statistical methods are invented from time to time, and statisticians may argue about their correctness and appropriateness. They even argue occasionally about the value and applicability of the old ones. By and large, however, the quantitative researcher can pretty confidently plug his or her data into any statistical formula taken from any book, and will not be challenged by anyone about the procedure itself, as long as it suits the type of data and the research question asked.

The situation is very different for the qualitative researcher.

First, 'qualitative research' means different things to different people. Each discipline seems to have its favorite type of qualitative research, and researchers in one are often not even aware of what 'qualitative' means in the others. For an educator, for instance, 'qualitative' may bring to mind 'ethnography' (which actually was imported from anthropology), for a psychologist it may conjure up 'phenomenology', while the sociologist may connect it with 'ethnomethodology'. Technically, the psychologist's early 'case study' and the sociologist's traditional 'participant observation' are also qualitative research. In addition, many other names have been used to describe number-less research, and individual scholars have conducted inventive qualitative studies without labelling their method. Each one made up her/his own way of analyzing data.

When we talk, therefore, about the analysis of qualitative data, we are not dealing with a monolithic concept like 'statistics'. No one has 'codified' the procedures for qualitative analysis, and it is not likely that anyone ever will. Qualitative researchers are quite adamant in their rejection of standardization. Whenever they describe their methods, they are usually eager to point out that this is just one way of doing it, which others should feel free to adopt as much as they see fit, and modify and embellish it according to their own needs and ideas. Thus, the notion of qualitative analysis is fluid and defies definition. It is applied to a wide variety of principles and procedures. The only agreement we would find among qualitative researchers is that analysis is the process of making sense of narrative data.

If we cannot even give a useful answer to what qualitative analysis is and how it works, then it seems rather incongruent to try and involve a computer, the very essence of precision and orderliness. Isn't qualitative analysis a much too individualistic and flexible an activity to be supported by a computer? Won't a computer do exactly what qualitative researchers want to avoid, namely standardize the process? Won't it mechanize and rigidify qualitative analysis? The answer to these questions is NO, and this book explains why.

Since it won't do you much good merely to become convinced of the usefulness of the computer in qualitative analysis, the book then goes on to describe what, exactly, the computer can do. You need not worry; this is not another 'hit the Enter-key' type of manual, in disguise. It will help you understand individual programs for the personal computer so you can use those you choose with the confidence of the initiated. Mostly, however, the book acquaints you with the rationales behind the programs, or, to become a tad more technical, the main functions they are designed to perform.

In the course of the explanations and descriptions in this book you can explore matters that are related to the primary content of the book, but that are not a prerequisite for understanding the main train of explication. In fact, you can jump around in this book quite a bit without harm; how to make that work is explained in the next section.

References

WERTZ, FREDERICK J. (1987, Winter) 'Meaning and research methodology: Psychoanalysis as a human science', *Methods*, 1, 2, pp. 91-135.

How to Read This Book

This book is both a narrative and an information base. The narrative guides you through basic reflections about the nature and the processes of qualitative analysis, and about the nature and the functions of electronic software that facilitate the mechanical tasks in the analysis process. The book begins with chapters that tell you about the principles involved and familiarizes you with the fundamentals. The information base consists mainly of the later chapters in the book that describe types of software or individual software packages. While the narrative should be read in sequence, the information base can be accessed in any order. There are also sections that you can disregard if they don't interest you, without disadvantage (such as the chapters on qualitative research in the various disciplines). On the other hand, it is recommended that you peruse the chapter on the basic structure and functions of analysis programs before you read the descriptions of individual programs.

In general, the book is arranged so that concepts or practices referred to in later chapters are explained in earlier ones. However, that should not keep you from beginning anywhere you want. If you encounter something that is unfamiliar to you, you can always skip back again to an earlier chapter. Often, the symbols < > lead you to the appropriate chapter. If you read, for instance, in the chapter on qualitative research approaches about a certain type of research, and its name is followed by <Sociology>, you could interrupt your reading if you are wondering what the name means, and go to the section on qualitative research approaches in sociology. Then, when you have satisfied yourself that you have learned what you wanted to learn, return to the place in the chapter where you left off. Likewise, if you read about the various search procedures analysis programs use, and you are curious how The Ethnograph, for instance, implements these procedures, you could go to the section on The Ethnograph and look it up.

If your habit is to read a book thoroughly page by page, you can still do so with this book. But I invite you to let yourself explore. You won't be wasting time. The method takes into account two phenomena of our modern world. First, there is the information explosion. Even if you didn't do much of anything else, you can't possibly read all you'd like to know or are interested in within your lifetime. We have to learn to be selective. There might be a lot in this book that won't do you any good. If you don't own a Macintosh computer, don't read the section on the Macintosh program. You would be deplenishing a non-renewable resource: your time. No matter how much of a perfectionist you are, this doesn't make sense. There is no logical reason to read an informational book from cover to cover. It's just a habit. So don't feel compelled.

The other phenomenon is the 'everything-is-linked-to-everything' discovery. (I think everything always was, but we were so pleased with our modern efficient compartmentalizing of the intellectual world - the academic disciplines, for instance - that we did not discover this fact until recently.) Writing and reading about things in a one-dimensional sequential order is a miserable method of dealing with the world of ideas and thought. Anyone who has ever struggled with putting thoughts on paper for others to read and understand has realized that the mind can juggle many notions at once, and that 'everything is deeply intertwingled', as the delightfully brilliant Theodor Nelson proclaims (Nelson, 1974). The real world of ideas is to the artificial world of pen and paper as the three-dimensional, colorful world of nature is to a black and white photograph. In the rare case of the gifted artist the photograph might be even more impressive, but for most of us ordinary beings most of the time something gets lost in the process of capture. Nelson is far from having invented the color motion picture, but he did coin the term hypertext. Hypertext is the first step toward multi-dimensionality. It's non-sequential writing - writing that goes beyond and above the constructing of what we ordinarily consider plain text. The idea may seem more familiar if you simply call it 'branching'; but you'll have to think of a tree that grows in all directions, including down and back toward itself. From any given point, there are several ways in which to continue, - or you can go back and select a different path from the previous point. The branches represent links among related concepts or among pieces of information. If such a text existed, you could decide at every point which one you want to read about next.

We are so used to reading sequentially that a notion like hypertext seems not only far-fetched, but confusing. How would we know, for instance, when we have finished the book? Perhaps the answer is: finishing doesn't matter. Browsing might be all we want to do. At any rate, the 'book' is not meant to be a book with pages and two covers. Hypertext is meant to be electronic. The concept can only be implemented in a computer. In the meantime, however, the idea can begin to liberate our reading, even in a traditional book. Branching is done, to a very moderate degree, when we attach a footnote to a text. We want the information to be available for the reader who is interested in it, but it should not distract the reader who is not. This book takes branching a little farther (see the schematic Table of Contents), without losing the familiar structure of following a train of thought from A to Z.

You can get better acquainted with the idea by taking another look at the Table of Contents chart. How about taking a plunge and starting this book not with the chapter that immediately follows this introduction, but with any of the side branches? If you are an educator, for instance, you might be interested in the types of qualitative research that have been employed by educators. Then come back and begin reading the main strand. Check off on the schematic Table of Contents what you have already read. It would be rather irritating to discover that you have read the same section twice, wouldn't it? At any rate, here is your chance to break out of the familiar mold.

References

NELSON, THEODOR H. (1974) *Dream Machines (The Flip Side of Computer Lib)*, South Bend, Indiana, Theodor Nelson.

History of Qualitative Research

Qualitative research is as old as social science itself: well over a hundred years. 1842 is regarded as the birth year of sociology by those who consider Auguste Comte its founder; in 1871 anthropology matured into a discipline with Edward Tylor's work *Primitive Culture* (Encyclopedia Britannica, 1974, vol. 16, p. 985), and in 1878 William James established the first course in psychology (Encyclopedia Britannica, 1974, vol. 6, p. 372). Education as a discipline did not surface until the twentieth century. From the beginning tension arose between those scholars within each field who were believers in the admirably 'objective' results achieved in the much older natural sciences, and those who felt that the 'human' sciences needed a different approach because of their complexity and the existence of a phenomenon unknown in the mechanical world: consciousness. Except in anthropology, there were always social scientists who aspired to the clean and clear rules that physics and chemistry could produce, and others who argued that human beings were not things and did not function according to such simple causal laws. (Amedeo Giorgi describes the history of this tension very vividly in his 'Status of qualitative research in the human sciences', 1986.) The debate is still with us.

Those social scientists who wished to adopt the methods of the natural sciences had an undeniable advantage. They could imitate. Furthermore, their philosophical stance is the respectable and hopeful sounding 'positivism' (a term made popular by Saint-Simon of the French enlightenment movement), which refers to the 'positive' data of experience as the basis of all science (Encyclopedia Britannica, 1974, vol. 14, p. 877). In contrast, those scholars who were soon known as anti-positivists were inspired by the German romantic movement, which 'recognized the life experience of humans, the emotional and vital feeling of life, and the engagement that humans have with others and with the world' (Polkinghorne, 1983, p. 21). This sounded rather fragile in comparison with the robustness of positivism. Not surprisingly, these early promoters of a humanistic social science were unable to produce a method of investigation that could rival the coherent and standardized natural science procedures of measurement and experimentation. Except in sociology, where some scholars combined statistical and 'journalistic' methods, non-positivistic researchers soon found themselves in a pitiful minority.

The 1927 publication of Edward Lee Thorndike's *The Measurement of Intelligence* opened the door for the notion that practically anything psychological could be measured, which in turn encouraged mathematicians to invent ways in which these measures could be compared, building on the theory of probability. With the help of the resulting 'statistical' formulas the relationships between the measured entities could be established. If the relationships were valid now, they would be so in the future, and therefore, one had discovered rules that permitted one to predict - just like the natural sciences did.

After Lee Cronbach published in 1949 the *Essentials of Psychological Testing*, and Robert L. Thorndike in 1951 his *Educational Measurement*, scores of statistics books appeared, and acknowledging positivism as the only legitimate form of inquiry in the social sciences became inevitable. 'The function of science', so lectured Braithwaite in 1953, 'is to establish general laws governing the behaviors of the empirical events or objects with which the science in question is concerned, and thereby enable us to connect together our knowledge of the separately known events, and to make reliable predictions of events as yet unknown' (1953, p. 11). In 1964 Fred Kerlinger, in his classic tome on the methodology for the social sciences, accepted this position and postulated the construction and testing of hypotheses as the only avenue for arriving at such general laws or explanations (Kerlinger, 1964, p. 16 ff.). As far as most social scientists were concerned, the case was settled.

Yet something remained irksome about this state of affairs. 'Scientists are not and cannot be concerned with the individual case' pondered Kerlinger fifteen years later (1979, p. 270). 'The unit of speech in science is always the set, the group. But behavioral scientists, and particularly psychologists, often talk as if the unit of speech were the individual. Psychological theories, for example, are sometimes enunciated as though they were explanations of what goes on inside a single individual' (*ibid.*, p. 275). This is dangerously unscientific, since 'the existential individual, the core of individuality, forever escapes the scientist. He is chained to group data, statistical prediction, and probabilistic estimates' (*ibid.*, p. 272). Science, therefore, was for scholars, not for 'clinicians, teachers, and other people whose . . . main interest in science is how it can help them cure or teach individuals' (*ibid.*, p. 270). It's a troublesome paradox, Kerlinger concluded, and he left it at that (*ibid.*, p. 275).

Worse, some scientists simply did not adhere to the principles described in Kerlinger's work, and produced undeniably convincing results nevertheless. Take, for instance, B.F. Skinner. He worked with individuals. He never compared groups. He did not ever properly formulate and test hypotheses. So that we wouldn't feel too safe about the remarkable insights Skinner had achieved about certain types of learning, Kerlinger sternly warned us: '. . .one has to have severe reservation about conclusions reached from one individual' (*ibid.*, p. 277).

Disturbingly, there were still other types of investigations that remained outside Kerlinger's canon of methods while yielding impressive enough results to be acknowledged by him: case studies and content analysis. He concluded that there could be only one explanation: They were not science (*ibid.*, p. 276/77).

Despite the dominance of positivistic methods, researchers in small niches of all social sciences had quietly continued to conduct non-positivistic studies. They did not construct concepts and measured variables. They observed, described, asked, listened, analyzed, and interpreted, and some even published accounts of their methods (Webb and Webb, 1932). Most had a harder time publishing their work, however, than authors whose results ended up being statistically insignificant. Sometimes they were compelled to include some numbers in their studies to be judged even marginally legitimate. (A famous example is the study of 'the experience of really feeling understood' by the phenomenologist Adrian van Kaam in 1959.) And then the course of scientific events took a new turn. While Kerlinger, a superb teacher whose contribution to research methodology is enormous, was struggling to defend his dangerously anorexic definition of science (the entire discipline of history was, according to him, not a science at all, *ibid.*, p. 269), reform movements swept through the fields of education and psychology. They first focussed on the practical realm and then reached the scholarly level as well. During that same period, new developments cropped up in theoretical sociology that soon influenced the way large groups of sociologists began to conduct their research.

In psychology, Abraham Maslow is probably the best known figure among the founders of 'humanistic' psychology. The slim volume that contains his thoughts on the conduct of inquiry, however, seems to have taken a back seat to his purely psychological writings. Published in 1966, *The Psychology of Science* distinguished between a mechanistic science (of the Kerlinger variety) and a humanistic science (of the Maslow variety). Mechanistic science, in Maslow's opinion, was 'not incorrect, but rather too narrow and limited' (Maslow, 1966 p. 5). 'A more inclusive conception of science' would be one that 'includes the idiographic, the experiential, the Taoistic, the comprehensive, the holistic, the personal, the transcendent, the final, etc. (*ibid.*, p. 63). In short, 'if there is any primary rule of science, it is . . . acceptance of the obligation to acknowledge and describe all of reality, all that exists, everything that is the case' (*ibid.*, p. 12). He could hardly have been more encompassing.

But how is this to be done? Maslow concedes that we don't know yet. For starters, if we wanted to know about people, we could ask them. 'By far the best way to learn what people are like is to get them, one way or another, to tell us, whether directly by question and answer . . . to which we simply listen, or indirectly by covert communications, paintings, dreams, stories, gestures, etc. which we can interpret' (*ibid.*, p. 12). Maslow's main point, however, was that science must not be method-centered, i.e., it must not confine itself to those problems for whose study legitimate methods existed. Quite to the contrary, science must be problem-centered and *invent* appropriate methods for investigating the problems of concern and puzzle. 'The first effort to research a new problem is most likely to be inelegant, imprecise and crude' (*ibid.*, p. 14). But there is no other way to conquer new frontiers. 'The assault troops of science are certainly more necessary to science than its military policemen. This is so even though they are apt to get much dirtier and to suffer higher casualties' (*ibid.*, p. 14). Therefore Maslow's message to social scientists was to supplement 'the caution, patience, and conservatism which are sine qua non for the scientist . . . by boldness and daring' (*ibid.*, p. 31).

Bold, daring, and dirty some became, even without Maslow's encouragement. Maslow had not been alone in his doubts about the entrenched definition of science. Inspired by Thomas Kuhn's (1962) startlingly persuasive thesis that certain views of knowledge production or 'paradigms' dominate the entire world of science at any given time until a crisis ushers in a new one, a crisis was declared by some impetuous scholars, and a 'new paradigm' proclaimed. While Paul Feyerabend shocked respectable people with his openly dirty treatise *Against Method: Outline of an Anarchistic Theory of Knowledge* (1975), the milder revolutionaries still went far enough to renounce Maslow's benevolent tolerance of mechanistic science as merely too narrow. The old and the new paradigms are contradictory, not complementary, they alleged, because positivism is 'based on an independent existing social reality that could be described as it really is' (Smith and Heshusius, 1986, p. 5). Such reality *does not exist*, and therefore certainty about it could never be achieved even if our methods were perfect. Instead, 'social reality is mind-dependent in the sense of mind-constructed. Truth is ultimately a matter of socially and historically conditioned agreement' (*ibid.*, p. 5). This means what we consider a fact depends on the way we have been socialized to see the world, i.e., it depends on our mental frame of reference. We could, for instance, assume that intelligence is a singular faculty that human beings possess, and that this faculty comes in degrees. Some people are known to have more of it than others. We could also become convinced (by Howard Gardner), however, that there exist several human mental competencies all of which could be labelled 'intelligence', such as logical-mathematical, linguistic, spatial, musical, intelligence, etc., and that 'they can be fashioned and combined in a multiplicity of adaptive ways by individuals and cultures' (Gardner, 1983, p. 9). We could hold that new paradigms in the scientific world follow each other as the results of scientific revolutions, or that scientists are progressing slowly and with some round-abouts toward the perfect method of knowledge production. The point is, in all cases both versions are *beliefs*, not certainty. That is what the scholars who came to be known as post-positivists, or human scientists, wanted to get across.

This last paragraph oversimplifies the matter vastly. Learned books could be written about the philosophical antecedents and implications of the two paradigms, and a number of authors have done just that. For the purposes of this overview, however, let us concentrate on the observation that the advantages of the natural-science imitators, although long-lasting, seem to have been temporary nevertheless. Some of the assault troops even turned the entire affair around, and instead of being content with defending their new position against the accusation of being less than science, used the heavy weapon of ideology to launch a surprise attack on positivistic thinking. This was accomplished by declaring positivistic science an outgrowth of capitalist technocracy. As such, its core was the 'mechanistic imperative' that reduced the human being to an object, took the social order as a given, and aimed at 'modifying and controlling undesirable behavior in the services of the social system' (Suransky, 1980, p. 167). A non-positivistic research stance, such as phenomenology, therefore, was not only proper scholarship, but necessarily turned into 'a weapon of social change' (*ibid.*, p. 177).

Be that as it may, not too many people became aware of this belligerent streak in the history of research in the social sciences. For most, the change became apparent gradually and peacefully as the emergence of alternatives in methodology.

Psychologists were lucky to find in Amedeo Giorgi a scientist dedicated to systematic and rigorous procedures who became committed to phenomenology, the branch of European philosophy that had been created as a reaction to the objectification efforts in the social sciences during their early years. Giorgi, who has done more than probably any other psychologist to illuminate the rather inaccessible tenets of phenomenology, did not stop with explaining principles. He described the method he used in his own studies in detail, and encouraged other phenomenological researchers to publish their accounts as well. His series of publications is called *Duquesne Studies in Phenomenological Psychology*, and began appearing in 1971. Later Giorgi became one of the initiators of the Human Science Research conference that has taken place every year since 1983 and provides an international forum for methodological discussion and innovation. Human science research, just as humanistic psychology, has remained, however, a side strand to the mainstream of American psychology. For the largest gathering of psychologists in the world, the annual meeting of the American Psychological Association, the existence of any type of qualitative research has not even been acknowledged yet in the subject index of the conference program (1988) <Psychology>.

Carl Rogers bridged the disciplines of psychology and education. His strong influence on teachers during the 1960's reform movement prepared the climate for the acceptance of non-positivistic research in education, although he himself did not propagate any particular method. Interestingly, education had had a short and ill-fated bout with an innovative research approach in the 1950's. Disappointed practitioners had begun to regard educational research with some contempt, since it failed to provide guidelines for the betterment of schools. When Stephen Corey in 1953 suggested in a book called *Action Research to Improve School Practices* that teachers themselves take up the business of research, many responded with enthusiasm. They had felt shoved aside. Now they were asked to state the goals of the research projects conducted in their classrooms themselves, rather than have them formulated by ivory-tower academicians. They were even invited to gather data and help interpret them. The teachers were to work in groups, advised and supervised by a university research expert.

Action research in education enjoyed a brief boom in the late 1950's and early 1960's, and then succumbed to the concerted onslaught of criticism from the *real* scientist who found the idea of lay research detestable and the practices sloppy. Only recently has action research begun to resurface, although not in the USA. The British educators Wilfred Carr and Stephen Kemmis regard it as the practical application of the idea of a 'critical social science' as demanded by Martin Heidegger, since it empowers those who are the research targets.

Phenomenological research in education entered the USA via the Netherlands, and soon connected with Giorgi's school of phenomenological psychology. It has remained as marginal in education as in psychology, although the interest in it is currently on the rise (Tesch, 1988).

The average educator, however, is much better acquainted with qualitative research than the average psychologist. Anthropologists had long been interested in education as the major vehicle for the transmission of culture, and the two disciplines had begun to produce joint research by the 1950's. George Spindler edited a volume in 1955 that assembled studies of school life from an anthropological perspective (Spindler, 1955). He continued to conduct ethnographic investigations in education (ethnography being the basic descriptive method of anthropology; the term was first used by Bronislaw Malinowski in 1922). Soon he was joined by Theodore Brameld (Brameld, 1957), who published the first anthropological article in a journal of the American Educational Research Association, *Review of Educational Research* (Brameld and Sullivan, 1961). Another influential advocate and practitioner of ethnographic methods is Ray Rist, who had received his anthropological training from the anthropologist Eleanor Leacock in the 1960's.

While this development did not come as a surprise, qualitative research had also slipped into education from an unexpected direction: educational evaluation. Egon Guba cautiously tested the water with 'The expanding concept of research' in 1967, just a year after Maslow's book had appeared. Guba was drawing on phenomenological thought, as well as on ethnography. When Denzin coined the phrase 'naturalistic inquiry' in 1971, Guba built on it and published in 1978 the slim but potent volume *Toward a Methodology of Naturalistic Inquiry in Educational Evaluation.* The term was here to stay. 'Naturalistic inquiry' entered the subject index of the convention program of the gigantic American Educational Research Association the same year and has remained there steadfastly ever since.

The early and mid 1970's saw a rapid succession of important qualitative publications in education. Frederick Erickson (1973), Louis Smith (1974), Harry Wolcott (1975), Ray Rist (1975), and Michael Q. Patton (1975), all began their qualitative/ethnographic writings around the same time (and so did I: Tesch, 1976). By 1977 it was time for Stephen Wilson to provide an overview of 'the use of ethnographic techniques in educational research'. The 'movement' caught on so rapidly that Ray Rist felt compelled, in his famous article 'Blitzkrieg ethnography' (1980), to caution educators not to hop on the bandwagon too eagerly, less the method be robbed of its sophistication by hasty enthusiasts with superficial training. Several thorough books on qualitative methods have appeared since (Patton, 1980; Dobbert, 1982; Bogdan and Biklen, 1982, Lincoln and Guba,1983; Goetz and LeCompte, 1984; Miles and Huberman, 1984), and a plethora of articles. In 1986 a Special Interest Group for qualitative researchers formed at the AERA convention, immediately counting about 100 members. The convention schedule now features large numbers of qualitative research sessions, including training workshops. In 1988 the first educational journal exclusively for qualitative research was launched: *The International Journal for Qualitative Studies in Education* <Education>.

By now it will come as no surprise that the gestation years for new methodologies in sociology were the second part of the 1960's, with 1967 turning out to become the birth year of fraternal twins. Glaser and Strauss published their *Grounded Theory: Strategies for Qualitative Research,* and Harold Garfinkel his *Studies in Ethnomethodology.* Herbert Blumer followed in 1969 with *Symbolic Interactionism* (having published an earlier article on the topic in 1967 as well). Unlike psychology and education, sociology had never been exclusively devoted to the worship of the natural sciences, due to the influence of the so-called Chicago School. The sociologists of this school were interested more in describing the patterns of life in different parts of society than in establishing social 'laws'. They called their preferred investigative method 'participant observation', which they conducted in 'the field'. Out of this school came some of the most powerful sociological works, all of them systematic descriptions of groups or types of people and their social interactions. Severyn Bruyn (1966) had just called attention to the *Human Perspective in Sociology*, which, as he saw it, was at the heart of participant observation, when Glaser and Strauss and Garfinkel added their new dimensions to the methodological debate. Webb *et al.,* had provided a systematic description of non-obtrusive methods of data collection in the same year, 1966. Thus, the 1967 works were not quite as significant a milestone in sociology as the appearance of qualitative writings was in psychology and education.

Sociologists who wished to learn about qualitative methods found a substantial number of resources already among the pre-1960 publications. The volume of methodological writings increased quite noticeably in the 1970's and 1980's, however. Among the most widely known books are Filstead's *Qualitative Methodology*(1970), Lofland's *Analyzing Social Settings* (1971), Schatzman and Strauss's *Field Research* (1973), Bogdan and Taylor's *Introduction to Qualitative Research Methods* (1975), Spradley's *The Ethnographic Interview* (1979) and *Participant Observation* (1980), and Hammersley and Atkinson's *Ethnography* (1983). A journal, *Qualitative Sociology*, has been published since 1978. Sessions involving qualitative methods are sprinkled liberally throughout the American Sociological Association's conference schedule as a matter of course. Thus qualitative methods in sociology have had both a less controversial history than in psychology and a less stormy one than in education <Sociology>.

Anthropology has been a descriptive science ever since its inception, and therefore largely escaped the qualitative-quantitative controversy. As new fields entered the academic arena, some of their researchers became attracted to qualitative methods as well. Most noticeable among them are nursing research and organizational research. Researchers in these social sciences did not invent new qualitative methods of their own, since they were aware of those developed in the older disciplines. They drew on what was already available and adapted the methods to their purposes. In 1985 Madeline Leininger provided directions for scholars in the nursing field with the volume *Qualitative Research Methods in Nursing* (Leininger, 1985), while Gareth Morgan's (1983) and John van Maanen's (1979) useful collections of methodological examples stimulated qualitative studies in organizations. In their own contributions to the volumes these authors also added significantly to the existing edifice of thought on qualitative methods and the world view behind them.

References

BLUMER, HERBERT (1967) 'Society as symbolic interaction', in MANIS, J. and MELTZER, B. (Eds.) *Symbolic Interaction*, Boston, Allyn and Bacon.

BLUMER, HERBERT (1969) *Symbolic interactionism,* Englewood Cliffs, NJ, Prentice Hall.

BOGDAN, ROBERT C. and TAYLOR, STEVEN J. (1975) *Introduction to Qualitative Research Methods: A Phenomenological Approach to the Social Sciences,* New York, John Wiley and Sons.

BOGDAN, ROBERT C. and BIKLEN, SARI K. (1982) *Qualitative Research for Education: An Introduction to Theory and Methods,* Boston, Allyn and Bacon, Inc.

BRAITHWAITE, R. B. (1953) *Scientific Explanation,* Cambridge, MA, Cambridge University Press.

BRAMELD, THEODORE (1957) *Cultural Foundations of Education,* New York, Harper and Row.

BRAMELD, THEODORE and SULLIVAN, EDWARD B. (1961) 'Anthropology and education', *Review of Educational Research,* 31, pp. 70-79.

BRUYN, SEVERYN T. (1966) *The Human Perspective in Sociology: The Methodology of Participant Observation,* Englewood Cliffs, NJ, Prentice Hall, Inc.

CARR, WILFRED and KEMMIS, STEPHEN (1986) *Becoming Critical: Education, Knowledge and Action Research,* Lewes, The Falmer Press.

COREY, STEPHEN M. (1953) *Action Research to Improve School Practices,* New York, Columbia University Press.

CRONBACH, LEE J. (1949) *Essentials of Psychological Testing,* New York, Harper and Row Publishers.

DENZIN, NORMAN K. (1971) 'The logic of naturalistic inquiry', *Social Forces,* 50, pp. 166-82.

DOBBERT, MARION L. (1982) *Ethnographic research,* New York, Praeger Publications.

ERICKSON, FREDERICK (1973) 'What makes school ethnography "ethnographic"?' *Anthropology and Education Quarterly,* 4, 2, pp. 10-19.

FEYERABEND, PAUL K. (1975) *Against Method: Outline of an Anarchistic Theory of Knowledge,* Atlantic Highlands, NJ, Humanities Press.

FILSTEAD, W. J. (Ed.) (1970) *Qualitative Methodology: Firsthand Involvement with the Social World,* Chicago, Rand McNally.

GARDNER, HOWARD (1983) *Frames of Mind: The Theory of Multiple Intelligences,* New York: Basic Books, Inc.

GARFINKEL, HAROLD (1967) *Studies in Ethnomethodology,* Englewood Cliffs, NJ, Prentice-Hall.

GIORGI, AMEDEO; FISCHER, WILLIAM, F. and VON ECKARTSBERG, ROLF (Eds.) (1971-83) *Duquesne Studies in Phenomenological Psychology,* Vols. 1-4, Pittsburgh, PA, Duquesne University Press.

GIORGI, AMEDEO (1986, Spring) 'Status of qualitative research in the human sciences: A limited interdisciplinary and international perspective', *Methods,* 1, 1, pp. 29-62.

17

GLASER, BARNEY G. and STRAUSS, ANSELM L. (1967) *The Discovery of Grounded Theory: Strategies for Qualitative Research*, Chicago, Aldine Publishing Company.

GOETZ, JUDITH P. and LeCOMPTE, MARGARET D. (1984) *Ethnography and Qualitative Design in Educational Research*, Orlando, FL, Academic Press.

GUBA, EGON (1967, April) 'The expanding concept of research', *Theory into Practice*, 6, pp. 57-65.

GUBA, EGON (1978) *Toward a Methodology of Naturalistic Inquiry in Educational Evaluation*, Los Angeles, CA, Center for the Study of Evaluation.

HAMMERSLEY, MARTYN and ATKINSON, PAUL (1983) *Ethnography: Principles in Practice*, New York, Tavistock Publications.

KERLINGER, FRED N. (1964) *Foundations of Behavioral Research*, New York, Holt, Rinehart and Winston.

KERLINGER, FRED N. (1979) *Behavioral Research*, New York, Holt, Rinehart and Winston.

KUHN, THOMAS S. (1962) *The Structure of Scientific Revolutions*, Chicago, University of Chicago Press.

LEININGER, MADELINE M. (1985) *Qualitative Research Methods in Nursing*, Orlando, FL, Grane and Stratton.

LINCOLN, YVONNA and GUBA, EGON (1983) *Naturalistic Inquiry*, Beverly Hills, CA, Sage Publications.

LOFLAND, JOHN (1971) *Analyzing Social Settings*, Belmont, CA, Wadsworth Publishing Company.

MALINOWSKI, BRONISLAW (1922) *The Argonauts of the Western Pacific*, London, Routledge and Kegan Paul.

MASLOW, ABRAHAM (1966) *The Psychology of Science*, New York, Harper and Row.

MILES, MATTHEW B. and HUBERMAN, A. MICHAEL (1984) *Qualitative Data Analysis: A Sourcebook of New Methods*, Beverly Hills, CA, Sage Publications.

MORGAN, GARETH (Ed.) (1983) *Beyond Method: Strategies for Social Research*, Beverly Hills, CA, Sage Publications.

PATTON, MICHAEL Q. (1975) *Alternative Evaluation Research Paradigm*, Grand Forks, ND, Study Group on Evaluation, University of North Dakota.

PATTON, MICHAEL Q. (1980) *Qualitative Evaluation Methods*, Beverly Hills, CA, Sage Publications.

POLKINGHORNE, DONALD (1983) *Methodology for the Human Sciences*, Albany: State University of New York Press.

Qualitative Sociology (1978 ff.) Editors: CONRAD, PETER and REINHARZ, SHULAMIT, New York, Human Science Press.

RIST, RAY C. (1975) 'Ethnographic techniques and the study of an urban school', *Urban Education*, 10, pp. 86-108.

RIST, RAY C. (1980) 'Blitzkrieg ethnography: On the transformation of a method into a movement', *Educational Researcher*, 9, 2, pp. 8-10.

SCHATZMAN, LEONARD and STRAUSS, ANSELM L. (1973) *Field Research*, Englewood Cliffs, NJ, Prentice Hall.

SMITH, JOHN K. and HESHUSIUS, LOUS (1986, January) 'Closing down the conversation: The end of the qualitative-quantitative debate among educational inquirers', *Educational Researcher*, 15, pp. 4-12.

SMITH, LOUIS (Ed.) (1974) 'Anthropological perspectives on evaluation', *AERA Monograph Series in Evaluation*, Chicago, Rand McNally.

SPINDLER, GEORGE (Ed.) (1955) *Education and Anthropology*, Palo Alto, CA, Stanford University Press.

SPRADLEY, JAMES P. (1979) *The Ethnographic Interview*, New York, Holt, Rinehart and Winston.

SPRADLEY, JAMES P. (1980) *Participant Observation*, New York, Holt, Rinehart and Winston.

SURANSKY, VALERIE (1980, May) 'Phenomenology: An alternative research paradigm and a force for social change', *Journal of the British Society for Phenomenology*, vol. 11, 2, pp. 163-179.

TESCH, RENATA (1976) *The Humanistic Approach to Educational Research*, Santa Barbara, CA, The Fielding Institute.

TESCH, RENATA (1988) 'The contribution of a qualitative method: Phenomenological research', paper presented at the annual meeting of the American Educational Research Association, New Orleans.

THORNDIKE, EDWARD LEE (1927) *The Measurement of Intelligence*, New York, Bureau of Publications, Teachers College, Columbia University.

THORNDIKE, ROBERT L. (Ed.) (1951) *Educational Measurement*, Washington, DC, American Council on Education.

VAN KAAM, ADRIAN L. (1959, May) 'Phenomenological analysis: Exemplified by a study of the experience of really feeling understood', *Journal of Individual Psychology*, pp. 66-72.

VAN MAANEN, JOHN (Ed.) (1979) *Qualitative Methodology*, Beverly Hills, CA, Sage Publications.

WEBB, S. and WEBB, B. P. (1932) *Methods of Social Study*, London: Longman.

WEBB, EUGENE J.; CAMPBELL, DONALD T.; SCHWARTZ, RICHARD D. and SECHREST, LEE (1966) *Unobtrusive Measures: Nonreactive Research in the Social Sciences*, Chicago, Rand McNally Publishing Company.

WILSON, STEPHEN (1977) 'The use of ethnographic techniques in educational research', *Review of Educational Research*, 47, 1, PP. 245-265.

WOLCOTT, HARRY (Ed.) (1975, Summer) 'Special issue on ethnography of schools', *Human Organization*.

Qualitative Research in Sociology

Before the term 'qualitative' was common, sociologists who had no interest in setting up experimental conditions or conducting quantifiable surveys simply called their activities 'fieldwork' and their method of data collection 'participant observation'. If they had been asked to label their approach, they probably would have called it 'anthropological'. Most of these early qualitative researchers were members or followers of the so-called 'Chicago School'. Chicago had the first sociology department in the United States. However, this department was not a sociology department as we know it today. Sociology in the US was much influenced by British 'social anthropology', and the department in Chicago was called 'Department of Social Science and Anthropology' (Kirk and Miller, 1986, p. 35). Thus, much of the distinction between anthropology and sociology in those days had to do with the locations in which the studies were conducted, either foreign/exotic or at home.

The person who probably had the greatest influence on the practices of young sociologists at the time was Robert Park. In an earlier career, he had been a newspaper reporter. His enthusiasm for first-hand data collection resulted in a host of studies that were based on direct observation accompanied by profuse note-taking and followed by narrative reporting. Chicago had attracted a large contingent of eminent scholars, and each had her/his own style and theoretical orientation, yet they did not differentiate their approaches sufficiently to attach distinct labels to them. 'There seems to have been a reasonably consistent paradigm of research methods' concludes Jack Douglas (1976, p. 43). He simply calls it 'the classical model of field research' (*ibid.*). Very rarely was the method captured in a manual or even textbook for novices. Instead, 'the Chicago tradition of field research methods was largely a word-of-mouth and apprentice tradition until the 1950's' (*ibid.*, p. 45).

This 'grand era of Chicago sociology' lasted from about 1920 to 1950 (*ibid.*, p. 44). Actually, it would be more accurate to say that it was gradually phased out by the 1960's. It had also undergone some differentiation. At least two types could be discerned: small group studies and large community surveys. The large studies usually required team work by several researchers, since they often covered entire cities. More importantly, the 'classic model' underwent internal changes of epistemological importance.

As Jack Douglas sees it, the Chicago school was not weakened and then displaced by 'control'-oriented researchers whose positivistic views gained more and more ground, but the mode itself turned more and more positivistic. 'Field research came increasingly to be seen as a set of highly rationalized and even systematized techniques' (*ibid.*, p. 50), because the classic field researchers 'assumed that the classic ideas of 'absolute objectivity' are more or less true and that sociological research methods such as theirs should generate such truth' (*ibid.*, p. 49). Therefore, they devised all kinds of 'accounting schemes' to exercise 'quality control'. A contemporary post-positivistic researcher would find few commonalities with the later 'classical' field researcher, except the nature of the data.

It was not until the 1960's that more distinguishable research directions evolved that assumed their own labels and methods. Except for grounded theory construction, these approaches were not particularly clearly defined. Ethnomethodology, for instance, was first introduced through the description of three research examples, rather than a set of axioms or goals and procedures (Garfinkel, 1967). As individual sociologists began working in the one or the other mode, they conducted their studies according to their own understanding and interpretation of the original writing. In the process, the various 'schools' became quite diverse and are difficult to describe as unified 'types' of research. Ethnomethodology, for instance has been viewed as 'a form of life to be lived' (Mehan and Wood, 1975, p. 6), 'a way of working which creates findings, methods, theories; it enables its practitioners to enter other realities, there to experience the assembly of world views (*ibid.*, p. 3). Quite to the contrary, Douglas believes that ethnomethodology makes sociology 'merely a branch of post-Chomsky linguistics' (Douglas, 1976, p. 53), while others point out the phenomenological features of ethnomethodology (Bogdan and Taylor, 1975, p. 23; Psathas, 1973).

Ethnomethodology (Garfinkel, 1967) and the closely related symbolic interactionism have in common that they both focus on common social interactions. Ethnomethodologists are language-oriented, and they usually employ mechanical recording devices to capture 'accounts' of everyday language. They try to discover how people make sense of their language interactions, especially how they deal with the taken-for-granted meaning changes of such ambiguous words as 'they', 'it', or 'that'.

Mary Rogers distinguishes situational ethnomethodologists (how people talk about and make sense of behavioral episodes, for example), and linguistic ethnomethodologists (Rogers, 1983, p. 106). The latter conduct 'conversational analysis', an activity that became one of the roots of

discourse analysis. Modern discourse analysis is an interdisciplinary research branch that investigates 'the many dimensions of text, talk, and their cognitive, social and cultural contexts' (van Dijk, 1985, p. xiii). Not surprisingly, no single method has evolved in discourse analysis, since it draws on sociolinguistics, cognitive psychology, social psychology, artificial intelligence studies, linguistics, anthropology, and communication studies. So far, methodological texts have not attended to the principles and practices of discourse analysis in a prescriptive manner, but have been collections of research examples (van Dijk, 1985). In sociology it is difficult to draw a clear line between ethnomethodologically influenced conversational analysis and sociolinguistic discourse analysis.

As mentioned above, **symbolic interactionism**, which had been around as a concept since 1937 (Bogdan and Biklen, 1982, p. 14), and had become shaped into a research approach around the same time as ethnomethodology (Blumer, 1967 and 1969), shares some of the ethnomethodologist's concerns with interaction. In fact, occasionally ethnomethodology is seen as a type of symbolic interactionism (Meltzer *et al.*, 1975). The label refers to the fact that 'humans . . . live in a symbolic environment as well as a physical environment, and they act in response to symbols as well as to physical stimuli' (Jacob, 1987, p. 27). The symbols are the language and actions of others. Thus, 'people are constantly in a process of interpretation and definition as they move from one situation to another (Bogdan and Taylor, 1975). Their own actions are a result of their interpretation of the situation. The goal of symbolic interactionists, consequently, is to discover 'how this process of designation and interpretation is sustaining, undercutting, redirecting, and transforming the ways in which the participants are fitting together their lines of action' (Blumer, 1969, p. 53).

Both ethnomethodology and symbolic interactionism were influenced by phenomenological philosophy. A third direction in sociological research, **grounded theory construction**, was not only inspired by it, but took an explicitly phenomenological stance (Glaser and Strauss, 1967). One of the tenets of phenomenology is to 'bracket' existing notions about a phenomenon, and let the phenomenon speak for itself. Barney Glaser and Anselm Strauss suggested to take that tenet seriously.

Rather than considering the field collection of naturally occurring data sufficiently phenomenological, Glaser and Strauss advised researchers to discontinue their practice of bringing theories to the field and gathering data with the goal of disconfirming or verifying those theories. Instead, they described a method in which the process would be reversed: While the researcher suspended all prior theoretical notions, data relevant to a particular sociological problem area would be collected, and then inspected to discover whether any theory or at least hypothesis could be developed directly from the patterns found in the data. The method for discovering such patterns was called by Glaser and Strauss 'constant comparison'. This term refers to the fact that data are ordered into preliminary categories according to their conceptual context, and then constantly compared within a category to establish consistency, and across categories to establish clear boundaries. The concept in each category could be refined into a theoretical notion, and the researcher could then explore whether several concepts were connected which each other, thus forming hypotheses, based on or 'grounded in' the data.

While grounded theory was a reaction against the overemphasis on theory verification, other qualitative sociologists began to be increasingly concerned with the 'dehumanization' effect that was created by 'too much statistics' applied by their colleagues in the positivistic tradition (Lofland, 1971, p. 6). Rather than relying exclusively on statistical surveys and social experimentation, 'the social world should be studied in its 'natural state', undisturbed by the researcher. Hence, 'natural' settings, not 'artificial' settings like experiments or formal interviews, should be the primary source of data' (Hammersley and Atkinson, 1983, p. 6). This view became known as the 'naturalistic' perspective (Lofland, 1967; Denzin 1970). It signaled, according to Hammersley and Atkinson, a 'renaissance of interpretive sociology' (1983, p. 10), and thereby a gradual reappearance of a more holistic form of ethnography than the earlier 'classic field model'.

Holistic ethnography is described in detail in the chapter on educational research, since it began to flourish in the 1960's when the federal government began to fund qualitative studies, especially in schools (see Bogdan and Biklen, 1982, p. 19). The main methodological difference between the earlier forms of anthropological sociology and more modern ethnography was the increasing inclusion of interview techniques, which then became less and less structured, and more and more 'creative' (Douglas, 1985). The only methodological text within sociology that explicitly uses the term ethnography in its title is by Hammersley and Atkinson (1983), both of whom are British. Their ethnography is holistic in the sense that 'the ethnographer participates . . . in people's daily lives for an extended period of time, watching what happens, listening to what is said, asking questions; in fact collecting whatever data are available to throw light on the issues with which he or she is concerned' (*ibid.*, p. 2).

In the US, the developments within ethnography took a more structured turn. While, according to Gubrium, 'the tradition of the field' had been to 'classify and highlight the social organization and distribution of subjective meanings as native and diverse field realities' (1988, pp. 24, 26), in the 1970's the 'classification and highlighting' began to concentrate on language. This type of structural ethnography seeks to describe systematically the 'meaning systems' that cultural groups and subgroups have created and in which they live. Structural ethnographers see culture 'as a cognitive map' which is revealed in the language through which people communicate (Spradley, 1979, p. 7). It is 'a shared system of meaning' (*ibid.*, p. 6), that 'serves as a guide for action and for interpreting our experience' (*ibid.*, p. 7). Therefore, culture is studied 'through the way people talk' (*ibid.*, p. 9), and particularly the way 'native terms and phrases' are used. 'The end product of doing ethnography is a verbal description of the cultural scene studied' (*ibid.*, p. 21).

In **ethnoscience** (or 'cognitive ethnography'), which was inspired by Spradley's work (Werner and Schoepfle, 1987, vol. 1, p. 15), the focus on language becomes exclusive. Its methods are 'lexicographic in spirit' (Werner and Schoepfle, 1987, vol. 2, p. 16). Since the analysis process resembles the operations of map-making (*ibid.*, p. 24), the end product is the construction and graphic depiction of 'lexical/semantic fields of linked propositions' (*ibid.*, p. 38). The classic form of this graphic depiction is the inverted tree drawing that represents a taxonomy. In its most basic version it contains linguistic terms that are related to each other through the formula 'b is a kind of a', where 'a' would be situated at the top of the graph, and 'b' at the end of a branch below it. Such elemental relationships are discovered through what Werner and Schoepfle call the 'structural analysis' of the language under study (*ibid.*, chapter 2). Ethnoscientists work with more complex analysis types and diagrams as well, and they also use various statistical techniques to explore linguistic patterns.

Oswald Werner and G. Mark Schoepfle, the scholars who described ethnoscience, are not sociologists; they are anthropologists (linguistic and cultural, respectively). Ethnoscience, therefore, is not a primary sociological method. The intensive examination of language, however, is reminiscent of a method with a long tradition in sociology: classical **content analysis**. Although not restricted to sociology, but shared with journalism, political science and social psychology, content analysis has been known to sociologists as long as fieldwork and participant observation. Since the method is largely numeric, it cannot properly be called a type of qualitative research. Yet its conclusions are not statistical; they are substantive. Furthermore, in its historical development content analysis has grown to include qualitative strategies, and today 'the best content analytic studies utilize both qualitative and quantitative operations on text' (Weber, 1985, p. 10).

Although the first content analytic studies date back to the beginning of the century (Barcus, 1959), the method seems to have come to prominence in the 1930's and 1940's. The *American Journal of Sociology* and *Social Forces* both published numerous studies of the content of radio programs and newspapers during those years (the former even of its own content). By now the data sources have become more diverse and the methods more sophisticated. Among the sources are ethnographic materials such as folktales and other verbal traditions. The methods have gone beyond the simple counting of words to the categorization of words and phrases according to their meaning, the determination of word usage through context extraction, and even limited use of artificial intelligence (Weber, 1985, pp. 70f.).

A fusion of quantitative and qualitative methods is advocated by David Altheide, who suggests viewing appropriate documents as ethnographic material, thus creating **ethnographic content analysis**. The materials are appropriate insofar as they are 'products of social interaction' (Altheide, 1987, p. 66). The 'distinctive characteristic [of ethnographic content analysis] is the reflexive and highly interactive nature of the investigator, concepts, data collection and analysis' (*ibid.*, p. 68). For instance, categories for sorting of data pieces are not established prior to the analysis, but partially emerge from the data, the context is taken into account, and 'data are often coded perceptually, so that one item may be relevant for several purposes' (*ibid.*, p. 69). Data are collected while the study is in progress, and the analysis sometimes leads to reconceptualizations which, in turn, require additional data. The inclusion of new data is, of course, possible only where data are contemporary, not historical. Ethnographic content analysis is, therefore, best suited to current affairs such as news media coverage and policy analysis.

The kind of reflexive researcher interaction with documents that is used in ethnographic content analysis is not without a model. In fact, some of the earliest sociological studies were based on documents, specifically, biographical materials. The example most cited is Thomas and Znaniecki's (1918) study of the Polish peasant, in which the data consisted of letters. Thomas and Znaniecki considered 'life records' 'the perfect type of sociological material' (*ibid.*, p. 1833). They used large numbers of these records to discover 'data and facts' that can 'be treated as mere instances of more or less general classes of data or facts, and can thus be used for the determination of laws of social becoming' (*ibid.*, p. 1832). Sociologists, by and large, don't seem to have accepted that argument. However, the vivaciousness of individual case descriptions has always attracted individual scholars, and today they are valued not so much as 'a supplementary source of data to infer cultural patterns' (Watson, 1976, p. 96) as they are for an application of phenomenological principles to sociological research. (For phenomenology see the chapters on psychology and education.) 'In line with the broad tradition of Verstehen sociology, the life history technique documents the inner experiences of individuals, how they interpret, understand and define the world around them' (Faraday and Plummer, 1979, p. 776). In this vein, **life history studies** no longer are limited to biographical and autobiographical documents, diaries, and letters, but include in-depth interviewing and some focussed observation.

Life history studies have also been called 'biographical ethnography' (Werner and Schoepfle, 1987, vol. 1, p. 48). As such, they represent a deviation from the usually quite static sociological descriptions of patterns and systems. They include the dimension of time: Life histories must take into account the chronological order of events. A small group of sociologists have made chronological sequences their explicit focus of investigation: they perform **event structure analysis**. People cause certain events to happen by making choices in the actions they take. In the same way they prevent other events from occurring. But each situation offers only a limited number of choices, and certain events cannot occur before their prerequisites have taken place. Thus for any situation abstract logical structures of events can be generated and compared with actual event sequences. The results could provide clues about people's priorities or about norms in a culture. Event analysis can be applied not only to actual incidents, but to folk tales and other cultural narratives (Heise, 1988).

Summary

Qualitative Research in Sociology

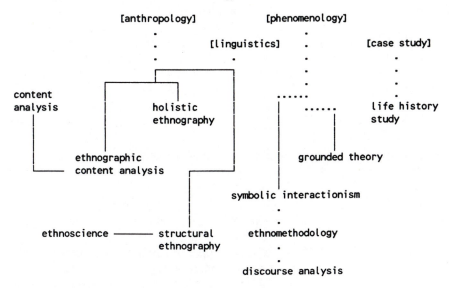

Purposes of Qualitative Sociological Research

content analysis, classical   'making replicable and valid inferences from data to their context' (Krippendorf, 1980, p. 21)
'objective, systematic, and quantitative description of the manifest content of communication' (Berelson, 1952, p. 489)

'making inferences by systematically and objectively identifying specified characteristics within text' (Stone *et al.*, 1966, p. 5)

content analysis, ethnographic

'the reflexive analysis of documents' (Altheide, 1987, p. 65)

'used to document and understand the communication of meaning, as well as to verify theoretical relationships' (Altheide, 1987, p. 68)

discourse analysis

'the linguistic analysis of naturally occurring connected spoken or written discourse' (Stubbs, 1983, p. 1)

providing 'insight into the forms and mechanisms of human communication and verbal interaction' (van Dijk, 1985, p. 4)

ethnography (holistic)

'to describe and analyze all or part of a culture or community by describing the beliefs and practices of the group studied and showing how the various parts contribute to the culture as a unified, consistent whole' (Jacob, 1987, p. 10)

ethnography (structural)

'classifies and highlights the social organization and distribution of subjective meanings as native and diverse field realities' (Gubrium, 1988, p. 26), being 'concerned with . . . cataloging their forms and relationships in time and space' (*ibid.*, p. 26)

where we 'think of culture as a cognitive map' (Spradley, 1979, p. 7), and where 'both tacit and explicit culture are revealed through speech' (*ibid.*, p. 9)

ethnomethodology

to 'study how members of society, in the course of ongoing social interaction, make sense of 'indexical' expressions. Indexicals are terms whose meaning is not universal, but is dependent upon the context' (Bailey, 1978, p. 249)

'how members of situations assemble reasonable understandings of the things and events of concern to them and, thereby, realize them as objects of everyday life' (Gubrium, 1988, p. 27)

'how people in society organize their activities in such a way that they make mutual sense, how people do things in such ways that others can recognize them for what they are' (Sharrock and Anderson, 1986, p. 56)

ethnoscience   (cognitive anthropology)

'to understand participants' cultural categories and to identify the organizing principles that underlie these categories . . . through the study of semantic systems' (Jacob, 1987, p. 22)

'to define systematically the meaning of words, or labels - in short the names of things in the context of their use' (Werner and Schoepfle, 1987, vol. 2, p. 29) in order to 'construct lexical-semantic fields of linked propositions' (*ibid.*, p. 38)

event structure analysis

to examine and represent series of events as logical structures, i.e., as elements and their connections (including the assumptions that govern these connections) that can serve as explanatory models for interpreting actual or folkloristic sequences of events (Heise and Lewis, 1988)

grounded theory construction

to 'discover theory from data' through the 'general method of comparative analysis' (Glaser and Strauss, 1967, p. 1)

life history study, document case study

an 'unstructured and non-quantitative' approach using personal documents (Bailey, 1978, p. 273), often resulting in typologies or 'through which to examine and analyze the subjective experience of individuals and their construction of the social world' (Jones, 1983, p. 147)

| symbolic interactionism | 'to see how the process of designation and interpretation [participants are defining and interpreting each other's acts] is sustaining, undercutting, redirecting and transforming the ways in which the participants are fitting together their lines of action' (Blumer, 1969, p. 53) |
| | 'understanding how individuals are able to take one another's perspective and learn meanings and symbols in concrete instances of interaction' (Jacob, 1987, p. 29) |

References

ALTHEIDE, DAVID L. (1987) 'Ethnographic content analysis', *Qualitative Sociology*, 10, 1, Spring, pp. 65-77.

BAILY, KENNETH D. (1987) *Methods of Social Research*, New York, The Free Press.

BARCUS, F. E. (1959) *Communications Content: Analysis of the Research 1900-1958*, University of Illinois, Doctoral dissertation.

BERELSON, B. (1952) *Content Analysis in Communications Research*, New York, Free Press.

BLUMER, HERBERT (1967) 'Society as symbolic interaction', in MANIS, J. and MELTZER, B. (Eds.) *Symbolic Interaction*, Boston, Allyn and Bacon.

BLUMER, HERBERT (1969) *Symbolic Interactionism*, Englewood Cliffs, NJ, Prentice Hall.

BOGDAN, ROBERT C. and TAYLOR, STEVEN J. (1975) *Introduction to Qualitative Research Methods: A Phenomenological Approach to the Social Sciences*, New York, John Wiley and Sons.

BOGDAN, ROBERT C. and BIKLEN, SARI K. (1982) *Qualitative Research for Education: An Introduction to Theory and Methods*, Boston, Allyn and Bacon, Inc.

DENZIN, NORMAN K. (1970) *Sociological Methods: A Sourcebook*, Chicago, Aldine, Atherton.

DOUGLAS, JACK D. (1976) *Investigative Social Research*, Beverly Hills, CA, Sage Publications.

DOUGLAS, JACK D. (1985) *Creative Interviewing*, Beverly Hills, CA, Sage Publications.

FARADAY, ANNABEL and PLUMMER, KENNETH (1979) 'Doing life histories', *Sociological Review*, 27, 4, pp. 773-98.

GARFINKEL, HAROLD (1967) *Studies in Ethnomethodology*, Englewood Cliffs, NJ, Prentice-Hall.

GLASER, BARNEY G. and STRAUSS, ANSELM L. (1967) *The Discovery of Grounded Theory: Strategies for Qualitative Research*, Chicago, Aldine Publishing Company.

GUBRIUM, JABER (1988) *Analyzing Field Reality*, Beverly Hills, CA, Sage Publications.

HAMMERSLEY, MARTYN and ATKINSON, PAUL (1983) *Ethnography: Principles in Practice*, New York, Tavistock Publications.

HEISE, DAVID R. (1988, Spring) 'Computer analysis of cultural structures', *Social Science Computer Review*, 6, 1, pp. 183-97.

HEISE, DAVID R. and LEWIS, ELSA M. (1988) *Introduction to ETHNO*, Raleigh, NC, National Collegiate Software Clearinghouse.

JACOB, EVELYN (1987, Spring) 'Qualitative research traditions: A review', *Review of Educational Research*, 57, 1, pp. 1-50.

JONES, GARETH R. (1983) 'Life history methodology', in MORGAN, G. (Ed.), *Beyond Method*, Beverly Hills, CA, Sage Publications.

KIRK, JEROME and MILLER, MARC L. (1986) *Reliability and Validity in Qualitative Research*, Beverly Hills, CA, Sage Publications.

KRIPPENDORF, KLAUS (1980) *Content Analysis: An Introduction to Its Methodology*, Beverly Hills, CA, Sage Publications.

LOFLAND, JOHN (1967) 'Notes on naturalism', *Kansas Journal of Sociology*, 3, 4, pp. 45-61.

LOFLAND, JOHN (1971) *Analyzing Social Settings*, Belmont, CA, Wadsworth Publishing Company.

MEHAN, HUGH and WOOD, HOUSTON (1975) *The Reality of Ethnomethodology*, New York, John Wiley and Sons.

MELTZER, B. N.; PETRAS, J. W. and REYNOLDS, L. T. (1975) *Symbolic Interactionism: Genesis, Varieties and Criticism*, London, Routledge and Kegan Paul.

PSATHAS, GEORGE (Ed.) (1973) *Phenomenological Sociology: Issues and Applications*, New York, John Wiley and Sons.

ROGERS, MARY F. (1983) *Sociology, Ethnomethodology, and Experience*, Cambridge, MA, Cambridge University Press.

SHARROCK, W. and ANDERSON, B. (1986) *The Ethnomethodologists*, New York, Tavistock Publications.

SPRADLEY, JAMES P. (1979) *The Ethnographic Interview*, New York, Holt, Rinehart and Winston.

STONE, PHILLIP J., DUNPHY, DEXTER C., SMITH, MARSHALL S. and OGILVIE, DANIEL M. (1966) *The General Inquirer: A Computer Approach to Content Analysis*, Cambridge, MA, M.I.T. Press.

STUBBS, MICHAEL (1983) *Discourse Analysis: The Sociolinguistic Analysis of Natural Language*, Chicago, The University of Chicago Press.

THOMAS, WILLIAM I. and ZNANIECKI, FLORIAN (1918) *The Polish Peasant in Europe and America*, Boston, Richard G. Badger.

VAN DIJK, TEUN A. (Ed.) (1985) *Handbook of Discourse Analysis, Vol. 4.*, London, Academic Press.

WATSON, LAWRENCE, C. (1976, Spring) 'Understanding a life history as a subjective document', *ETHOS*, 4, 1, pp. 95-131.

WEBER, ROBERT PHILIP (1985) *Basic Content Analysis*, Beverly Hills, CA, Sage Publications.

WERNER, OSWALD and SCHOEPFLE, G. MARK (1987) *Systematic Fieldwork, Vol. 1.*, Beverly Hills, CA, Sage Publications.

WERNER, OSWALD and SCHOEPFLE, G. MARK (1987) *Systematic Fieldwork, Vol. 2.*, Beverly Hills, CA, Sage Publications.

Qualitative Research in Psychology

The use of the word 'qualitative' is rare in American psychology (it is used more widely in Europe). When psychologists think of research that is descriptive and interpretive, they usually associate it with the term 'humanistic'. The typical humanistic psychologist, however, is not known for her/his interest in research ('Humanistic psychologists who are interested in research constitute a minority in the Association for Humanistic Psychology', Massarik, 1986, p. 19). It is, instead, the 'human scientists' who are the most active in dealing with theoretical and methodological issues in research. (To my knowledge, the term 'human sciences' was first used as a translation of the German 'Geisteswischenschaften' in Stephan Strasser's work in 1963.)

In theory, 'human sciences' is a term used merely to distinguish sciences that explore the world of humans in contrast to exploring the rest of nature. It could be substituted for 'social sciences' (Giorgi, 1986, p. 34). In practice, however, human sciences has come to mean: those approaches in the social sciences that do not imitate the natural sciences.

The term that comes to mind first when considering the human sciences approach in psychology is 'phenomenology'. Phenomenology is a philosophy and Edmund Husserl, the gentleman credited with having invented this branch of philosophy, had much to say about the nature of knowledge, but he did not provide detailed instructions for researchers. It was up to individual scholars to translate Husserl's writings into concrete research procedures.

Existential-phenomenological Approaches

Adrian van Kaam was probably the first psychologist who set out to study mundane experiences and to describe how he gathered and analyzed his data. Coming from a Rogerian client-centered perspective, he explored in his Ph.D. research in 1958 the phenomenon of 'feeling understood' (von

33

Eckartsberg, 1977, p. 26). His method was to ask students to describe in great detail situations in which they felt really understood, and particularly their feelings at the time. He then analyzed, or 'explicated' these descriptions with the intent to determine 'the necessary and sufficient constituents of this feeling' (van Kaam, 1966, p. 301). Van Kaam went on to organize the graduate program in phenomenological psychology at Duquesne University.

Van Kaam and his approach attracted Amedeo Giorgi, who had in 1958 earned his doctorate in experimental psychology, to Duquesne. Giorgi, and his colleagues Paul Colaizzi, William and Constance Fischer, and Rolf von Eckartsberg were the formulators of phenomenological methodology in psychology. They built on van Kaam's work and added variations of their own. Their writings, and those of their students, are collected in the four volumes of the *Duquesne Studies in Phenomenological Psychology*, the first of which appeared in 1971. Another Duquesne-inspired volume of phenomenological studies that can serve as methodological examples was edited by Valle and King in 1978: *Existential-phenomenological Alternatives for Psychology* (Valle and King, 1978).

Giorgi's main deviation from van Kaam's work was that frequencies of 'constituents' were no longer counted, as van Kaam had done, and rather than working back and forth across all descriptions to discern commonalities, Giorgi stayed with one case at a time until the 'meaning units' were exhausted, before making comparisons. In addition, he usually does not elicit written descriptions, but conducts interviews which are later transcribed verbatim.

Although van Kaam used the term 'existential' to describe his work, while Giorgi prefers 'phenomenological', the two philosophies are so closely related that the former is often implied in the latter, or the two words are connected with a hyphen (**existential-phenomenological**). Within the approach, however, various schools have evolved. Colaizzi points out that a distinction must be made between researchers who use their own experience as data (a **reflexive** form of **phenomenology**) and those who use descriptive protocols from many subjects, which he calls an **empirical** form of **phenomenology**. Colaizzi considers himself and his Duquesne colleagues empirical phenomenologists. It fell to William Fischer to clarify how phenomenological empiricism differs from that of the natural scientist. Both scholars work with data experienced by the senses, he states, but 'traditional natural scientific psychology is empirical to the extent that it is open to phenomena insofar as they show themselves to the researcher' (Fischer, in Valle and King, 1978, p. 168). 'As an empirical phenomenological psychologist, however, I understand empirical to mean that the researcher is open to all perceivable dimensions and profiles of the phenomenon that is being researched. Hence, the experiences of the subjects, as well as those of the researcher, are . . . acknowledged as potentially informative' (*ibid.*).

One special form of reflexive research is **heuristic** research. This is the name Clark Moustakas gave to what he considers essentially a 'discovery process', as distinguished from 'verification and corroboration' (Moustakas, 1981, p. 207). The emphasis in this method is on the process more than the outcome. Research begins with 'inner searching for deeper awareness' (*ibid.*, p. 209), as achieved in meditation, self-searching, and 'intuitive and mystical reaching'. The experiences of others are then listened to, 'not taking notes and making records', but with objectivity and warmth, 'keeping the focus . . . on the essence of the experience through the person's rendering of it and relating of it' (*ibid.*, p. 210). Toward the end of the process the researcher might also delve into any piece of literature that can deepen the understanding. Instead of defining and categorizing the researcher is involved in a 'search for a pattern and meaning' (*ibid.*, p. 211), in which he or she becomes completely immersed. The result of the quest is a narrative 'portrayal' of the experience.

A separate type of empirical research results from situations in which it is difficult for the phenomenologist to gather her/his data in the usual manner of intensely interviewing or eliciting detailed descriptions. Some 'psychological phenomena . . . are beyond human experiential awareness or . . . cannot be communicated; among these are, for example, broad social events, infant, child, and animal behavior, and predominantly bodily activity which we cannot penetrate by conscious experience' (Colaizzi, in Valle and King, 1978, p. 65). In these cases the researcher observes, but not by recording isolated events, as the traditional observer does. The phenomeno-logical observer perceives in a 'primitive' way (primitive in the sense of primordial, as Merleau-Ponty has taught us to distinguish). He or she allows the objects 'to take hold of us before we ever begin to mobilize our cognitive objectifying power of perceptual denotation' (McConville, in Valle and King, 1978, p. 106). Of course, as a mature human being, the researcher cannot defy cognition. What we can do in the process of objectifying the observed is to try as much as possible to be suspicious of what we think we have seen, i.e., ensure 'that the results of analytic knowledge are not interposed between our seeing and the seen' (Colaizzi, in Valle and King, 1978, p. 67). Colaizzi calls this type of phenomenological work **perceptual description.**

Some scholars felt uncomfortable with the strict distinction between 'reflective' and 'empirical' forms of phenomenological researching, claiming that personal experience is always involved when trying to make sense of someone else's account. They suggest that phenomenologists reflect on their own experience and explicitly create multiple descriptions of it, as experienced in changing situations. They then use these reflections and descriptions, as produced in an internal dialogue, to enter into a dialogue with others about their experience of the same phenomenon. This **dialogal phenomenology** was articulated by Strasser in 1969 (Strasser, 1969), and employed by Constance Fischer in her study of the experience of privacy (Fischer, in Giorgi *et al.*, 1971, pp. 149-63). Fischer not only dialogued once, but engaged in a progressive mutual exploration with others, with the intention of refining her grasp on the phenomenon, as everyone involved refined their grasp as well. The desired outcome of such dialogal process is consensus on the description of the phenomenon, - a result that she found not difficult to achieve.

From dialogal phenomenology it is not a big step to a reciprocal involvement of both researcher and subject. Such a relationship would involve learning and even personal growth for both parties. Rolf von Eckartsberg suggested an intimate collaboration between the person who collects the data and those who provide them in the process of making sense of the self-reports elicited (Eckartsberg, *ibid.*, pp. 66-79). He realized that in this process 'both partners co-constitute their reality with reciprocal effects' (*ibid.*, p. 74). Accordingly, 'ongoing change in both partners is a necessary concomitant' (*ibid.*).

Jim Barrell went even further by proposing to fuse research and self-development (Barrell and Barrell, 1975; Barrell, 1986). Since 'an investigator has no direct access to any experience but his own' (Barrell and Barrell, 1975, p. 65), Barrell advises the researcher to start by describing her/his own experience. He termed this brand of phenomenology the **experiential method.** Rather than merely dialoguing with others about a particular type of experience, the researcher trains participants in self-observation (as distinguished from introspection, which concentrates on mental aspects), and asks them to note the commonalities in different situations that are the occasions for the same kind of experience (for instance, jealousy). Thus the participants begin to engage in some of the activities that in other research approaches would be the prerogative of the researcher.

A few years earlier, John Heron had created a very similar research mode in England, which he also labelled 'experiential' (Heron, 1971). For him the distinction between researcher and research participant disappears still further: there are only co-researchers (Heron, 1981, p. 156). Interestingly, although both Barrell and Heron remain firmly within the existential-phenomenological tradition, they both speak of hypotheses. The investigative process for Heron is guided by a 'hypothetical' phenomenological mapping of the topic researched, which then is accepted, modified, or rejected as the study concludes. Barrell's research results in 'definitional hypotheses', which are 'statements about the necessary and sufficient factors for the occurrence of a given phenomenon'; and 'functional hypotheses', which are 'statements about the relationships between these experiential factors' (Price and Barrell, 1980, p. 81). In limited ways, the outcomes of an experiential study can even be quantified.

One variation of phenomenological research in psychology distinguishes itself from others by the nature of the data rather than the methodological approach. The data are myths, etymology, literature and other art forms. These human creations are especially rich in images that can reveal to the skilled researcher their hidden wisdom about psychological life. Archetypal and depth psychology are drawn on to gain insights, and the approach has come to be known as **imaginal** (Aanstoos, 1987, p. 17). Robert Romanyshyn and his students at the University of Dallas have been especially productive in imaginal research.

Other Qualitative Forms of Psychological Research

While phenomenological research is probably the most actively conducted type of qualitative research in psychology at this time, it is not the only way to be non-quantitative, or even the oldest. Ever since Freud, psychologists have produced 'case studies'. One of the most famous is Binswanger's *The Case of Ellen West* (Binswanger, 1958). The **case study**, most likely because of its respectable age and closeness to psychological practice, is much less controversial with conventional researchers than phenomenological research, and therefore it is often the only acceptable kind of qualitative research where quantitative research is the norm.

Somewhat related to phenomenology is another tradition that has influenced qualitative research in psychology: **hermeneutics**. It is much older than phenomenology. Essentially a form of exegesis, it was developed for the examination of biblical texts. Dictionaries define it as the art and science of interpretation. Martin Heidegger and then Paul Ricoeur masterfully appropriated hermeneutics for the social sciences by suggesting and demonstrating that human actions resemble the way a written text appears to the reader. 'The hermeneutic approach seeks to elucidate and make explicit our practical understanding of human actions by providing interpretations of them' (Packer, 1985, p. 1088). Unlike phenomenology, hermeneutics is not concerned with 'the experienced intention of the actor', but takes 'action as an access through which to interpret the larger social context of meaning within which it is embedded' (Aanstoos, 1987, p. 15). In that sense it is more interested in the social than the individual meaning of actions. Like phenomenology, hermeneutics attempts 'to describe and study meaningful human phenomena in a careful and detailed manner as free as possible from prior theoretical assumptions' and aims at 'progressive uncovering and explication' (Packer, 1985, pp. 1081, 1089).

In the course of the growing disenchantment with experimental psychology in the fertile 1960's <History>, one of the first critics was Roger Barker. He did not base his criticism as much on philosophical notions as on practical considerations: laboratory research studies phenomena in an artificial environment. Therefore, all conclusions drawn are valid only in artificial environments, he decided. If we want to know about human beings

in their natural 'habitat', we have to study them in their normal surroundings. Barker called this type of investigation **ecological psychology**. It has
in common with phenomenological research the inclusion of the 'life-world'
of the individual, i.e., it operates in the concrete setting of people's life.
However, Barker makes a clear distinction between the 'milieu', which is the
objective environment, and the 'psychological habitat', which is the subjective
environment. The latter is accessible in terms of the individual's emotional
reactions to her/his surroundings. Unlike phenomenologists, ecological
psychologists are interested in the interdependence of the two (Jacob, 1987,
p. 4). They believe that certain behavioral laws result from this interaction,
and they often use descriptive statistics to specify them.

Two more types of qualitative research deserve mention. One is a
relatively old sociological method that is being introduced into psychology
by David Rennie: **grounded theory** <Sociology>. The other is **critical
emancipatory** research, based on Habermas' work, whose notion of a 'critical
social science' has activated scholars in various fields. Such a science would
demonstrate 'why individuals have the distorted self-understanding that they
do, and how they can be corrected' (Carr and Kemmis, 1986, p. 137). Theo
de Boer has clarified how such an approach can be applied to psychology
(de Boer, 1983). It would 'track down automatic mechanisms in thinking
and acting that have a cultural origin. It would reveal dispositions that rest
on culture and tradition . . . a person's manner of life could be called into
question through reflection' (de Boer, *ibid.*, p. 162). Critical emancipatory
psychology has not yet produced a substantial body of research, but the basic
notion of accepting and even making use of value stances of the researcher
is beginning to seep into other disciplines as well. To some, it seems to
signal the advent of the next paradigm, leaving not only quantitative, but
also qualitative-interpretive research approaches behind <Education>.

Summary

Qualitative Research in Psychology

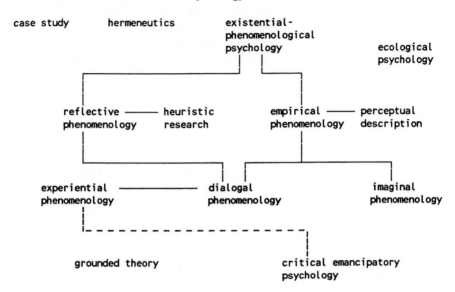

Purposes of Qualitative Psychological Research

case study	intensive and detailed study of one individual or of a group as an entity, through observation, self-reports, and any other means
critical emancipatory research	to 'disclose self-evident and unnoticed biases, habits of thinking, customary conventions, and so forth' through dialogue (de Boer, 1983, p. 155)
dialogal phenomenology	to study human experiences as articulated in language, taking 'stories [as] starting points for all further thinking and theory building' (von Eckartsberg, in Valle and King, 1978, p. 186)
ecological psychology	to 'describe behavior and discover the laws of behavior' (Jacob, 1987, p. 5) through 'studying the "behavior stream" that constitutes itself as "behavioral episodes" as nested in socially defined "behavioral settings"' (von Eckartsberg, in Valle and King, 1978, p. 199)

empirical phenomenology   to 'understand the general psychological meaning of some particular human way of being-in-a-situation, . . . through a number of descriptions of this way of being-in-a-situation from people who have lived through and experience themselves as so involved [called protocols]' (W. Fischer, in Valle and King, 1978, p. 177)

existential-phenomenological psychology   to 'reveal the structure of experience through descriptive techniques', thereby 'disclosing the nature of structure in the form of meaning', structure being 'the commonality running through the many diverse appearances of the phenomenon' (Valle and King, 1978, pp. 15, 17, 16)

experiential phenomenology   '. . . the investigators question, explore, and arrive at conclusions regarding psychological processes within themselves [so as] to generate testable experiential hypotheses' (Price and Barrell, 1980, p. 76)

grounded theory   to 'discover theory from data' through the 'general method of constant comparison' (Glaser and Strauss, 1967, p. 1)

hermeneutics   textual interpretation, applied to human action 'to elucidate and make explicit our understanding . . . by providing an interpretation of them' through 'progressive uncovering and explication' (Packer, 1985, p. 1088, p. 1089)

heuristic inquiry   'to know the essence of some aspect of life through the internal pathways of the self' (Douglas and Moustakas, 1985, p. 39)

imaginal phenomenology   'seeks to understand psychological life by going to those sources most regnant with imaginative potency' through 'metaphorical refiguring' (Aanstoos, 1987, p. 17, p. 18)

perceptual description   to investigate 'psychological phenomena which either are beyond human experiential aware-

ness or which cannot be communicated'
through 'the observation of lived events'
(Colaizzi, in Valle and King, 1978, p. 65, p.
62)

reflective phenomenology   'aims at a descriptive understanding of
psychological phenomena by reflectively
disclosing their meaning' 'through the imaginative presence to the investigated phenomenon' (Colaizzi, in Valle and King, 1978, p. 68,
p. 62)

References

AANSTOOS, CHRISTOPHER M. (1987, Winter) 'A comparative survey of
human science psychologies', *Methods,* 1, 2, pp. 1-36.

BARKER, ROGER G. (1968) *Ecological Psychology: Concepts and Methods
for Studying the Environment of Human Behavior,* Stanford, CA,
Stanford University Press.

BARRELL, JAMES J. and BARRELL, J. E. (1975) 'A self-directed approach for
a science of human experience', *Journal of Phenomenological
Psychology,* pp. 63-73.

BARRELL, JAMES J. (1986) *A Science of Human Experience,* Acton, MA,
Copley.

BINSWANGER, L. (1958) 'The case of Ellen West', in MAY, R.; ANGEL, E.
and ELLENBERGER, H. F. (Eds.) *Existence,* New York, Basic Books.

CARR, WILFRED and KEMMIS, STEPHEN (1986) *Becoming Critical: Education, Knowledge and Action Research,* Lewes, The Falmer Press.

DE BOER, THEO (1983) *Foundations of a Critical Psychology,* Pittsburgh, PA,
Duquesne University Press.

DOUGLAS, BRUCE G. and MOUSTAKAS, CLARK (1985, Summer) 'Heuristic
inquiry: The internal search to know', *Journal of Humanistic Psychology,* 25, 3, pp. 39-55.

GIORGI, AMEDEO; FISCHER, WILLIAM, F. and VON ECKARTSBERG, ROLF
(Eds.) (1971) *Duquesne Studies in Phenomenological Psychology, Vol.
1,* Pittsburgh, PA, Duquesne University Press.

GIORGI, AMEDEO; FISCHER, CONSTANCE and MURRAY, EDWARD (Eds.)
(1975) *Duquesne Studies in Phenomenological Psychology, Vol. 2,*
Pittsburgh, PA, Duquesne University Press.

GIORGI, AMEDEO; KNOWLES, RICHARD and SMITH, DAVID L. (Eds.) (1979)
Duquesne Studies in Phenomenological Psychology, Vol. 3, Pittsburgh,
PA, Duquesne University Press.

GIORGI, AMEDEO; BARON, A. and MAES, C. (Eds.) (1983) *Duquesne Studies in Phenomenological Psychology, Vol. 4*, Pittsburgh, PA, Duquesne University Press.

GIORGI, AMEDEO (1986, Spring) 'Status of qualitative research in the human sciences; A limited interdisciplinary and international perspective', *Methods*, 1, 1, pp. 29-62.

GLASER, BARNEY G. and STRAUSS, ANSELM L. (1967) *The Discovery of Grounded Theory: Strategies for Qualitative Research*, Chicago, Aldine Publishing Company.

HEIDEGGER, MARTIN (1962) *Being and Time*, New York, Harper and Row. (Originally published in 1927.)

HERON, JOHN (1971) *Experience and Method: An Inquiry Into the Concept of Experiential Research*, Human Potential Research Project, University of Surrey, England.

HERON, JOHN (1981) 'Experiential research methodology', in REASON, PETER and ROWAN, JOHN (Eds.) *Human Inquiry: A Sourcebook of New Paradigm Research*, New York, John Wiley and Sons.

JACOB, EVELYN (1987, Spring) 'Qualitative research traditions: A review', *Review of Educational Research*, 57, 1, pp. 1-50.

MASSARIK, FRED (1986) 'Forschung in der humanistischen Psychologie; ein Gespräch (geführt mit Gerhard Fatzer)', *Jahrbuch der Zeitschrift für humanistische Psychologie, Forschung I*, pp. 9-22.

MOUSTAKAS, CLARK (1981) 'Heuristic research', in REASON, PETER and ROWAN, JOHN (Eds.) *Human Inquiry: A Sourcebook of New Paradigm Research*, New York, John Wiley and Sons, pp. 207-17.

PACKER, MARTIN J. (1985) 'Hermeneutic inquiry in the study of human conduct', *American Psychologist*, 40, 10, pp. 1081-93.

PRICE, DON D. and BARRELL, JAMES J. (1980) 'An experiential approach with quantitative methods: A research paradigm', *Journal of Humanistic Psychology*, 20, pp. 75-95.

RENNIE, DAVID L.; PHILLIPS, JEFFREY R. and QUARTARO, GEORGIA (1987) 'Grounded Theory: A Promising Approach to Conceptualizing Psychology', Unpublished manuscript, York University.

RICOEUR, PAUL (1971) 'The model of the text: Meaningful action considered as text', *Social Research*, 38, pp. 529-62.

STRASSER, STEPHAN (1963) *Phenomenology and the Human Sciences*, Pittsburgh, PA, Duquesne University Press.

STRASSER, STEPHAN (1969) *The Idea of Dialogal Phenomenology*, Pittsburgh, PA, Duquesne University Press.

VALLE, RONALD S. and KING, MARK (Eds.) (1978) *Existential-Phenomenological Alternatives for Psychology*, New York, Oxford University Press.

VAN KAAM, ADRIAN L. (1966) *Existential Foundations of Psychology*, Pittsburgh, Duquesne University Press.

VON ECKARTSBERG, ROLF (1977) *Psychological Research Methods at Duquesne*, unpublished monograph, Duquesne University.

Qualitative Research in Education

In 1969 William Gephart took stock of the available 'research methodologies' in education, and found there were six (historical, case study, descriptive, quasi-experimental, unobtrusive-measure experiment, and experimental), to which he added two hypothetical ones (Gephart, 1969, p. 9). In the introduction he mentions in a single sentence an additional one which he does not further allude to: 'the aexperimental method' (*ibid.*, p. 2). The aexperimental method was, he informs us, suggested by Egon Guba. (Gephart's 'descriptive method' is not qualitative, but classified as traditionally quantitative, namely 'the determination of the manner in which a population is distributed on a variable or variables' (*ibid.*, p. 4).) This aexperimental method has come to be known as **naturalistic inquiry**.

The nature of naturalistic inquiry is difficult to describe. It has 'its root in ethnography and phenomenology' (*ibid.*, p. 1). The term was first used in psychology (Willems and Raush, 1969) and in sociology (Denzin, 1970), and it was introduced into education as 'an approach which has considerable promise . . . for evaluation particularly' (Guba, 1978, p. 1). Although in 1978 still referred to as a method (*ibid.*), it was later viewed more broadly as a method for getting at the truth (Guba and Lincoln, 1981, p. 53). By 1985 it had become 'the naturalistic paradigm' (Lincoln and Guba, 1985, p. 36). While in 1978 naturalistic inquiry was contrasted with 'conventional inquiry (which ordinarily is experimental inquiry . . .)' (Guba, 1978, p. 11), in 1985 it was contrasted with positivism and viewed as 'a particular postpositivist paradigm' (Lincoln and Guba, 1985, p. 36).

In a sense, therefore, naturalistic inquiry is a term parallel to the term qualitative research, where qualitative research is meant to denote all research not concerned with variables and their measurement. Most types of qualitative research described in this book, at least those that employ interpretational qualitative analysis, share all or some of the fourteen characteristics that define naturalistic inquiry:

Natural setting; human instrument; utilization of tacit knowledge; qualitative methodology; purposive sampling [instead of random]; inductive data analysis; grounded theory; emergent design; negotiated outcome [negotiated with the study participants]; case study reporting mode; idiographic interpretation; tentative application [instead of generalization]; focus-determined boundaries; special criteria for trustworthiness. (*ibid.*, pp. 39-43, square brackets inserted by this author)

Thus, according to the tenets of naturalistic inquiry 'qualitative' merely is one of the characteristics of the naturalistic paradigm (*ibid.*, p. 40), although quantitative data are not excluded (*ibid.*, p. 250). From a definitional point of view it does, in fact, make more sense to say that using qualitative methods is a way of conducting naturalistic inquiry, rather than to say that using naturalistic inquiry is a way of doing qualitative research. One reason why the terms are rarely used that way may be that Yvonna Lincoln and Egon Guba have provided detailed directions regarding the design of naturalistic inquiry, its implementation, data processing, and so forth. For many researchers, therefore, naturalistic inquiry appears to be simply a way of doing qualitative research, rather than a philosophical stance. At the same time, as mentioned in the introduction to this book, the term qualitative research as a paradigm description displays a tenacity that defies logic.

If we compare naturalistic inquiry as a way of doing research with other types of qualitative research, it stands out through its emphasis on 'the human as instrument' (*ibid.*, p. 250). This notion is based on the old fieldwork concept in which the researcher simply used her/his eyes and ears and made notes in unstructured fashion, then reflected upon them and distilled them into a narrative. In naturalistic inquiry this image becomes expanded and refined. 'Humans [are] the major form of data collection device.' As instruments, they 'can be developed and continuously refined' (*ibid.*, p. 250). In fact, 'there is no reason to believe that humans cannot approach a level of trustworthiness similar to that of ordinary standardized tests' (*ibid.*, p. 195).

It is interesting that naturalistic inquiry was first advocated as an alternative to conventional methods in the field of educational evaluation. The development seems to have begun with Parlett and Hamilton's (1972) **illuminative evaluation** idea in Britain, and Robert Stake's (1975) definition of 'responsive' evaluation in the US. These, as well as Egon Guba's 1978 publication, were occasional papers or monographs with limited circulation. The 'big splash' was made by Michael Quinn Patton in 1980 with the appearance of *Qualitative Evaluation Methods*. As we now know, the term 'qualitative' was going to stick, and even to become appealing. Thus, while in 1979 qualitative methods were seen merely as 'a needed perspective in evaluation research' (Filstead, 1979), by 1988 David Fetterman could proclaim 'a silent scientific revolution' in the sense of a paradigm shift (Fetterman, 1988, p. 4). This assessment of the situation is probably accurate, considering that 30% of the members of the American Evaluation Association chose 'qualitative methods' as their Topical Interest Group in 1987 (Evaluation Practice, 8, 4, p. 74). The cause was much advanced by the 1984 publication of two important volumes: *Ethnography in Educational Evaluation* by David Fetterman, and *Qualitative Data Analysis* by Matthew Miles and Michael Huberman (in this book their approach is labelled **transcendental realism**).

Since a large proportion of studies in the field of education are evaluative, qualitative research might be said to have made its entry into the field by way of evaluation. However, that would be only half correct. Long before Mr Gephart discovered aexperimental research, a subgroup of educators had been doing nothing else but qualitative research. Their field of interest overlapped with another discipline, anthropology. Anthropology of education, or educational anthropology is the other gate through which qualitative research entered.

Educational anthropology is a field with a long tradition. Already in 1913 the great educator Maria Montessori brought the two disciplines together in her work *Pedagogical Anthropology* (Montessori, 1913). Many anthropologists studied children and matters of education in the first half of the century. In the 1950's, however, educators themselves began to study education from an anthropologist's point of view and with an anthropologist's tools. George Spindler began publishing his work in 1955. During the reform-oriented 1960's, many educators began to question the traditional research methods that relied on measurements only, and narrative accounts of what was going on in schools and classrooms appeared on the scene (most notable perhaps Philip Jackson's (1968) *Life in the Classroom* and Elizabeth Eddy's (1969) *Becoming a teacher*). The journal *Review of Educational Research* had published a paper on *Anthropology and Education* (Brameld and Sullivan, 1961) as early as 1961. Even American federal research projects became more exploratory during this time and used interviews and participant observation (Bogdan and Biklen, 1982, p. 19). Young researchers involved in these projects, as well as students from the 'Spindler school' continue to carry on this type of qualitative work, which by now is customarily referred to as **ethnography**, anthropology's well-established qualitative method.

The term ethnography would soon become just about synonymous with 'qualitative research' in American education. Encouraged by the formation of the Council on Anthropology and Education in 1968, many individual research projects in the 1970's were based on ethnographic methods. Most of them were not yet published in mainstream educational journals, but in *Anthropology and Education*, which began circulation in

1969. Occasionally, ethnographic papers successfully reached the general educational audience, as when the *Educational Researcher* published a paper on 'The use of anthropological field methods' in 1974 (Lutz and Ramsey, 1974), and the *Review of Educational Research* printed Stephen Wilson's account of 'Ethnographic techniques in educational research' in 1977. In 1978 Ray Rist organized the first symposium on ethnography for the annual meeting of the American Educational Research Association, and in the year thereafter he provided a research training course in ethnographic methods for AERA. The course was promptly repeated in 1980; ethnography was in.

Educational researchers with an interest in ethnography were much helped when two books appeared that described the method in detail: Dobbert's *Ethnographic Research* in 1982, and Goetz and LeCompte's *Ethnography and Qualitative Design in Educational Research* in 1984. Marion Dobbert addressed her book to educators and evaluators alike, and remained predominantly within the framework of cultural anthropology. Judith Goetz and Margaret LeCompte took a somewhat broader approach. They define the process of ethnography as:

> Ethnography is . . . a way of studying human life. Ethnographic design mandates investigatory strategies conducive to cultural reconstruction. First, the strategies used elicit phenomenological data; they represent the world view of the participants being investigated, and participant constructs are used to structure the research. Second, ethnographic research strategies are empirical and naturalistic. Participant and nonparticipant observation are used to acquire firsthand, sensory accounts of phenomena as they occur in real world settings, and investigators take care to avoid purposive manipulation of variables in the study. Third, ethnographic research is holistic. Ethnographers seek to construct descriptions of total phenomena within their various contexts and to generate from these descriptions the complex inter-relation-ships of causes and consequences that affect human behavior toward and belief about the phenomena. Finally, ethnography is multimodal or eclectic; ethnographic researchers use a variety of research techniques to amass their data (Wilson 1977). (Goetz and LeCompte, 1984, pp. 3-4)

Except for the emphasis on 'cultural reconstruction', this description of ethnographic research has many aspects in common with naturalistic inquiry (see above). In methodological discussions, however, another difference has been pointed out: while Goetz and LeCompte continue to use the traditional vocabulary for assessing the quality of an ethnographic study (reliability and validity), but propose different criteria, Lincoln and

Guba reject the traditional labels and replace them with the term 'trust-worthiness', which is composed of a cluster of criteria for which they also use non-traditional vocabulary.

In Britain, the term ethnography was less prominent, but the idea of qualitative research in education had taken hold in the late sixties and early seventies as well. Researchers used the old terms 'field research' and 'participant observation'. As in the US, a strong impetus came from evaluation. In 1970, the Centre for Applied Research in Education (CARE) opened under the directorship of Lawrence Stenhouse. Its aim was'to describe naturalistic educational settings, to illuminate them with the account of educational members, and to be applied knowledge rather then stop at observation' (Reynolds, 1988, p. 148). The Centre pioneered qualitative methods (Atkinson *et al.*, 1988). Especially helpful to researchers were the methodological texts authored by Walker on case studies (1974 and 1983). While some researchers in Britain borrowed symbolic interactionism from their colleagues in sociology, others were interested in what they called the social anthropology of education (*ibid.*, p. 235/36). In the early 1980's additional methodology books began to appear, most notably the series on field research edited by Robert Burgess. The first volume was a source book and manual called *Field Research* (1982), which was soon followed by Burgess' *In the Field* (1984a) and three collections of qualitative research examples (1984b, 1985a, 1985b).

Within American ethnography, some researchers paid particular attention to language and began using some of the methods developed in sociolinguistics. Their work has been labelled 'microethnography' or **ethnography of communication.** It is based heavily on 'machine-recording' of naturally occurring interactions, where every moment can be 'revisited' by replaying it. Audio and audiovisual recordings enable the researcher to pay attention to details easily overlooked otherwise, because they are associated with rare events rather than with the usually observed frequently re-occurring events (Erickson, 1986).

While ethnographers and naturalistic researchers were occupying the center stage in educational qualitative research, much important qualitative work was accomplished by another group of educators who worked quietly in the background within small pockets throughout the US and Canada. They were influenced by developments in Europe, particularly in the Netherlands. The Dutch educator Martinus Langeveld had tried to put into practice the philosophical principles of Edmund Husserl, the creator of phenomenology. His student Ton Beekman established through Loren Barritt a relationship with the University of Michigan at Ann Arbor in the late 1970's. Soon, a group of researchers from Ann Arbor conducted **phenomenological** studies, providing models for others who learned from them and eventually formed a solid research community. (Phenomenological researchers now meet annually at the Human Science Research conference.)

Phenomenological research differs from naturalistic and ethnographic approaches in its emphasis on the individual, and on subjective experience. Rather than studying the impact of a program designed to facilitate the integration of minority students, for instance, or studying the culture of the multi-racial classroom, or the interactions among children of different races, phenomenology would study what the experience of being in a multi-racial classroom is like, or what the experience of being a minority student (or majority student) in an integrated classroom is like. 'Phenomenology is the systematic investigation of subjectivity' (Bullington and Karlson, 1984, p. 51). Its aim is 'to study the world as it appears to us in and through consciousness' (*ibid.*, p. 51). The value of a phenomenological study is measured in terms of its power to let us come to an understanding of ourselves, and 'an understanding of the lives of those for whom we bear pedagogic responsibility' (Langeveld, 1983, p. 7).

There are many similarities in the conduct of phenomenological studies with naturalistic inquiry. The differences are: in phenomenology more emphasis is placed on 'bracketing out preconceived ideas' (Barritt *et al.*, 1985, p. 20), on non-directiveness in interviewing, and the 'essential' themes that 'constitute' the phenomenon. The result of a phenomenological study is a narrative that delineates a pattern, or, expressed phenomenologically, a description of 'the structural invariants of a particular type of experience' (Dukes, 1984, p. 201).

In some respects not unlike phenomenological research, but with no apparent epistemological connection, is **educational connoisseurship and criticism.** A concept introduced to educational evaluation by Elliot Eisner (1975), it is rooted in the arts, where a connoisseur is a person 'with refined perceptual apparatus, knowledge of what to look for, and a backlog of previous relevant experience' (Guba, 1978, p. 39). Its similarity with phenomenological research lies in the fact that 'the interpretive aspect of educational criticism represents an effort to understand the meaning and significance that various forms of action have for those in a social setting' (Eisner, 1988, p. 146), i.e., what their experience is like. Educational connoisseurship requires 'an ability to participate empathetically in the life of another' (*ibid.*, p. 146). Like phenomenological research, it 'is closer in character to a hermeneutic activity than a technical one' (Eisner, 1981, p. 8). (For hermeneutics see the chapter on qualitative research in psychology.) Its contribution is 'a heightened awareness of the qualities of [classroom] life so that teachers and students can become more intelligent within it' (Eisner, 1988, p. 142).

To provide teachers and students with more 'intelligence' about their situation is precisely the goal of another 'critical' approach to educational research. This one, however, is not based on art, but on the philosophical notion of critical theory, particularly the work of Jürgen Habermas. I am referring to the **critical educational science** described and advocated by the

British and Australian educators Wilfred Carr and Stephen Kemmis (1986). Their goal is the revival of **action research** as empowerment. Emancipatory action research is 'a form of self-reflective enquiry undertaken by participants in social situations in order to improve the rationality and justice of their own practices, their understanding of these practices, and the situations in which the practices are carried out' (*ibid.*, p. 162). As such, it is juxtaposed to 'technical action research' whose aim is 'efficient and effective practice, judged by reference to criteria which may not themselves be analyzed in the course of the action research process' (*ibid.*, p. 202).

Since emancipatory action research 'organizes practitioners into collaborative groups for the purpose of their own enlightenment' (*ibid.*, p. 200), it is often also called **collaborative** research. Various groups in the US have begun to introduce collaborative action research, for instance at the University of Georgia in Athens, at The Teachers College of Columbia University, at East Texas State University in Commerce, and in the Education Department of Clemson University in South Carolina. (For an example see Allen *et al.*, 1988.)

One last type of qualitative research deserves mention, since it is likely to gain in importance for educators. It is called **phenomenography**, a type of research growing out of the work of the Swedish educator Ference Marton (1986). Unlike phenomenology, phenomenography is not the application of a philosophical method to research; the name was chosen in 1979 after the approach had been developed, since it 'aims at description, analysis, and understanding of experiences' (Marton, 1981, p. 180). The experiences are conceptual experiences of the world around us. Led by Marton, a group of researchers at the University of Gothenburg began to concentrate on the study of learning and thinking, focussing on people's common sense conceptions with which they explain the physical and social world.

Marton contends that just as, over the course of history, the understanding changes that science provides us about phenomena such as velocity, proportions (in mathematics), pricing (in economics), etc., so do individual understandings within learners. Rather than studying the process of thinking and learning on some abstract structural level, he proposes to study the content of thinking, i.e., the explanations people carry around in their heads for the various aspects of reality they encounter. There exists, he suggests, only 'a relatively limited number of qualitatively different ways' in which any given phenomenon is conceptualized (Marton, 1981, p. 181). Therefore, it is possible to describe and categorize these conceptions, although, of course, a complete and 'ultimate' description of the substance of human thinking can never be achieved (*ibid.*, p. 197), especially since new forms of explanations and conceptions are continually introduced by science.

49

Summary

Qualitative Research in Education

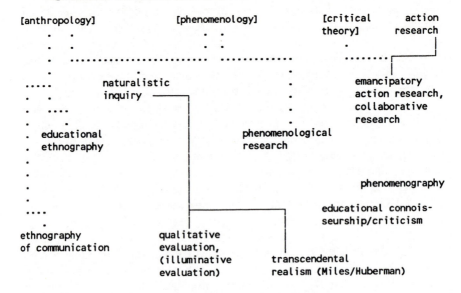

Purposes of Qualitative Educational Research

action/collaborative research	improving practices by or in cooperation with practitioners
emancipatory action research	enlightenment for emancipation
educational connoisseurship and criticism	critically describing (disclosing), interpreting, and evaluating social phenomena (similar to arts appreciation)
ethnography of communication	describing the patterns of interaction of the members of a cultural group (related to sociolinguistics)
ethnography	describing and analyzing practices and beliefs of cultures or communities (as consistent wholes)
naturalistic inquiry	a non-positivistic approach to research in which the researcher is the instrument, and

	the focus is on understanding the meaning the people under study give to their experiences
phenomenography	describing conceptually perceived qualities of a phenomenon through contextual analysis
phenomenological research	illuminating intersubjective human experiences by describing the essence of the subjective experience
qualitative/illuminative evaluation	evaluation that employs the tenets of naturalistic inquiry and emphasizing the process by which outcomes are produced rather than merely judging the outcomes
transcendental realism	describing as precisely as possible the range and the local and historical contingencies of social regularities in social behavior

References

ALLEN, JOBETH; COMBS, JACKIE; HENDRICKS, MILLIE; NASH, PHYLLIS and WILSON, SUSAN (1988) 'Studying change: Teachers who become researchers', *Language Arts*, 65, 4, pp. 379-87.

ATKINSON, PAUL; DELAMONT, SARA and HAMMERSLEY, MARTYN (1988) 'Qualitative research traditions: A British response to Jacob', *Review of Educational Research*, 85, 2, p. 250.

BARRITT, LOREN; BEEKMAN, TON; BLEEKER, HANS and MULDERIJ, KAREL (1985) *Researching Education Practice*, Grand Forks, ND, University of North Dakota, Center for Teaching and Learning.

BOGDAN, ROBERT C. and BIKLEN, SARI K. (1982) *Qualitative Research for Education: An Introduction to Theory and Methods*, Boston, Allyn and Bacon, Inc.

BRAMELD, THEODORE and SULLIVAN, EDWARD B. (1961) 'Anthropology and education', *Review of Educational Research*, 31, pp. 70-9.

BULLINGTON, JENNIFER and KARLSON, GUNNAR (1984) 'Introduction to phenomenological psychological research', *Scandinavian Journal of Psychology*, 25, pp. 51-63.

BURGESS, ROBERT G. (Ed.) (1982) *Field Research: A Sourcebook and Field Manual*, London, Allen and Unwin.

BURGESS, ROBERT G. (1984a) *In the Field*, London, Allen Lane.

BURGESS, ROBERT G. (Ed.) (1984b) *The Research Process in Educational Settings: Ten Case Studies*, Lewes, The Falmer Press.

BURGESS, ROBERT G. (1985a) *Field Methods in the Study of Education*, Lewes, The Falmer Press.

BURGESS, ROBERT G. (Ed.) (1985b) *Strategies in Educational Research*, Lewes, The Falmer Press.

CARR, WILFRED and KEMMIS, STEPHEN (1986) *Becoming Critical: Education, Knowledge and Action Research*, Lewes, The Falmer Press.

DENZIN, NORMAN K. (Ed.) (1970) *Sociological Methods: A Sourcebook*, Chicago, Aldine Atherton.

DOBBERT, MARION L. (1982) *Ethnographic Research*, New York, Praeger Publications.

DUKES, SHEREE (1984) 'Phenomenological methodology in the human sciences', *Journal of Religion and Health*, 23, 3, pp. 197-203.

EDDY, ELIZABETH M. (1969) *Becoming a Teacher: The Passage to Professional Status*, New York, Teachers College Press.

EISNER, ELLIOT W. (1975) 'The perceptive eye: Toward a reformation of educational evaluation', invited address, annual meeting of the American Educational Research Association, Washington D.C.

EISNER, ELLIOT W. (1981, April) 'On the differences between scientific and artistic approaches to qualitative research', *Educational Researcher*, 10, 4, pp. 5-9.

EISNER, ELLIOT W. (1988) 'Educational connoisseurship and criticism: Their form and function in educational evaluation', in FETTERMAN, DAVID M. (Ed.) *Qualitative Approaches to Evaluation: The Silent Scientific Revolution*, New York, Praeger.

ERICKSON, FREDERICK (1986) 'Qualitative methods in research on teaching', in WITTROCK, MERLIN C. (Ed.) *Handbook of Research on Teaching*, Third edition, New York, Macmillan Publishing Company.

EVALUATION PRACTICE (1987) 'Reports from TIGs', *Qualitative Methods*, 8, 4, Beverly Hills, CA, Sage Publications.

FETTERMAN DAVID M. (1984) *Ethnography in Educational Evaluation*, Beverly Hills, CA, Sage Publications.

FETTERMAN DAVID M. (Ed.) (1988) *Qualitative Approaches to Evaluation: The Silent Scientific Revolution*, New York, Praeger.

GEPHART, WILLIAM (1969) 'The eight general research methodologies: A facet analysis of the research process', Center on Evaluation Development and Research: Phi Delta Kappa Occasional Paper.

GOETZ, JUDITH P. and LECOMPTE, MARGARET D. (1984) *Ethnography and Qualitative Design in Educational Research*, Orlando, FL, Academic Press.

GUBA, EGON (1978) *Toward a Methodology of Naturalistic Inquiry in Educational Evaluation*, Los Angeles, CA, Center for the Study of Evaluation.

GUBA, EGON and LINCOLN, YVONNA (1981) *Effective Evaluation*, San Francisco, CA, Jossey-Bass Inc.

JACKSON, PHILIP W. (1968) *Life in the Classroom*, New York, Holt, Rinehart and Winston.

LANGEVELD, MARTINUS (1983) 'Reflections on phenomenology and pedagogy', *Phenomenology and Pedagogy*, 1, 1, pp. 5-7.

LINCOLN, YVONNA and GUBA, EGON (1985) *Naturalistic Inquiry*, Beverly Hills, CA, Sage Publications.

LUTZ, FRANK W. and RAMSEY, MARGARET A. (1974) 'The use of anthropological field methods in education', *Educational Researcher*, 3, 10, pp. 5-9.

MARTON, FERENCE (1981) 'Phenomenography - Describing conceptions of the world around us', *Instructional Science*, 10, pp. 177-200.

MARTON, FERENCE (1986, Fall) 'Phenomenography - A research approach to investigating different understandings of reality', *Journal of Thought*, 21, 3, pp. 28-48.

MILES, MATTHEW B. and HUBERMAN, A. MICHAEL (1984) *Qualitative Data Analysis: A Sourcebook of New Methods*, Beverly Hills, CA, Sage Publications.

MONTESSORI, MARIA (1913) *Pedagogical Anthropology*, (trans. by Frederic Taber Cooper), New York, Stokes.

PARLETT, MALCOLM and HAMILTON, DAVID (1972) 'Evaluation as illumination: A new approach to the study of innovatory programs', Occasional paper, Edinburgh: Centre for Research in the Educational Sciences, University of Edinburgh.

PATTON, MICHAEL Q. (1980) *Qualitative Evaluation Methods*, Beverly Hills, CA, Sage Publications.

REYNOLDS, DAVID (1988) 'British school improvement research: the contribution of qualitative studies', *International Journal of Qualitative Studies in Education*, 1, 2, pp. 143-54.

SPINDLER, GEORGE (Ed.) (1955) *Education and Anthropology*, Palo Alto, CA, Stanford University Press.

SPINDLER, GEORGE (1955) 'Education in a transforming American culture', *Harvard Educational Review* 25, 145-56.

STAKE, ROBERT E. (1975) 'Program evaluation, particularly responsive evaluation', Occasional Paper #5, The Evaluation Center, Western Michigan University.

WALKER, R. (1974) 'Classroom research: A view from SAFARI', in *Innovation, Evaluation Research and the Problem of Control*, Norwich, University of East Anglia.

WALKER, R. (1983) 'The use of case studies in applied research and evaluation', in HARTNET, A. (Ed.) *The Social Sciences and Educational Studies*, London, Heineman, pp. 190-204.

WILLEMS, EDWIN P. and RAUSH, HAROLD L. (1969) *Naturalistic Viewpoints in Psychological Research*, New York, Holt, Rinehart, and Winston.

WILSON, STEPHEN (1977) 'The use of ethnographic techniques in educational research', *Review of Educational Research*, 47, 1, pp. 245-65.

Types of Qualitative Research

Introduction

Strictly speaking, there is no such thing as qualitative research. There are only qualitative *data*. In many studies both quantitative and qualitative data are used; so if we wanted to distinguish research according to data types, there should be a third one: 'mixed'. Of course, everyone would consider this quite ridiculous. 'Qualitative' research, as the term is used by many scholars, means a certain approach to knowledge production. It does not refer only to data. For the purposes of this book, however, it is useful to take 'qualitative' literally and consider qualitative research any research that uses qualitative data.

Qualitative data is any information the researcher gathers that is not expressed in numbers. If we accept this definition, the range of qualitative data includes information other than words. Pictures are qualitative data, too. Drawings, paintings, photographs, films, and videotapes are qualitative data if used for research purposes, and even music and sound tracks can be considered data. There are almost no limits to the human creations and productions one could study. Some researchers have even worked with household garbage (Rathje, 1984).

In this book we will not examine research using non-verbal qualitative data. Even if we concentrate on words, the focus will still be broad enough to include more types of research than are easy to deal with. Consider, for instance, that words can be looked at individually as symbols that are meant to convey a concept with certain meanings, or they can be looked at as building blocks of a narrative. There even is a way of looking at words quantitatively, and I don't mean counting them. Statisticians sometimes treat words quantitatively because they can be placed in categories. A common example is gender. 'Male' and 'female' are attributes that the variable 'gender' may take on, and these two attributes can be assigned numbers (like '1' for category 'male' and '2' for category 'female'), that can be manipulated statistically. Another name for these data is 'categorical', and another is 'nominal'. Special statistical procedures have been designed to deal with them. Halsted Press published a book in 1975 on *Analyzing Qualitative Data* (Maxwell, 1975). It's a statistics book.

The term 'qualitative' data, then, denotes a variety of data, not a single kind, and the distinction from 'quantitative' is not crisp, but somewhat arbitrary. To make things still more complicated, the use of the two different types of data does not coincide with the two research approaches which scholars commonly distinguish today: traditional (or positivistic), and 'new paradigm' (post-positivistic or human science) research <History>. Researchers were working with words long before we had heard of 'qualitative' data, while modern 'positivistic' scholars don't feel they have left their territory when they sometimes use open-ended responses to question-naires or interviews. On the other hand, as a senior researcher friend of mine once reminded me, qualitative researchers use numbers, too. How else would they find out about a 'pattern' in their data if they didn't establish for how many cases in their study a certain result holds true? One could easily get into hairsplitting here, but that would not be productive. Let's just accept that even seemingly clear-cut scholarly terms can be fuzzy. To get anywhere, we sometimes need to act as if they were discrete and unam-biguous (an assumption to which we will return later <Organizing systems>.)

In this book the term 'qualitative' will refer to words, and 'qualitative research' will mean those kinds of research that predominantly or exclusively use words as data.

Working with Words

Words are parts of language. There are two basic ways of studying language: as a structure and as communication. When language as a **structure** is studied by linguists, the interest is in its syntax, the forms of words, etc. When it is studied as a structure by anthropologists, the interest is in the way words and phrases embody a system of cultural knowledge. Linguists would determine, for instance, what endings a certain word stem can have and how the various forms are used; anthropologists would explore what meaning a word has in a culture, usually by relating it to other words in that culture.

When language is studied as **communication**, it can also be examined in more than one way. The main two are: exploring language as an art form and exploring it as information. Literary criticism would be concerned with word usage by certain authors or at certain historical periods, for instance, while social scientists may want to find out what a particular text tells about social or psychological conditions. A third form of dealing with language as communication is interpretation. If the same narrative is read by several people, not everyone will understand it exactly as everyone else does. This recognition is as old as the Bible. Except for the most primitive forms of communication, the path between what is said and what is perceived is not direct. It can be so mysterious, in fact, that scientists still haven't figured out exactly how to establish with certainty what a text means. At best they may agree on what it should be taken to mean.

Stripped to their basics, the above distinctions could be depicted in the following way:

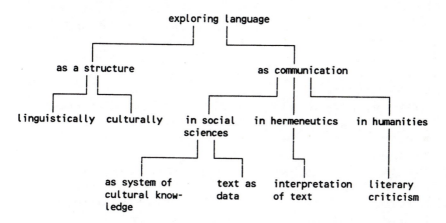

These distinctions help to narrow down further the boundaries of the material covered in this book. Linguistic analysis and literary criticism, the types of research that appear on the far left and the far right on the chart below, are not included in our description. The emphasis will be on the center of this diagram: language studied by social scientists as narrative data, with some excursions into the adjacent areas of interpretation, and of structural treatment of language as the embodiment of culture.

Words as Data in the Social Sciences

Sociology, psychology, education, and anthropology each has its own tradition of qualitative research <Sociology, psychology, education>. Usually, there is a mainstream, i.e., a favorite way of conducting qualitative research that most scholars in the field subscribe to. In education, for instance, ethnography has become the dominant mode. Researchers who work within that mode not infrequently view it as *the* way of doing qualitative research, and must be reminded that there are other ways as well. There are plenty of other ways, and especially of other labels. To give you an idea what various researchers in the social sciences have called their brand of qualitative research, consider the list below:

action research

case study

clinical research

cognitive anthropology

collaborative inquiry

content analysis

dialogical research

conversation analysis

Delphi study

descriptive research

direct research

discourse analysis

document study

ecological psychology

educational connoisseurship and criticism

educational ethnography

ethnographic content analysis

ethnography

ethnography of communication

ethnomethodology

ethnoscience

experiential psychology

field study

focus group research

grounded theory

hermeneutics

heuristic research

holistic ethnography

imaginal psychology

intensive research

interpretive evaluation

interpretive interactionism

interpretive human studies

life history study

naturalistic inquiry

oral history

panel research

participant observation

participative research

phenomenography

phenomenology

qualitative evaluation

structural ethnography

symbolic interactionism

transcendental realism

transformative research

The problem with this list is not only that it is far too long, but that some of the terms overlap with or are synonyms for others, and not all terms are on the same conceptual level. Some terms describe the perspectives qualitative researchers adopt (for instance 'naturalistic', 'interpretive', 'experiential', 'clinical'), or the tradition in the field on which they base their stance (such as 'ethnography', 'phenomenology', 'symbolic interactionism', or 'ethnomethodology'). Other terms refer to the research approach used ('discourse analysis', 'case study', 'action research', etc.), or merely to the type of data, method, or research location ('document study', 'participant observation', 'field research', 'oral history').

Even this grouping of terms is forced. Sometimes it is difficult to distinguish clearly between labels that denote an epistemological stance and those that refer to method. Ethnomethodology or symbolic interactionism are 'general conceptions . . . of the nature of explanations of social activity' (Halfpenny, 1981, p. 565) at the same time as embodying directions for appropriate research strategies. Grounded theory is simultaneously a set of assumptions about the production of knowledge and a set of guidelines for empirical research work. Thus it is impossible to sort the labels above neatly into categories according to 'types' of qualitative research.

Yet most of the terms have something in common with others, and since we will turn our attention to the process of analysis in the next chapter, it would help to reduce this multiplicity at least somewhat. Otherwise, it would be quite impossible to talk sensibly about the ways data are analyzed; this book would resemble a telephone book in structure. Therefore, the following is an attempt to bring a measure of order to the list above. (It might still look less like a structured narrative and more like a telephone book to you. You have every right to use it that way; just browse through and see who's in it!) You won't find all labels represented, since some labels are idiosyncratic and used by only one or very few authors. The ones included are further explained in the sections on the various disciplines <Sociology, psychology, education>.

In this case the order will be presented as a cognitive map. The map is laid out in terms of the research interest, by which I mean the more general analytic objective that lies behind the specific purpose of a research project. (For a list of research purposes see the sections on the disciplines.) Maps help to orient oneself in an unfamiliar territory. Yet they also have shortcomings. Since, by necessity, they must reduce objects, the objects lose their details. In fact, on a map every town looks like every other town, except when they are different enough in size to warrant a different size dot. The same holds true for most cognitive maps: they are simplifications. Worse, unlike geographic maps, most cognitive maps don't deal with discrete objects. The entities or concepts they depict usually don't have clear-cut boundaries. Their boundaries overlap or are fuzzy, and their location on the map is, therefore, at best an approximation. Still, as long as we keep that in mind, cognitive maps come in handy as intellectual tools wherever there are too many things to apprehend at once.

Here is the beginning of our map of qualitative research types:

The research interest is in . . .

| the characteristics of language | —— | the discovery of regularities | —— | the comprehension of the meaning of text/action | —— | reflection |

My first distinction is among these four major types. They are presented in a line, rather than a column, because one could think of them as lined up along a continuum. From left to right the types of research become less structured and more holistic. Those kinds of research that are mostly paying attention to language, for instance, deal with discrete parts of language, such as words or phrases, and the research process consists of very orderly procedures. In fact, some of the procedures for analysis may well be quantitative. On the other hand, those types of research that rely mostly on scholarly reflection treat the data holistically, allowing the analysis to build on intuition and on insight that are achieved through deep immersion in and dwelling with the data. The characteristics of these two types at the extremes blend into the types that are adjacent to them.

In turn, of course, the separation line between qualitative research in which the researcher is interested in discovering regularities, and in which s/he is concerned with what texts or actions mean is also not stark and straight. I have distinguished between these two types because in the former it is important to researchers to discover a structure in the data, either as a pattern or as a network of relationship among the parts. The result might be tentative hypotheses or propositions. Where the researcher is mostly interested in 'meaning', on the other hand, s/he interprets and looks for 'themes', some of which might not be directly expressed in the data, but emerge from them upon intensive analysis. Rather than seeking relationships, the researcher looks for commonalities across and uniquenesses within the themes. The result is usually a succinct description on a somewhat abstracted and therefore more 'general' level that highlights the essential constituents of the phenomenon studied.

Let us now pay attention to each of the four major types in turn. Each section will begin with a map that covers one 'research interest'; all of these maps are combined into one 'over-all' map at the end of this chapter. The names for specific research approaches mentioned in the sections will be followed by a letter within triangular brackets, for instance <S>. The letter is the abbreviation of the chapter about a discipline in which that type of research is discussed in more detail. <S> stands for sociology, <E> for education, and <P> for psychology.

Research that Studies the Characteristics of Language

The main division is between those types of research where language is mostly considered a means of communication, and those where language is viewed as a manifestation of the culture in which it serves as the communication instrument. An example of the former is the study of political documents to see how the rhetoric of one party differs from that of the other. An example of the latter is the identification of a system of terms that are shared among members of a subculture who attach to those terms certain meanings which remain obscure to outsiders.

The distinction is depicted in the map on the next page.

Each of the two main divisions has two subdivisions. When dealing with **language as communication**, one could be interested in the content of texts, as in the example above. The type of research that traditionally has used this approach is known as **content analysis** <S>. One could, however, also be interested in the process of communicating itself, i.e., 'in the forms and mechanisms of human communication and verbal interaction' (van Dijk, 1985, p. 4). This is a definition of **discourse analysis** <S>, or conversation analysis. How do people use language to present themselves in a certain (favorable) way to others, for example? How is discourse constrained by the presence of a person in power? These are the types of questions discourse analysts address. Of course, these questions cannot be answered without a cultural context, and so there should also be a line to the term 'culture' in our map. (The reason why there is not is that this is not the only case where a connection other then the one depicted is possible. If all of the weaker links were drawn in, the map would become too congested to be useful.)

The research interest is in . . .

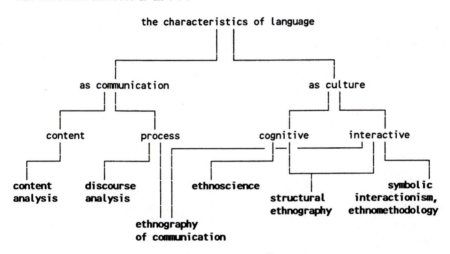

```
                    the characteristics of language


            as communication                    as culture


        content          process          cognitive        interactive


content      discourse                ethnoscience                    symbolic
analysis     analysis                                                 interactionism,
                                                  structural          ethnomethodology
                                                  ethnography
                        ethnography
                        of communication
```

There is another type of research listed under 'communication', and this one does have a strong link to 'culture': **ethnography of communication** <E> or microethnography. Here researchers explicitly 'focus on the patterns of social interaction among members of a cultural group' (Jacob, 1987, p. 18). Ethnographers of communication include non-verbal communication, i.e., behavior, in their study. What goes on in the typical therapy interaction? Or what are the interaction patterns of students and teachers in a certain classroom situations? These are examples of the kinds of questions ethnographers interested in communication might ask.

As with our first branch in the map, there are again at least two ways in which *language as culture* can be studied. Although the distinction between the two poles here is sharp, there is also one type of research that bridges the two. At the one pole we find those scholars who study culture strictly in terms of 'lexical/semantic relations and the lexical/semantic fields that the relations comprise' (Werner and Schoepfle, 1987, vol. 2, p. 15). This type of research is commonly called **ethnoscience** <S> (it is practically the same as cognitive anthropology). The results are often the development of structures that can be viewed as models of the cognitive structure of the culture as mirrored in its language. These models are then diagrammed, much like the cognitive map above. A simple example might be an inverted tree-type diagram of the terms used in a culture to distinguish between types of occupations or of foods, or any other sub-aspect of the culture.

At the other pole of the cultural aspect of language study are **symbolic interactionism** <S> and **ethnomethodology** <S>. These have in common that they both question how human beings make sense of their interactions with each other. One concentrates on the symbolic environment, i.e., things and actions as interpreted by others with whom one is in interaction, and the other, ethnomethodology, concentrates on how people make sense of 'indexical expressions' in communication. 'Indexicals are terms whose meaning is not universal but is dependent upon the context' (Baily, 1987, p. 273). In the preceding sentence the indexical term is 'whose'. Without context, we would not know that it stands for 'terms'. In another sentence it might stand for 'researchers'. Similarly, there are 'indexical actions'. Of course, in my example the context is clear; in real life interactional situations are often very complicated, while people's skills in making sense of them are taken for granted. This astonishing everyday occurrence is the study domain of the ethnomethodologist.

Structural ethnography <S> uses classification of cultural terms and concepts as a research tool, as ethnoscience does, and at the same time, it focusses on interpersonal meaning. Thus it resides at the overlap of ethnoscience and symbolic interactionism. The term structural ethnography is relatively new (Gubrium, 1988, p. 24), and is used to describe the 'traditional' way of conducting ethnography in sociology. Traditional here refers to the kinds of studies that began with Malinowski, who reported his inferences about people's 'implicit cultural knowledge, - beliefs and perspectives that were so customary . . . that they were held outside conscious awareness and thus could not be readily articulated by informants' (Erickson, 1986, p. 123). Structural ethnography 'classifies and highlights the social organization and distribution of subjective meanings as native and diverse field realities' (Gubrium, *ibid.*, p. 26).

That concludes our brief review of language-oriented research. All of the research approaches that concentrate on language as a mirror of culture seek to detect regularities, and therefore one could argue that they belong with our next group, 'research that aims at the discovery of regularities'. The reason why they were treated separately is that in ethnoscience, structural ethnography, ethnography of communication, symbolic interactionism, and ethnomethodology the regularities explored are those of language and language use as it commonly occurs. In our next review we will look at types of research where regularities in action, experience, or attitudes and beliefs are observed, in short in cultural expressions where language is the transmitter of the phenomenon studied, not the object of study.

Research that Aims at the Discovery of Regularities

In this group we find the types of research that are most likely to be called simply 'qualitative' or perhaps 'ethnographic' in the methodological literature. I have divided them into two groups (see map below). Although one could say that in both groups researchers are interested in the structure of the data, the difference is more than one of degree. Some scholars carve out entities from the data that they regard as 'properties', 'concepts', or even 'variables'. In most cases they assume that there might be connections or relationships among them that are to be discovered. The *regularities* are viewed *as a system of conceptual order.* Other researchers are oriented more toward insightful description, where the structure is manifested in commonalities in the data, i.e., *as certain patterns that repeat across data.*

Let's take a look at the map:

The research interest is in . . .

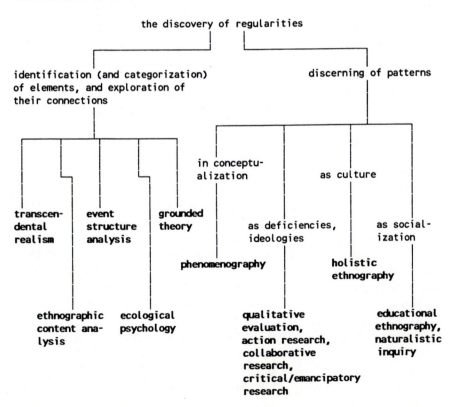

The main two kinds of research in the first group (finding connections between/among categories) are **transcendental realism** <E> and grounded theory. While the later is a commonly known name, the former is almost totally obscure. I chose it for the type of research that is associated with the names Miles and Huberman. Their important book about qualitative analysis (1984) describes a certain approach to qualitative research that they did not further identify, but for which we need a distinctive label here to distinguish it from other approaches. The term I adopted comes from their chapter 'Assessing local causality in qualitative research' in Berg and Smith (1985, p. 353). Their aim is to construct from qualitative data 'causal networks', which are 'visual rendering[s] of the most important independent and dependent variables in a field study and of the relationships among them' (*ibid.*, p. 364).

A quite similar approach is taken by Glaser and Strauss (1967) who seek to discover theory, i.e., 'generalized relations among . . . categories and their properties' (p. 35). In this **grounded theory** <S> method the researcher sorts incidents s/he finds in qualitative data into categories and then, through constantly comparing the content of them, defines the properties of the categories until they have taken on an abstract form, i.e., until a typical incident for the category could be defined conceptually in terms of the category's properties. These conceptual categories, in turn, are then related to each other according to the discoveries made in the data.

Ethnographic content analysis <S> 'is used to document and understand the communication of meaning, as well as to verify theoretical relationships' (Altheide, 1987, p. 68). This type of content analysis uses many of the traditional content analysis procedures, but also the back-and-forth movement between concept development and data analysis, and the constant comparison that grounded theory applies.

Just as ethnographic content analysis builds on a quantitative method, **event structure analysis** <S>, is an enrichment of the usually statistically treated 'sequential analysis' (Bakeman and Gottman, 1986). The researcher's focus of interest in both forms of analysis is the dynamic aspects of phenomena, such as interactions between or among people or the unfolding of folk tales and other stories. The objective is to discover the structure of these processes, i.e., the 'rules' that govern the sequence of interactions or events. Quantitative researchers use statistics like transitional probability or time-series analysis to discover regularities in the sequence of events. Qualitative researchers are more interested in the conceptual logic of event structures, i.e., in 'models' that show the relationships among events. David Heise calls these logical structures 'production grammars' (1988, p. 187), since they are a set of rules. A production grammar is expressed either as a list of relations among events or depicted in a diagram.

The dynamic nature of human affairs is central also to another type of research. In **ecological psychology** <P> researchers study 'streams of behavior' in order 'to produce detailed, objective descriptions of naturally occurring behavior' (Jacob, 1987, p. 3). These descriptions may be quantified by counting frequencies or making statistical comparisons, but the main goal of the ecological psychologist is to relate behaviors to the environment in which they occur. People 'behave' not in a neutral situation, but in specific physical and social settings to which they react emotionally. Rather than examining the inner logic of events or behaviors, as sequential analysts do, ecological psychologists aim to discover the rules that govern the influence of environmental settings on behavior.

Now let's look at the right side of our map. Here I have listed the types of research in which scholars do not look for regularities in terms of lawful order, but in terms of commonalities. They are trying to discern *patterns* in the data. One line goes to a type of research in which patterns *in conceptualization* are explored. It is called **phenomenography** <E>. Since a phenomenon is 'an item of experience or reality' (Webster's, 1964, p. 1696), the name implies the description of such items. That comes close. According to its founder, phenomenography 'is a research method for mapping the qualitatively different ways in which people experience , conceptualize, perceive, and understand various aspects of, and phenomena in, the world around them' (Marton, 1986, p. 31). The emphasis is on the HOW, on the 'way things work', and the 'world' may mean anything from physical to political phenomena. Phenomenographers study how people explain to themselves (and others) what goes on around them, and how these explanations or conceptualizations change.

The next branch of our map leads to a cluster of research approaches under the heading of 'discerning *patterns as deficiencies*'. This is shorthand for saying that these types of research are not used for the development of theoretical notions, but for practical scrutiny of human situations, and often also for the formation of alternative solutions where problems are found to exist.

The best known label in this cluster is probably **evaluation research** <E>. It seeks to determine whether an action has the results it is meant to have. Most commonly, the 'actions' that are reviewed are the programs implemented by public service agencies, and traditionally they have been studied through the use of experimental designs (Suchman, 1967). Qualitative researchers, however, have found ways of evaluating the outcomes of programs through the description and comparison of cases, the development of typologies, classification ('what things fit together', Patton, 1980, p. 311) and cross-classification, the proposition of 'linkages' between processes and outcomes, and even the translation into metaphors. Some qualitative evaluation is purposely not directed toward 'effects' in a narrow sense, but more broadly toward 'illumination' (Parlett and Hamilton, 1972).

Action research <E> is also oriented toward outcomes, but much less passive. While evaluation research at best is 'formative', i.e., suggestive of ways and means that would help to achieve the intended results of a program where they had been found to fall short, action research is explicitly geared toward improvement of unsatisfactory situations. Its main characteristic, however, is the involvement of 'practitioners' in research processes that concern their own affairs. Action research is meant to overcome the passiveness of the research process by turning research itself into a transformative activity.

In the sense that people are involved in research about their own situation, action research is self-study. Some researchers have made self-study the defining characteristic of their research approach. Where the people who work together in some kind of organization or other social setting form a 'community of inquiry' (Torbert, 1983, p. 276) in order to systematically 'increase personal or institutional effectiveness' (*ibid.*, p. 374), they are engaged in **collaborative inquiry**. They collect and interpret information that is considered 'valid' if it 'generates increasingly intelligent, self-corrective action' (*ibid.*, p. 289).

The concepts of action research as participatory and collaborative engagement lend themselves easily to fertilization by the notions of a critical social science as espoused by the philosopher Jürgen Habermas. The result is a type of action research called **emancipatory** <E>, since the generation of knowledge in this type of research is a process of enlightenment 'by which participants in a situation reach authentic understandings of their situation' (Carr and Kemmis, 1986, p. 158). Furthermore, they develop 'critiques of social conditions which sustain dependence, inequality or exploitations' (*ibid.*, p. 164). Unlike collaborative inquiry, emancipatory research does not aim at the improvement of practice, but at liberation that permits actors to make choices without ideological constraints. Like collaborative research, emancipatory action research is successful to the degree in which the knowledge produced results in the improvement of practices.

While the cluster of research types above is improvement-oriented, the varieties of research that are called ethnographic are purely descriptive. Since some of them were mentioned earlier because they examine mostly a culture's language, we will here adopt Evelyn Jacob's term for multi-faceted exploration of *cultural patterns*: holistic ethnography <S, E>. Ethnography has its origin in anthropology, where it was used mainly to study exotic cultures. Social scientists then recognized that groups within cultures form their distinctive subcultures, and that these are sufficiently unique to warrant intensive examination and portrayal. 'Holistic ethnographers seek to describe and analyze all or part of a culture or community by describing the beliefs and practices of the group studied and showing how the various parts contribute to the culture as a unified, consistent whole' (Jacob, 1987, p. 10).

A special kind of ethnography is the one that concerns itself with a distinct part of human cultures: the *patterns in the socialization process* we call schooling. The purpose of **educational ethnography** <E> is given by Goetz and LeCompte as 'provid[ing] rich, descriptive data about the contexts, activities, and beliefs of participants in educational settings. . . . The results of these processes are examined within the whole phenomenon; isolation of outcomes is rarely considered' (Goetz and LeCompte, 1984, p. 23). Except for its focus on education, and in particular on schooling, educational ethnography is understood and conducted much like holistic ethnography. The results are descriptions of the components and dynamics of 'cultures' within educational settings, and sometimes comparisons across settings.

Naturalistic inquiry <E>, which is listed together with educational ethnography, is actually not a type of research, but the label for an entire knowledge producing paradigm. It is intended to denote one of the paradigms that developed in reaction to positivism. Not many scholars, however, seem to think in terms of multiple post-positivistic paradigms. Here we will simply consider the methods of naturalistic inquiry. They are much like ethnography, and especially educational ethnography, except that more procedural diversity is encouraged. Special attention is paid to the researcher as 'the major form of data collection device' (Lincoln and Guba, 1985, p. 250). The researcher needs thorough training for naturalistic inquiry in order 'to operate as an effective instrument' (*ibid.*, p. 250).

Research that Seeks to Discern Meaning

First, our map:

The research interest is in . . .

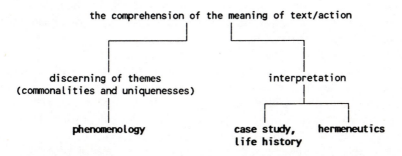

The left branch of this chart is quite close to the kinds of research that seek to discern patterns; in fact, often the comprehension of meaning is likened to the discovery of 'the pattern which connects' (Bateson, 1978). However, the pattern here does not consist of regularities in the sense of order, but in the sense of 'essence'. The researcher seeks to understand the nature of the text or phenomenon in front of her/him; s/he endeavors to gain insight.

The process of meaning-making is usually thought of as 'interpretation'. The reason why I assigned this label to only one of the branches is the need to distinguish between *interpretation* as exegesis and the type of research that uses a unique way of penetrating to the meaning of a phenomenon: *probing for 'themes'.*

Phenomenology <P, E>, similar to naturalistic inquiry, is by some considered a paradigm rather than a research strategy. It began as a school of philosophy. In the course of applying this philosophy to the scientific exploration of the social world, however, scholars developed explicit investigative methods. Phenomenological researchers study the ordinary 'life-world': they are interested in the way people experience their world, what it is like for them, how to best understand them. In order to gain access to others' experience phenomenologists explore their own, but also collect intensive and exhaustive descriptions from their respondents. These descriptions are submitted to a questioning process in which the researcher is open to themes that emerge. A theme is something 'akin to the content, or topic, or statement, or fact in a piece of data' (Tesch, 1987, p. 231). Finding commonalities and uniquenesses in these individual themes allows the researcher to crystallize the 'constituents' of the phenomenon (Giorgi, 1975, p. 74). The result is a description of the 'general structure' (*ibid.*, p. 75) of the phenomenon studied.

As an inquiry process, phenomenology is closely related to **hermeneutics** <P>. In fact, a branch exists in phenomenology that is called 'hermeneutic phenomenology'. In this school of thought scholars apply 'the interpretive tradition . . . to the empirical world by likening the world to a text which must be read' (Barritt *et al.*, 1985, p. 22). Hermeneutics itself is a very old type of text study that was originally confined to theological documents. The word simply means 'interpretation'. Over time, the strategies of hermeneutics have undergone various reformations. Today most scholars adopt Schleiermacher's hermeneutical canons, 'where a singular event is understood by reference to whatever it is a part of . . .' (Polkinghorne, 1983, p. 221), and the analyst moves back and forth between individual elements of the text and the whole text in many cycles, called the 'hermeneutic spiral'. Unlike most qualitative researchers, hermeneutic researchers make sure to include in their considerations the historical context which every experience is 'part of' (Rowan and Reason, 1981, p. 132 ff.).

The historical dimension is at the center of a type of research that concentrates on following the development of events and experiences over time: **life history studies** <E>. Naturally, the methods are related to those historians employ, particularly to the practice of explication, which Barzun aptly describes as 'worming secrets out of manuscripts' (Barzun and Graff,

1977, p. 94). A sociologist, psychologist, or educator who does historical research, however, would go beyond explication toward interpretation, since s/he is concerned more with understanding the dynamics of human affairs than with historical documentation. In principle, two different sources of data are available: documents and oral narratives. **Oral history** is the practice of eliciting memories from elderly people in order to capture the culture of a bygone era. **Document study** allows the researcher to travel even further back when trying to gain 'insight into how those circumstances we experience as contemporary "reality" have been negotiated, constructed and reconstructed over time' (Goodson, 1985, p. 126).

Case studies <P, E> are studies in which researchers concentrate on a single 'case'. Sometimes a few individual cases are aggregated in one research report. According to Yin they rely 'on many of the same techniques as a history, but . . . add two sources of evidence not usually included in the historian's repertoire: direct observation and systematic interviewing' (Yin, 1984, p. 19). They have been listed here under the rubric 'interpretation' because the early researchers who conducted case studies 'interpreted' their observations in the very basic sense of reflecting on their data until they achieved a better understanding of what they meant. (Furthermore, Donald Campbell, in his foreword to Yin's book on case study research connects case studies with hermeneutics.) While these early case studies never included quantitative analysis, the 'single case' has by now spawned an entire branch of statistics. Yet the traditional case study still remains firmly within the domain of the qualitative researcher.

Research that is Based on Reflection

Research that seeks to 'understand', to comprehend meaning, is, of course, not devoid of reflection. As with all previous divisions among groups of research types, the boundaries are fluid. Reflection, in this last segment, however, refers to a special kind of reflection: the one informed largely by intuition. Instead of intuition, one could also refer to 'tacit knowledge', that 'whole system of acceptances that are logically prior to any particular assertion of our own' (Polanyi, 1962, p. 268). It is reflection as introspective contemplation, at the confluence point of the social sciences and the humanities. It is the 'examining with a sense of wonder' (Barritt *et al.*, 1985, p. 25).

The map is simple:
(see next page)

The research interest is in . . .

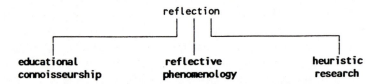

According to Elliot Eisner, there are two ways in which social science phenomena could be studied: scientifically, and artistically (Eisner, 1981, p. 5). By 'artistically' Eisner does not mean that research results should be fantasy, but that the research methods could resemble those used in artistic **connoisseurship** <E> and criticism. 'Connoisseurship is the art of appreciation [and] criticism is the art of disclosure' (Eisner, 1976, p. 141). Just as is the artist, the researcher is interested in the particular, not the general, 'because of the belief that the general resides in the particular' (Eisner, 1981, p. 7). Therefore, the artistically oriented researcher tries to 'imaginatively project himself into the life of another' (*ibid.*, p. 6), and rather than seeking truth, s/he seeks to create 'images that people will find meaningful and from which their fallible and tentative views of the world can be altered, rejected, or made more secure' (*ibid.*, p. 9).

To immerse oneself wholly in one's own experience and that of others is the hallmark of **heuristic research** <P>. The word heuristic is often used to describe a means by which someone is stimulated and helped to find out more or learn more on her/his own. Heuristic research carries farthest the notion that the researcher is the research instrument: 'It requires a subjective process of reflecting, exploring, sifting and elucidating the nature of the phenomenon under investigation' (Douglas and Moustakas, 1985, p. 40). Research is not done in an intellectual or academic manner, but becomes 'an integrative, living form', where the researcher is 'being involved, committed, interested, concerned' and open to 'intuitive visions, feelings, sensings that [go] beyond anything [one] could record or think about or know in a factual sense' (Moustakas, 1981, p. 212). In addition to empathetic listening, poetry, music, literature and other art forms are sources for increased understanding of the phenomenon.

The description of heuristic research above would fit quite well also the type of phenomenological research whose means for the attainment of knowledge is 'imaginative presence' (Colaizzi, 1978, p. 67). It is called **phenomenological reflection** <P>, since the researcher does not rely heavily on 'data', i.e., the experiential accounts of others, but on her/his own contemplation (*ibid.*, p. 68). The phenomenon rises to clearer awareness by approaching it from different angles, for instance from a metaphorical, or a mythical, or a poetic perspective. Phenomenological reflection is a process of 'wondering about' and searching, delving into a phenomenon, awakening to it, and letting oneself be inspired.

Finale

2b différents types

The lengthy list of descriptions above contains twenty-six different types of qualitative research. They are ordered, and graphically depicted in that order. The cognitive maps we constructed place into physical proximity those types of research that have something in common, and all four maps put together result in an awesome picture, reproduced on pp. 80/81. *72/73*

The map has a flow from those kinds of research on the top that have certain resemblances to natural science research to those at the bottom that have certain resemblances to the arts. It all looks beautifully orderly.

However, this graph is but one way of seeing qualitative research. Another way would be to see research through a metaphor. Think of a painter's palette. There are certain basic colors. They can be mixed to form an unending variety of shades. Every individual researcher could do a study of a unique 'shade'. Just because someone has given her/his shade a name and written about it or even defined how it differs from other shades (and thereby is likely to have warranted its inclusion in the above diagram), does not mean that it is an established type of research that now has to be used exactly that way by other researchers, keeping each of its tenets intact. To be sure, some types of research and some labels catch on more strongly than others or already have a longer tradition than others. But basically, there is only one requirement for research: that you can persuade others that you have indeed made a credible discovery worth paying attention to. *place pour ✳✳ adaptation*

This isn't easy. Scholars are by profession critics. Although no one seems to claim any longer that there is an absolute truth to be discovered, various canons of 'trustworthiness' have been established for qualitative research that cannot be ignored easily by any research practitioner. In fact, the research types located toward the bottom of the diagram do not adhere to some of these canons, and you will have to decide for yourself whether you want to consider them to be 'legitimate'. Similarly, the ones on the top are so close to quantitative research that you might not want to accept them either. The purpose of this chapter has been to provide a sense of the diversity and colorfulness of qualitative research, to shed light on some of the shades, not to categorize types in a immobile structure. The diagram at the end of this chapter is a heuristic device, one that we need as a background for learning about qualitative analysis. In itself, it has no 'validity'. Or better: the diagram (which is a device cherished by researchers whose place is on top of the diagram) is no more valid than the palette metaphor (a device cherished by those on the bottom). Both serve to illuminate, and both distort.

Graphic Overview of Qualitative Research Types

The research interest is in . . .

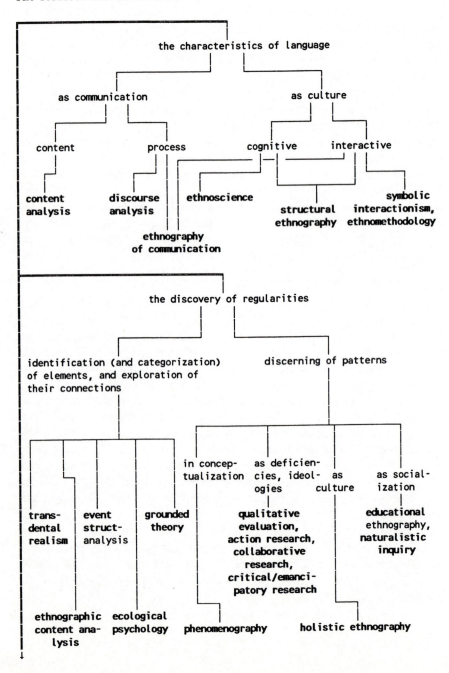

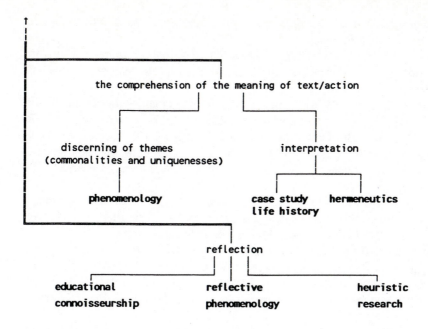

References

ALTHEIDE, DAVID L. (1987, Spring) 'Ethnographic content analysis', *Qualitative Sociology*, 10, 1, pp. 65-7.

BAILY, KENNETH D. (1987) *Methods of Social Research*, New York, The Free Press.

BAKEMAN, ROGER and GOTTMAN, JOHN M. (1986) *Observing Interaction: An Introduction to Sequential Analysis*, Cambridge, MA, Cambridge University Press.

BARRITT, LOREN; BEEKMAN, TON; BLEEKER, HANS and MULDERIJ, KAREL (1985) *Researching Education Practice*, Grand Forks, ND, University of North Dakota, Center for Teaching and Learning.

BARZUN, JACQUES and GRAFF, HENRY F. (1977) *The Modern Researcher*, New York, Harcourt Brace Jovanovich, Inc.

BATESON, GREGORY (1978, Summer) 'The pattern which connects', *Co-Evolution Quarterly*, pp. 5-15.

BERG, DAVID N. and SMITH, KENWYN K. (Eds.) (1985) *Exploring Clinical Methods for Social Research*, Beverly Hills, CA, Sage Publications.

CARR, WILFRED and KEMMIS, STEPHEN (1986) *Becoming Critical: Education, Knowledge and Action Research*, Lewes, The Falmer Press.

COLAIZZI, PAUL F. (1978) 'Psychological research as the phenomenologist views it', in VALLE, RONALD S. and KING, MARK (Eds.) *Existential-*

Phenomenological Alternatives for Psychology, New York, Oxford University Press.

DOUGLAS, BRUCE G. and MOUSTAKAS, CLARK (1985, Summer) 'Heuristic inquiry: The internal search to know', *Journal of Humanistic Psychology*, 25, 3, pp. 39-55.

EISNER, ELLIOT W. (1976) 'Educational connoisseurship and criticism: Their form and function in educational evaluation', *The Journal of Aesthetic Education*, The University of Illinois Press, pp. 135-50.

EISNER, ELLIOT W. (1981, April) 'On the differences between scientific and artistic approaches to qualitative research', *Educational Researcher*, 10, 4, pp. 5-9.

ERICKSON, FREDERICK (1986) 'Qualitative methods in research on teaching', in WITTROCK, MERLIN C. (Ed.) *Handbook of Research on Teaching*, Third edition, New York, Macmillan Publishing Company.

GIORGI, AMEDEO (1975) 'Convergence and divergence of qualitative and quantitative methods in psychology', in GIORGI, AMEDEO; FISCHER, CONSTANCE and MURRAY, EDWARD (Eds.) *Duquesne Studies in Phenomenological Psychology*, Vol. 2, 72-9, Pittsburgh, PA, Duquesne University Press.

GLASER, BARNEY G. and STRAUSS, ANSELM L. (1967) *The Discovery of Grounded Theory: Strategies for Qualitative Research*, Chicago, Aldine Publishing Company.

GOETZ, JUDITH P. and LECOMPTE, MARGARET D. (1984) *Ethnography and Qualitative Design in Educational Research*, Orlando, FL, Academic Press.

GOODSON, IVOR (1985) 'History, context and qualitative method in the study of curriculum', in BURGESS, ROBERT G. (Ed.) *Strategies of Educational Research: Qualitative Methods*, Lewes, The Falmer Press, pp. 121-52.

GUBRIUM, JABER (1988) *Analyzing Field Reality*, Beverly Hills, CA, Sage Publications.

HALFPENNY, PETER (1981, November) 'Teaching ethnographic data analysis in postgraduate courses in sociology', *Journal of the British Sociological Association*, 15, 4, pp. 564-70.

HEISE, DAVID R. (1988, Spring) 'Computer analysis of cultural structures', *Social Science Computer Review*, 6, 1, pp. 183-97.

JACOB, EVELYN (1987, Spring) 'Qualitative research traditions: A review', *Review of Educational Research*, 57, 1, pp. 1-50.

LINCOLN, YVONNA and GUBA, EGON (1985) *Naturalistic Inquiry*, Beverly Hills, CA, Sage Publications.

MARTON, FERENCE (1986, Fall) 'Phenomenography - A research approach to investigating different understandings of reality', *Journal of Thought*, 21, 3, pp. 28-48.

MAXWELL, A. E. (1975) *Analyzing Qualitative Data*, New York, Halsted Press.

MILES, MATTHEW B. and HUBERMAN, A. MICHAEL (1984) *Qualitative Data Analysis: A Sourcebook of New Methods*, Beverly Hills, CA, Sage Publications.

MOUSTAKAS, CLARK (1981) 'Heuristic research', in REASON, PETER and ROWAN, JOHN (Eds.) *Human Inquiry: A Sourcebook of New Paradigm Research*, New York, John Wiley and Sons, pp. 207-17.

PARLETT, MALCOLM and HAMILTON, DAVID (1972) 'Evaluation as illumination: A new approach to the study of innovatory programs', Occasional paper, Edinburgh: Centre for Research in the Educational Sciences, University of Edinburgh.

PATTON, MICHAEL Q. (1980) *Qualitative Evaluation Methods*, Beverly Hills, CA, Sage Publications.

POLANYI, MICHAEL (1958) *Personal Knowledge*, Chicago, IL, The University of Chicago Press.

POLKINGHORNE, DONALD E. (1982, Summer) 'What makes research humanistic?' *Journal of Humanistic* Polkinghorne, Donald E. (1983) *Methodology for the Human Sciences*, Albany, State University of New York Press.

RATHJE, W. L. (1984) 'The garbage decade', *American Behavioral Scientist*, 28, 1, pp. 9-29.

ROWAN, JOHN and REASON, PETER (1981) 'On making sense', in REASON, PETER and ROWAN, JOHN (Eds.) *Human Inquiry: A Sourcebook of New Paradigm Research*, Chichester, NY, John Wiley and Sons.

SPRADLEY, JAMES P. (1979) *The Ethnographic Interview*, New York, Holt, Rinehart and Winston.

SPRADLEY, JAMES P. (1980) *Participant Observation*, New York, Holt, Rinehart and Winston.

SUCHMAN, E. A. (1967) *Evaluative Research: Principles and Practice in Public Service and Social Action Programs*, New York, Russell Sage Foundation.

TESCH, RENATA (1987) 'Emerging themes: The researcher's experience', *Phenomenology + Pedagogy*, 5, 3, pp. 230-41.

TORBERT, WILLIAM R. (1983) 'Initiating collaborative inquiry', in MORGAN, GARETH (Ed.) *Beyond Method*, Beverly Hills, CA, Sage Publications.

VAN DIJK, TEUN A. (Ed.) (1985) *Handbook of Discourse Analysis, Vol. 4*, London, Academic Press.

Webster's Third New International Dictionary (1964) Springfield, MA, G. and C. Merriam Company.

WERNER, OSWALD and SCHOEPFLE, G. MARK (1987) *Systematic Fieldwork, Vol. 2*, Beverly Hills, CA, Sage Publications.

Types of Qualitative Analysis

Introduction

The fact that distinctions can be made among at least twenty-six different kinds of approaches to qualitative research may seem discouraging. Does it mean that we have to learn about twenty-six different data analysis procedures as well? The answer is: no. The world of research is not tidy enough to provide us with a neat one-to-one correspondence between research interests and analysis procedures. For some approaches with a long tradition, such as ethnography or content analysis, the analysis process has become quite well defined. In more recent ones, such as collaborative inquiry or discourse analysis (which dates back only to the 1970's), researchers are still exploring and inventing individually. In some cases, scholars have adopted analysis procedures of related approaches, and in still others researchers use their own terminology, but their steps and modes are in effect quite similar to some others that have been described in different words.

If individual research approaches don't each have their characteristic and unique analysis procedures, is there at least some correspondence between the four basic qualitative research groups we have distinguished and their dominant analysis strategies? Even here matters are not as clear-cut as one might wish. However, there are at least a few basic observations that can be made about each group. Researchers who have the same fundamental interests when working with words do treat their data in somewhat similar ways. Let us recall the major distinctions. To achieve a better overview at one glance, we will translate part of our original 'map' into another form. This time it is a structured listing, or what has come to be called an 'outline' format:

The research interest can be in:

1. **the characteristics of language**
   a. as communication
      i. with regard to its content
      ii. with regard to its process
   b. as it mirrors culture
      i. in terms of the cognitive structure
      ii. in terms of the interactive process
2. **the discovery of regularities**
   a. as the identification and categorization of elements and the establishment of their connections
   b. as the identification of patterns
3. **the comprehension of the meaning of text or action**
   a. through the discovery of themes
   b. through interpretation
4. **reflection**

As you may remember, the sequence of the items in this outline is not arbitrary. From the top to the bottom the approaches to research become less structured, less formal, and more 'humanistic' both in terms of the human sciences (as non-positivistic) as well as in terms of the humanities. At the extreme at the top (under 1), some of the studies are so structured that they are more quantitative in nature than qualitative.

In stark contrast to those types of research that are formalized to the point of being quantifiable stand those listed under 4 (the research interest is in reflection), where there is no formal data analysis procedure at all. This being so, not much can be said about the way data are analyzed. The practitioners of these kinds of research, if asked, probably would inform us that the analysis requires, in addition to imaginative activities, a great deal of disciplined thinking. However, I was unable to find any detailed description of the way this systematic 'reflection' works. In fact, in one case (phenomenological reflection) we are told by an otherwise extremely clear and articulate author: 'For reasons intrinsic to reflecting activity and thinking in general, this method cannot be articulated separate from its results; it can be communicated only by providing examples of it' (Colaizzi, 1978, p. 68). Consequently, we are excused from the task of describing the analysis procedures for 'reflective' types of research.

The two middle portions of the outline (2 and 3: research that deals with the discovery of regularities, and research where the interest is in the comprehension of the meaning of text or action) are the most homogenous in terms of the analysis processes used in each. As usual, there are overlaps between the two groups, and even some overlap with the 'language characteristics' group.

In the remainder of this chapter, you will find brief descriptions of the analysis procedures of each research approach <Research types> in groups 1 to 3. At the end, there is a summary, where we have distilled some criteria according to which major analysis types can be grouped together or distinguished from each other. To read the main corpus of this chapter is not essential for understanding the summary at the end. You may read on for an overview, or skip to only those types of analysis that interest you, or you may go directly to the summary.

Analysis in Types of Research where the Interest is in the *Characteristics of Language* as Communication or as the Cognitive Representation of Culture

The labels in this group are **content analysis, discourse analysis, ethnoscience, ethnography of communication, structural ethnography, symbolic interactionism,** and **ethnomethodology**. The span from content analysis to ethnomethodology is a long one; except for the fact that both are focussing on language, there is not much they have in common. The qualitative dimensions of content analysis are limited, while symbolic interactionism and ethnomethodology are seen by some as 'falling within the phenomenological tradition' (Bogdan and Taylor, 1975, p. 13), a 'meaning-oriented' type of research. Among the approaches in the middle group, discourse analysis and the ethnography of communication have some commonalities with respect to analysis, and ethnoscience and structural ethnography do as well. Thus, we will divide this cluster into four groups: a. content analysis, b. discourse analysis and ethnography of communication, c. ethnoscience and structural ethnography, and d. symbolic interactionism and ethnomethodology.

Content analysis

'A central idea in content analysis is that the many words of the text are classified into much fewer content categories' (Weber, 1985, p. 7). While the 'recording units' are sometimes larger than words (sentences, paragraphs, or themes), the basic procedure in content analysis is to design categories that are relevant to the research purpose and to sort all occurrences of relevant words or other recording units into these categories. For instance, someone doing a content analysis of this book could decide to sort words or sentences into the categories 'computer-related' and 'epistemology-related'. Then the frequency of occurrences in each category would be counted, and certain conclusions could be drawn about whether this book is more informative about computers or about the philosophical roots of research approaches. In actual studies, researchers have been able to infer from such frequency counts important propositions about the existence of propaganda in political documents, about differences in the attention focus between men and women in certain situations, about the psychological state of people or groups, and so on (*ibid.*, p. 9).

Another regularly used technique in content analysis is the taking of 'inventories' of words in a document or transcription. This is done by constructing exhaustive indices. Since the indices are then frequency ordered (usually with the most often used word at the top of the list), this strategy ends up also being numeric, as categorizing does. Inferences made from these inventories would also be similar to those drawn from the results of categorization. The only qualitative procedure in content analysis, i.e., the one in which numbers don't play any role at all, is the exploration of word usage, where researchers want to discover the range of meanings that a word can express in normal use. The method employed is the establishment of a 'key-word-in-context' index. The target words are extracted with a specified amount of text immediately preceding and following them. Researchers can then group together those words in which the meaning is similar and establish how broadly or narrowly a certain term is construed by the author of the text, or they may compare word uses among groups of authors.

Discourse analysis and ethnography of communication

Both discourse and the ethnography of communication are closely related to linguistics; they might even be called a form of sociolinguistics (Gumperz and Hymes, 1972). 'Sociolinguists study the routine speech and actions of people in social groups. They try to discover patterns of communication that have functional relevance for those people' (Florio-Ruane, 1987, p. 186). Discourse analysis usually is less context-imbedded, i.e., it focusses directly and solely on conversations or other language interactions, whereas the ethnography of communication keeps in mind the 'others in the scene' who constitute the actors' 'social ecology' (Erickson, 1986, p. 128). Otherwise, however, the topics chosen are much alike, and so are the analysis processes.

The analysis is done by 'index[ing] the whole recorded corpus' of data (*ibid.*, p. 145), or otherwise breaking down the 'record' (an actual audio or video recording) or 'protocol' (a transcription) into 'instances' that can be compared with others in the same data corpus and sorted. The goal is to either discover the 'structure' of the language interaction in terms of regularities that can then be described in more general terms as a 'model' and perhaps represented graphically, or to find 'linkages' so that the researcher can make 'assertions'. Examples of discourse analysts' assertions are: 'Those in lesser status roles display more question copy [i.e., they repeat the question they were asked] and less elaboration, suggesting that the form of response marks or conveys the respondent's view of his status relative to the questioner' (Urmston, 1984, p. 225). Or, 'there is some indication that strong disagreement is easier to declare in writing than face to face' (Mulkay, 1985, p. 201).

A communications ethnographer, on the other hand, may assert that: 'School difficulties of Indian children [can be traced] to differences in their cultural based, tacit understanding of appropriate ways of getting along with peers and learn from adults' (Florio-Ruane, 1987, p. 190). These assertions are 'general' descriptions, as compared to mere 'particular' descriptions, and are based on a 'pattern' found in the data. Sometimes, the linkages between the 'universal' instances (universal within the body of data) can be represented in diagrams or some other graphic form <ETHNO>.

Ethnoscience and structural ethnography

Both ethnoscience and structural ethnography are based on the proposition that 'because language is the primary means for transmitting culture from one generation to the next, much of any culture is encoded in linguistic form' (Spradley, 1979, p. 9). The two approaches are distinguished merely by a greater emphasis among ethnoscientists on reduction as an analysis principle and the view that the application of statistical procedures constitutes a desirable expansion of their work (Werner and Schoepfle, 1987, vol. 2, pp. 25, 37), while structural ethnographers pay more attention to the definitional meanings in language and see their work as culminating in the discovery of cultural themes as larger patterns within, or 'world views' of, cultures (Spradley, *ibid.*, pp. 156, 186). For structural ethnographers 'the end product of doing ethnography is a verbal description of the cultural scenes covered' (*ibid.*, p. 21), whereas ethnoscientists equate the end product with 'an expert system - a data base to which anyone interested in the lives of the natives can refer' (Werner and Schoepfle, 1987, vol. 2, p. 23). These differences are more pronounced in the scholars' rhetoric, however, than in their practice. The analytic procedures for ethnoscience and structural ethnography are quite similar.

The characteristic data gathering device is the elicitation of material through direct questioning. The ethnographer begins the process with a 'friendly conversation', and the ethnoscientist also includes 'conversational interviews' as 'samples of native language'; but in both approaches, most data come as responses to questions about 'naming units' (words and phrases) and 'the relationships between naming units' (Werner and Schoepfle, 1987, vol. 2, p. 30). For example, when studying the academic culture, the naming units could be 'ethnography' and 'ethnoscience', and the researcher would infer what the relationship is between these two terms by asking members of that culture how they use the terms. The task of the analyst is to deduce the structure of the culture's cognitive universe from these data. This structure is seen specifically as a 'folk system of classification' (*ibid.*, p. 31), or a 'lexical/semantic field' (*ibid.*, p. 15).

The first step usually is to identify 'folk terms' that may be 'cover terms', i.e., 'terms that are being used for more than one thing' (Spradley, 1979, p. 104), such as 'qualitative research'. Then the researcher would explore what the semantic relationships are between the cover term and its related terms, such as 'X is a kind of Y, X is a result of Y, X is a part of Y, X is used for Y, X is a stage in Y, X is a characteristic of Y', and so on (*ibid.*, p. 111). These relationships are often depicted in diagrams, such as grids or other structured boxes, outline- or tree-shaped taxonomies (much like the ones for qualitative research approaches in this book), flow charts, decision tables, overlapping circles, star burst charts (with one term in the center and the related terms around the periphery), causal chains or networks, or anything else the researcher can invent. All of them can be thought of as cognitive maps (Werner and Schoepfle, 1987, p. 24). The analysis process has broken 'down the sequential, linear order of texts into the non-linear, network-like semantic structures that underlie these texts' (*ibid.*, p. 30).

Symbolic interactionism and ethnomethodology

While the analysis processes in ethnoscience and structural ethnography have been described explicitly and almost exhaustively (Werner and Schoepfle, 1987, Spradley, 1979), little is available that tells scholars exactly how to go about conducting an ethnomethodological or symbolic interactionist research project. Ethnomethodologists have even been accused of an 'admitted inability - or at least reluctance - . . . . to adequately describe their methods' (Rogers, 1983, p. 104).

There are, however, specific techniques that ethnomethodologists employ. One is to have people write down verbatim an actual conversation and then add at each point what they understood the other person to have said (Garfinkel, 1967, p. 25). The most distinctive ethnomethodological technique, however, is the 'incongruity procedure'. Since the ethnomethodologist is interested in the aspects of daily life that are most taken for granted, i.e., how people achieve the implicit 'shared agreement' apparent in their dealings with each other and the world, one way to expose the *how* is to shatter the agreement. 'By producing confusion, anxiety, bewilderment, and disorganized interaction, [the ethnomethodologist] attempts to discover what is otherwise hidden: the common sense everyday rules of social interaction' (Bogdan and Taylor, 1975, p. 127). For example, in a field experiment, the researcher disrupts the common sense understanding by having someone act explicitly outside of the 'rules', such as trying to bargain in a store rather than paying the set price, getting physically too close to another person in a conversation, or displaying other unusual and provocative behaviors (*ibid.*, p. 127). The researcher then observes how the actors in the situation 'repair' the incongruity. How to analyze the resulting records is left to the individual researcher; there is no handbook for ethnomethodology. Occasionally, one can find vague reference to phenomenological procedures in ethnomethodological writings, particular to the 'invariant' characteristics of the observed events. We will describe phenomenological procedures later.

The analysis process of symbolic interactionism is easier to describe, since some members of the 'Chicago School' of sociologists, with which this term is usually associated, have provided detailed accounts of their methods (Bogdan and Biklen, 1982, p. 32; Jacob, 1987, p. 27). Interactionists assume that 'people are constantly in a process of interpretation and definition as they move from one situation to another' (Bogdan and Taylor, 1975, p. 14). This is not a conscious process that anyone can simply describe when asked. The researcher has to infer the salient features of this operation by collecting all kinds of data (by interviewing, examining personal documents, but particularly by observing) and then extracting from these records the material that is relevant to the question the researcher asks. Such a question could be: What are the varying perspectives of medical students during the course of their school career? A study of this kind was done by Howard Becker and his colleagues (Becker *et al.*, 1961), and these researchers are the scholars who have taken most care in describing their methods. The following is taken mostly from one of their accounts.

The end result of a symbolic interactionist study, according to Blumer (whose name is intimately related to the beginnings of symbolic interactionism), is the formulation of propositions about relationships among categories of data, which the researcher weaves into a 'theoretical scheme' (Blumer, 1969, p. 48). The process that leads to such propositions is comprised of three steps. First the researcher constructs tentative propositions from her/his observations about the existence of a phenomenon and perhaps about the co-occurrence and possible relationship between two observed phenomena (Becker and Geer, 1982, p. 241). In a second stage, the researcher finds out whether the events that prompted the development of these propositions and their potential relationships are 'typical and widespread' (*ibid.*, p. 242). Lastly, the concrete individual findings are used to confirm, disconfirm, or modify the propositions, resulting in 'a descriptive model which best explains the data [the researcher] has assembled' (*ibid.*, p. 243).

In practice, the three stages are not distinct. Concrete data are gathered and analyzed throughout the entire project. The 'running summary' of field notes is broken down into separate incidents. An incident is a 'complete verbal expression of an attitude, or complete acts by an individual or groups', which the researcher summarizes (*ibid.*, p. 245). Each summarized incident is marked 'with a number or numbers that stand for the various areas to which it appears to be relevant' (*ibid.*). This is also called 'coding into categories', and one incident may be coded under several categories. Categories (or interpretive 'perspectives') have been tentatively identified during the beginning stages of the research project. When they become 'filled' with data, the researcher is able to 'formulate a more differentiated statement of the content' of the category (*ibid.*, p. 246). Once each category is properly characterized, the researcher finds out how frequent the occurrence of that 'perspective' is, how widely distributed it is (its 'range'), and how much it is shared among the group of people studied. The researcher also looks for 'negative cases' whose lack would assure the validity of the 'perspective'. The findings are presented as a set of statements about 'the necessary and sufficient conditions for the existence of some phenomenon', statements that some phenomenon is an 'important' or 'basic' element in the organization, or 'statements identifying a situation as an instance of some process or phenomenon described more abstractly in sociological theory' (*ibid.*, p. 243).

This concludes our survey of the analysis procedures of language-oriented types of qualitative research. As you might have noticed, toward the end of this section we have gained more and more distance from the emphasis on language, and instead began dealing with the study of social entities. The analysis procedures described most recently are, as we will show, not applicable only to symbolic interactionism, but could be used in other types of research as well, especially those that we have grouped under the heading of 'interest in the discovery of regularities'. That is the cluster of research types we will look at next.

Analysis in Types of Research where the Interest is in the *Discovery of Regularities* as the Identification and Categorization of Elements and the Establishment of their Connections, or as the Identification of Patterns

The two subgroups within this cluster of research approaches are distinguished from each other mostly by one feature: For some researchers it is important to establish linkages between/among the elements that they have identified and classified, while others aim mostly at systematic and insightful description of the phenomenon under study.

Establishing relationships is commonly considered by researchers to be the first step in theory-building. Since symbolic interactionists consider theory-building, or the development of conceptual schemes, a desirable outcome, it should not come as a surprise that their procedures for conducting data analysis, as we have just described them, are quite similar to the ones used by researchers who are interested in 'connections'. In fact, Anselm Strauss, one of the two scholars who are viewed as the inventors of the grounded theory approach (the other is Barney Glaser), was a student of Blumer's and a co-researcher with Howard Becker in the symbolic interactionist study in medical school. To some extent, the analysis methods used in the types of research listed in this group are variations of symbolic interactionism procedures. All of them seem to have some basic processes in common, although they are not necessarily derivations of each other. However, if each were described separately, there would be quite a bit of repetition. Therefore, I will sketch out the basic process first, and then report on the variants.

Research in which Connections among the Identified and Categorized Elements are Sought

As mentioned earlier, the difference between this group of research types (**grounded theory, transcendental realism, ethnographic content analysis, event structure analysis,** and **ecological psychology**) and the 'pattern' group is that those researchers who seek 'connections' seek 'explanations'. They try to find out more than just *what is*; they also try to find out *why* it is. Seeking explanations is the same as 'theorizing'. The analysis procedures used in this cluster of research approaches, therefore, must be designed to facilitate theorizing. A single research project does not produce an entire social theory, but it can develop a set of theoretical propositions. Explanatory propositions are statements about relationships, such as 'X exists because. . .; given X, then Y will follow; X is necessary but not sufficient for Y to occur; X causes Y' (Miles and Huberman, 1984, p. 72). Consequently, the researcher's first analysis goal is to find the entities that s/he will call X or Y.

In **grounded theory** construction these entities are called 'categories'. Such categories may be derived from existing theories, but that procedure is tolerated more than it is encouraged (Glaser and Strauss, 1967, p. 45/46). In fact, the entire point of theory construction is 'to produce concepts that seem to fit the data' (Strauss, 1987, p. 28). These concepts are provisional at first. They are developed in a process called 'open coding' (*ibid.*), in which the analyst looks at the data line by line for 'empirical indicators', consisting of 'behavioral actions and events, observed and described in documents and in the words of interviewees and informants' (*ibid.*, p. 25). S/he 'asks of the data a set of questions' (*ibid.*, p. 30), one of which is, 'What category does this incident indicate?' (*ibid.*). A provisional code name is given to that category, and codes proliferate quickly. 'But the process later begins to slow down through the continual verifying that each code really does fit. . .' (*ibid.*, p. 32). 'Theoretical memos' which form a 'running record of insights, hunches, hypotheses, discussions about the implications of codes, additional thoughts, whatnot' (*ibid.*, p. 110), are kept by the researcher and 'move the analyst further from the data and into a more analytic realm' (*ibid.*, p. 32). Once the researcher has become sure of a category, s/he may engage in 'axial coding', which 'consists of intense analysis done around one category at a time. . . This results in cumulative knowledge about relationships between that category and other categories and subcategories' (*ibid.*). Using specific criteria, the analyst eventually chooses one or more categories as the 'core' categories. At this point, 'selective' coding begins, i.e., 'the analyst delimits coding to only those codes that relate to the core codes in sufficiently significant ways as to be used in a parsimonious theory' (*ibid.*, p. 33).

Glaser and Strauss coined the terms 'constant comparison' to describe the process of progressive category clarification and definition, and the term 'theoretical sampling' to refer to the decision 'what data to collect next and where to find them' (Glaser and Strauss, 1967, p. 45).

Many of the principles underlying grounded theory construction were employed in the studies that yielded the material for Miles and Huberman's book on *Qualitative Data Analysis* (1984) - although Strauss (1987, p. 55) feels that these authors misunderstood some of the grounded theory technology. Miles and Huberman also explicitly wish 'to interpret and explain . . . phenomena and have confidence that others, using the same tools, would arrive at analogous conclusions' (Miles and Huberman, 1984, p. 20). The authors' stance is characterized by the term **transcendental realism**. Their book is not so much an explication of one approach, however, as a compilation of individual methods for collecting, sorting, displaying, and comprehending data that are useful for researchers who wish to develop theoretical propositions. It is a 'sourcebook', as the authors quite fittingly mention in the subtitle.

As in symbolic interactionism and grounded theory, researchers do not wait to begin analyzing their data until *after* all of them are collected. The two processes run parallel to each other and are informed by each other. Data collecting dominates the earlier phases, while data analyzing dominates the later ones; the first analytic steps, however, are taken by the researcher as soon as an initial set of data is gathered.

The analysis units are 'segments of text' (or 'incidents' in grounded theory and symbolic interactionist terminology) <Interpretational analysis>. Segments are 'classified' by 'coding' them <Qualitative analysis programs>. 'Codes are categories. . . . They are retrieval and organizing devices that allow the analysis to spot quickly, pull out, and then cluster all the segments relating to the particular question, hypothesis, concept, or theme. Clustering sets the stage for analysis' (Miles and Huberman, 1984, p. 56). The codes are not numbers, however, as used by symbolic interactionists; they consist of a few letters symbolizing the substance of the category. They are indicators, so to speak, of the content of a segment.

The categories for which these codes stand are generated from the researcher's questions or hypotheses, or from problem areas and key concepts s/he considers relevant at the outset of the study. They could also be derived from the data themselves (which is the preferred method in grounded theory creation). Not infrequently, both methods are combined, because 'other codes emerge progressively during data collection' (*ibid.*, p. 60), even when the study's conceptual framework has already yielded most of the codes.

A category is not untouchable once it has been developed. As the data collection and coding process unfolds, it will turn out that 'some codes don't work; others decay. . . . Other codes flourish, . . . Too many segments get the same code. This calls for breaking down codes into subcodes' (*ibid.*, p. 60).

In the types of research where connections among elements are sought, the analysis process must be accompanied by the researcher's constant search for configurations in the data that suggest that certain pieces of data belong together, or that an individual piece is an instance of a more general class of events or ideas. These emerging analytic notions are written down, as they occur, in researcher 'memos'. 'Memos are always conceptual in intent' (*ibid.*, p. 69). From them the researcher begins 'to identify an emergent theme, pattern, or explanation' (*ibid.*, p. 67), and generates ideas for further data collection, as well as category modification. 'Without memoing, there is little opportunity to understand how adequate the original framework is' (*ibid.*, p. 71).

When a considerable number of analytic memos has been accumulated, it is time to begin the conclusion-drawing process, i.e., the process that will lead to the formulation of the theoretical propositions the researcher has discovered in her/his data. The clustering of the data segments according to categories has set the stage for this activity. Each cluster, as a conceptual entity, could be called a 'variable'. The task for the researcher is to explore possible relationships of these variables (or 'categories' in grounded theory) to each other.

Miles and Huberman suggest 'an especially economic way to see [relationships]': the construction of matrix displays (*ibid.*, p. 225). Matrices are basically criss-crossed boxes in which one set of variables forms the headings for the columns, and another set (or time segments, role definitions, 'critical incidents', and so on) forms the headings for the rows. Other useful types of graphical displays are: process or sequence maps, where individual small boxes (one for each variable) are connected with arrows running from the left to the right, and sometimes branching; and context charts, flow charts, and causal maps, where the small boxes (or circles) are connected with arrows going in all directions, according to associative, temporal, or causal relationships.

Using these techniques, the researcher gets 'an initial sense of the main factors, plotting the logical relationships tentatively, testing them against the yield of the next wave of data collection, modifying and refining them into a new explanatory map, which then gets tested against new cases and instances' (*ibid.*, p. 228). After the researcher has employed a number of tactics to make sure that the postulated relationships are defensible (see Miles and Huberman, 1984, pp. 230-43), the 'chain of evidence' becomes confirmed, and the conclusions are cast into the form of conceptual statements that represent the results of the study.

While Glaser and Strauss and Miles and Huberman have provided extensive and thorough descriptions of their analysis procedures, only sparse information exists on how to handle data in other approaches. The descriptions in this book, therefore, must remain comparatively sketchy.

Ecological psychology's data are not general field notes or interview transcriptions, but behavior descriptions collected by trained observers during a 'behavior episode', called 'specimen records'. The person's surroundings and the events that occur during that period are recorded in parallel. The 'stream of behavior' is then divided into units ('episodes'), the features of which are painstakingly described. They are sorted and counted. The corresponding ecological units are called 'environmental force units'. The goal of the ecological psychologist is to discover the rule structure that governs the behavior of a typical actor, i.e., the laws of behavior (Jacob, 1987 pp. 5-9; von Eckartsberg, 1978, p. 199).

Ethnographic content analysis applies grounded theory to documents, although one researcher may use both quantitative methods (as described earlier) and qualitative ones. Unlike traditional content analysis, which employs fixed categories for coding of words and phrases, 'categories' and 'variables' initially merely guide the study, and others 'are allowed and expected to emerge throughout the study' (Altheide, 1987, p. 68).

Event structure analysis or qualitative sequential analysis uses 'events' as the unit of analysis. They are the elements among which the connections are sought. Events in real life or in stories happen in a chronological order. However, there is an underlying 'logical structure' according to which they happen. It would not make sense for some events to occur at certain points, because certain conditions have not been met. Furthermore, the story or actual event takes one turn every time a prior event is completed, when there are actually several possibilities of events that could occur instead. That is the kind of logical structure the event analyst is interested in.

David Heise calls these logical structures 'production grammars' (Heise, 1988, p. 187). Each element/event is isolated, and its connections to other events are listed (which events have to have happened for this event to become possible, and which other events are now possible because of the occurrence of this event). A preferred method of data display are 'directed graphs', in which 'nodes symbolize elements, and lines between nodes show relations' (*ibid.*, p. 185). These graphs usually take the form of dendograms, i.e., inverted tree diagrams. Once the logical structure is discerned and displayed, the researcher can raise the diagram to a higher abstraction level by replacing concrete events with the appropriate 'class' of events of which the concrete event is an instance. Thus, eventually, the researcher can draw conclusions about the rules that govern the action in specific cases, which (especially in folk stories) may be representative of a larger cultural theme.

Research in which the Identification of Regularities is Sought in the Form of Patterns

To be sure, the 'laws' or 'rules' mentioned in the previous section are often also called 'patterns' by scholars. It would not be a correct statement to say that researchers who use one of the research types in this current cluster do not look for connections (they might call them 'linkages'). Thus, it seems not quite fitting to make distinctions using these terms. The problem is that the distinctions indeed are fuzzy. They are artificial to the extent that they have been created by me as heuristic devices: It is less overwhelming to talk about groups of items that have something in common and then to explain the differences, than it is to describe item by item fully.

This group (**phenomenography, qualitative evaluation, action research, collaborative inquiry, critical /emancipatory research, holistic ethnography, educational ethnography** and **naturalistic inquiry**) is clearly distinguished from the previous group by two commonalities: 1) conceptual categories for organizing the data are never established beforehand but derived from the data, and 2) the goal of generating theory has to share the limelight with the goal of systematic description.

A few things must be said about each of the two statements above. As concerns the first, scholars who have been trained as anthropologists know about the existence of an entire set of categories that can be applied to the ordering of ethnographic data: the Outline of Cultural Materials, developed by G. P. Murdock (1971). It consists of almost eighty main categories with up to nine subcategories in each to which code numbers are assigned. This list, however, consists of descriptive categories (not conceptual ones) that refer to a dimension of the culture, such as 'food consumption', 'tools and appliances', 'social stratification', 'offenses and sanctions', and so forth. The list is used for cross-cultural analysis or 'ethnology'. Descriptive material gathered by various ethnographers in different cultures can be coded with these numbers, and the cultures can then be compared according to the various dimensions.

The ethnographers in this group of research approaches do not use a list like the Outline of Cultural Materials. Rather, they develop a categorizing system from 'certain words, phrases, patterns of behavior, subjects' way of thinking, and events [that] repeat and stand out' (Bogdan and Biklen, 1982, p. 156).

Regarding the second statement, we must understand that although most researchers in this group maintain that theory generation is the ultimate goal of social science research, they are cautious about how much of this can be done in an individual study. Rather than claiming that any theory has been derived, researchers 'construct hypotheses . . . and *attempt* to demonstrate support for those . . . hypotheses' (Bogdan and Taylor, 1975, p. 79, emphasis mine). Ethnographers establish 'way-stations on the road to theory' such as 'concrete descriptions, typologies, or models', but 'there is no obligation on the part of an ethnographer to travel all the way [to theory] in any particular study' (Hammersley and Atkinson, 1983, p. 201). The findings of a study result in no more and no less than 'a coherent, valid, and analytically sound "account"' (Halfpenny, 1979, p. 817).

The analytic procedures used by researchers who seek to discover patterns are quite similar to those described in the previous section. Therefore, the following description is a not as complete as it could be; I am seeking to avoid repetition. First, I will review the way analysis is perceived by researchers in ethnography and naturalistic inquiry, then I will explain how these differ from the evaluative/action research approaches and from phenomenography.

Naturalistic inquirers, holistic ethnographers, and **educational ethnographers** speak of their analyses as 'inductive', 'generative', and 'constructive' (Goetz and LeCompte, 1981). Inductive analysis begins with empirical observations and builds theoretical categories, instead of sorting data pieces deductively into pre-established classes. The units of analysis or data segments are not predetermined, but are carved out from the data according to their meaning. Rather than verifying given notions or hypotheses, the work of these scholars is 'generative', i.e., it seeks to discover constructs and propositions (*ibid.*, p. 53/54).

The analysis is conducted concurrently with data collection. It begins with a thorough first reading of the data to get a sense of their scope, and to check for 'topics that occur and reoccur' (Bogdan and Taylor, 1975, p. 83), for 'recurring regularities' (Guba, 1978, p. 53), or for 'emerging themes or patterns' (Taylor and Bogdan, 1984, p. 131). This activity is accompanied by copious note-taking, in which the researcher's observations (about the data), hunches, and ideas are captured. It is the first step toward the development of categories that can be applied as an organizing scheme to the data. Therefore, the researcher is especially alert to the items in the data that point to content 'labels'.

Individual researchers have different 'recipes' for arriving at a preliminary set of categories. Once they are developed, the next step is 'unitizing' (Lincoln and Guba, 1985, p. 344) or 'segmenting' (Hammersley and Atkinson, 1983, p. 167) the data, i.e., dividing them into 'the smallest piece[s] of information about something that can stand by itself' (Lincoln and Guba, *ibid.*, p. 345). Now the categories are applied to the segments. This process is customarily called 'coding'. Those researchers who are influenced by the symbolic interactionist tradition still use numbers as codes (each category is represented by a number), while others prefer abbreviations of the category names, i.e., mnemonic codes.

The purpose of coding is to aggregate all data about the same topic or theme, so that each category can be studied individually. However, before the researcher can take this last step, the organizing system must be refined. In the process of coding the researcher usually discovers that the originally developed categories do not always fit. They might need to be renamed, modified in content, subdivided, discarded, or supplemented by new ones. Checking the appropriateness of the categories is especially necessary every time a new batch of data is gathered. Eventually the refining process stops, as the researcher becomes satisfied with the congruence of the data and the organizing system. Some researchers prepare a careful list of all categories, including their subdivisions; they may take the form of an 'outline' or diagram.

The final application of the categories to the data segments yields that sought-for organization of the data in which they can be interpreted: each category contains all pieces from the entire data body that are relevant to that category. The researcher now looks for the configurations within each category in order to describe their content, and for linkages across categories. 'One looks to see whether any interesting patterns can be identified; whether anything stands out as surprising or puzzling; how the data relate to what one might have expected on the basis of common-sense knowledge, official accounts, or previous theory; and whether there are apparent inconsistencies or contradictions . . .' (Hammersley and Atkinson, 1983, p. 178). The results might be systematic 'thick' descriptions (Geertz, 1973, p. 26), typologies, freshly developed concepts, working hypotheses, or propositions.

Scholars who use research for the purpose of **evaluation** follow the described process more or less, but they do begin with a couple of initial categories that are part of every evaluative study: 'program process' and 'program impact' (Patton, 1980, p. 320). These categories, of course, are expanded greatly during the course of analysis. The results are more narrowly directed toward certain goals than those of general ethnographers; they will deal with relationships between needs and solutions, and the ways in which to modify and improve program designs. I have found no accounts by **action/collaborative** researchers and **critical science** researchers about their

91

data analysis, but since one of their goals is to discern regularities, they must be using procedures much like the ones I have described above.

Phenomenographers, on the other hand, have provided quite detailed reports (Marton, 1986). Their units of analysis are 'utterances'. Illustrative utterances from each interview (phenomenographers use primarily interviews) are selected as 'quotes', and these quotes are preliminarily sorted on the basis of their similarity. Groups of quotes are arranged and rearranged, the 'criterion attributes' of each group are made explicit, and eventually the meanings of each group begin to consolidate and to constitute a definite category (*ibid.*, p. 42/43). The research result is a sophisticated listing or 'mapping of the qualitatively different ways in which people experience, conceptualize, perceive and understand' those 'aspects of the world around them' that the study concentrated on (*ibid.*, p. 31).

The differences between the two subgroups in this section - researchers who primarily seek to establish relationships, and those who primarily seek to discover patterns - are slight. The former perhaps place more emphasis on the relation of the parts to the whole, and see memo-writing and category development as a first phase, code application as a second phase. But the distinctions between the two phases blur in practical application.

Analysis in Types of Research where the Interest is in the *Comprehension of the Meaning* of Text or Action

There are two subgroups in this cluster, which, in turn, encompass three types of research: phenomenology, case studies and life histories, and hermeneutics. Phenomenological analysis is already partly described by the subdivision in which I have placed this research approach: the discerning of themes. Let us see how this process differs from the ones we have already described.

Phenomenology: Not surprisingly, the analysis of data is begun in phenomenological research as soon as the first data are collected. They may consist of no more than a single interview. When the researcher gets ready to attend to her/his data, the first task is a conceptual one: the clarification of her/his own preconception of the phenomenon under study. In phenomenological terms this is called 'bracketing'. 'It means suspending as much as possible the researcher's meanings and interpretations and entering into the world of the unique individual who was interviewed' (Hycner, 1985, p. 281). Some researchers list their own presuppositions in writing, so that it becomes easier to hold them at bay. Of course, the phenomenological researcher knows that even then biases cannot be controlled completely.

Now the actual work with the data begins; first the researcher reads the entire data set. Phenomenological reading is more than a casual taking note of the content. The researcher immerses her/himself in the data, reads and rereads, and dwells with the data, so s/he may achieve closeness to them and a sense of the whole. When s/he is satisfied that the text has become accessible to her/him, two options are open for the next step. Some phenomenological researchers painstakingly delineate all 'meaning units' throughout the entire interview transcription and then decide which ones are relevant to the research questions asked (*ibid.*, p. 284; Giorgi, 1975, p. 87; Wertz, 1985, p. 167). Others look only for material that pertains to the phenomenon, then bound the meaning units that contain them (Colaizzi, 1978, p. 59; Barritt *et al.*, 1985, p. 41). A meaning unit is 'a part of the description whose phrases require each other to stand as a distinguishable moment' (Wertz, 1985, p. 165).

The content or 'theme' of each meaning unit is then restated by summarizing it or transforming it into a more professional (more abstract) language. If any of the meaning units from one interview protocol show similarities, they are clustered together. The researcher constantly goes back and forth between data and isolated themes, dialoguing with the text, so to speak, in order to achieve the most revelatory wording of a theme. Finally, the 'essential non-redundant themes' from one interview are 'tied together into a descriptive statement' (Giorgi, 1975, p. 88). This is a description on the 'specific' level, i.e., one that includes the specifics, or the concreteness of the one person's experience, in contrast to a 'general' description. A general description is obtained by comparing all specific descriptions and leaving out the particulars, centering instead on the 'transsituational' (*ibid.*, p. 88). This latter process is called by phenomenologists the 'identification of the fundamental structure' of the phenomenon (Colaizzi, 1978, p. 61). The result describes the 'constituents' of which the particular human experience that is being studied is comprised.

Although working with one data document at a time before comparing across cases seems to be a hallmark of phenomenological analysis, a few phenomenological researchers deviate from that practice (Barritt *et al.*, 1985, p. 43; Tesch, 1987, p. 233). 'The goal of the analysis is to find common themes' (Barritt *et al.*, 1985, p. 41), and even when phenomenologists summarize each protocol before going on to the next, there still is a lot of comparing done across protocols in order to find these common themes. Unlike most other researchers, phenomenologists also pay attention to unique themes that illustrate the range of the meanings of the phenomenon.

The characteristic mode of analysis of **hermeneutics, case studies**, and **life histories**, our last set of research types, is 'dialoguing with the data'. The three research approaches are considered together, because all call for 'interpretation'. Life histories are written text, and even in case studies the materials are written accounts of the 'story' of the case. They differ from all other types of research we have discussed (except content analysis and event structure analysis) in that the analysis is usually concerned with one piece of data and what it means, not with the regularities or patterns across many pieces of a similar kind.

The early producers of case studies left few accounts of their analytic procedures. They simply 'made sense' of the data they had collected, and the result of the analysis was an instructive 'portrait', the case having been selected for its 'typical' nature in the first place. (Some modern quantitative researchers identify variables within a single case and try to 'explain' them by proposing causal links among them.)

When researchers study and interpret a text hermeneutically, they try to discern what it means. They read the text in as thorough a fashion as possible. Just as in phenomenological analysis, the 'identification of aspects' is allowed to 'develop' (Packer, 1985, p. 1091). One of the main principles in doing hermeneutics is to consider each part of the text in relationship to the whole. The part receives its meaning from that whole. Once each part becomes better understood, through this association with the whole, the whole itself becomes more transparent. In the light of this new understanding of the whole the parts are interpreted again. This principle is called the 'hermeneutic circle'. Another hermeneutic principle is to place the text in its biographical context, i.e., to take into account not only the author and her/his personal circumstances, but the larger social and historical situation in which s/he found herself. The actual text is then reflected upon in the light of that context.

The result of a hermeneutical analysis is not a set of propositions, but 'clarification and elucidation', and 'greatly increased and differentiated sensitivity' to the substance of the text (*ibid.*, pp. 1089, 1091).

Summary

By now it may seem to you that there are too many types of qualitative research and too many different ways of handling qualitative data, and you are right. There are too many types to keep in mind all of them, which is what you will need to do when we go on to examine the role of the computer in qualitative data analysis. So, let us try to make things a bit easier.

There are several methods by which to achieve a better overview. One is to group the analysis types into fewer categories according to their similarities (to which we will return shortly). Another is to examine whether there are characteristics that all types of analysis have in common. For the latter, the condensed accounts I have provided in the preceding pages do not afford quite enough information. However, I have studied quite extensively the analysis descriptions that researchers and methodologists have supplied in their publications. In fact, I conducted what could be called a qualitative analysis of texts that describe qualitative analysis principles and procedures. I applied to the texts some of the same procedures described earlier in this chapter. From the moment I began to review the texts I took notes, tentatively derived categories, excerpted relevant portions, periodically scanned again the whole book or article to make sure I did not misinterpret the excerpts, continually compared excerpts from one text to those of others, refined my categories, collapsed or discarded some of them (there were thirteen at one point), played around with ideas about how to arrange and how to express my 'results', and then spent a lot of time finding a 'generalized' way of characterizing each item (category) succinctly.

I concluded that no characteristics are common to all types of analysis. The situation changes, however, if we narrow somewhat the range of analysis types. Look again at the tail- and front-ends of our chart at the end of the chapter on research types. At one pole of the continuum we find quite formal, partly quantitative types of research, on the other research in which the data analysis process cannot even be articulated. If we leave out those 'extremes', we have fewer constraints. Indeed, I found that there are at least ten principles and practices that hold true for the remaining types of analysis, from ethnomethodology to phenomenology (in addition, of course, to the usual principles of good scholarship such as honesty and ethical conduct).

1. **Analysis is not the last phase in the research process; it is concurrent with data collection or cyclic.** It begins as soon as a first set of data is gathered and does not only run parallel to data collection, but the two become 'integrated' (Glaser and Strauss, 1967, p. 109). They inform or even 'drive' each other (Miles and Huberman, 1984, p. 63).

2. **The analysis process is systematic and comprehensive, but not rigid.** It proceeds in an orderly fashion and requires discipline, an organized mind, and perseverance. The analysis ends only after new data no longer generate new insights; the process 'exhausts' the data.

3. **Attending to data includes a reflective activity that results in a set of analytical notes that guide the process.** 'Memos', as these analytical notes are often called, not only 'help the analyst move easily from data to a conceptual level' (Miles and Huberman, 1984, p. 71), but they record the reflective and the concrete process and, therefore, provide accountability.

4. **Data are 'segmented', i.e., divided into relevant and meaningful 'units',** yet the connection to the whole is maintained. Since the

human mind is not able to process large amounts of diverse content all at once, the analyst concentrates on sets of smaller and more homogeneous chunks of material at any one time. However, the analysis always begins with reading all data to achieve 'a sense of the whole'. This sense fertilizes the interpretation of individual data pieces.

5. **The data segments are categorized according to an organizing system that is predominantly derived from the data themselves.** Large amounts of data cannot be processed unless all material that belongs together topically is assembled conceptually and physically in one place. Some topical categories, relating to a conceptual framework or to particular research questions, may exist before analysis begins, but for the most part the data are 'interrogated' with regard to the content items or themes they contain, and categories are formed as a result. The process is inductive.

6. **The main intellectual tool is comparison.** The method of comparing and contrasting is used for practically all intellectual tasks during analysis: forming categories, establishing the boundaries of the categories, assigning data segments to categories, summarizing the content of each category, finding negative evidence, etc. The goal is to discern conceptual similarities, to refine the discriminative power of categories, and to discover patterns.

7. **Categories for sorting segments are tentative and preliminary in the beginning; they remain flexible.** Since categories are developed mostly from the data material during the course of analysis, they must accommodate later data. They are modified accordingly and are refined until a satisfactory system is established. Even then the categories remain flexible working tools, not rigid end products; 'no order fits perfectly' (Lofland, 1971, p. 123).

8. **Manipulating qualitative data during analysis is an eclectic activity; there is no one 'right' way.** The researchers who have described the procedures they have used to analyze text data usually are wary about 'prescriptions'. They wish to avoid standardizing the process, since one hallmark of qualitative research is the creative involvement of the individual researcher. There is 'no fixed formula' (Barritt *et al.*, 1985, p. 5). 'It is possible to analyze any phenomenon in more than one way' (Spradley, 1979, p. 92), and 'each qualitative analyst must find his or her own process' (Patton, 1980, p. 299).

9. **The procedures are neither 'scientific' nor 'mechanistic';** qualitative analysis is 'intellectual craftsmanship' (Mills, 1959). On the one hand, there are no strict rules that can be followed mindlessly; on the other hand, the researcher is not allowed to be limitlessly inventive. Qualitative analysis can and should be done 'artfully'

(Guba and Lincoln, 1981, p. 185), even 'playfully' (Goetz and LeCompte, 1984, p. 172), but it also requires a great amount of methodological knowledge and intellectual competence.

10. **The result of the analysis is some type of higher-level synthesis.** While much work in the analysis process consists of 'taking apart' (for instance, into smaller pieces), the final goal is the emergence of a larger, consolidated picture. This could be a 'composite summary' (Hycner, 1985, p. 296), a description of 'patterns and themes' (Patton, 1980, p. 302), a 'final order' (Lofland, 1971, p. 118), an 'identification of the fundamental structure' of the phenomenon studied (Colaizzi, 1978, p. 61), a 'provisional hypothesis' (Turner, 1981, p. 237), a new concept or 'theoretical category' (Lazarsfeld, 1972, p. 225), or a 'substantive theory' (Glaser and Strauss, 1967, p. 113).

These ten principles are not simply an additive summary or a collection of excerpts. Authors of texts on methods conceptualize their operations differently, use different terminologies, emphasize different aspects of the process, and some spell out explicitly what is left implicit by others. Nonetheless, it was possible to identify these commonalities. While they constitute no 'final order' or 'fundamental structure', they do make explicit a pattern and are a 'composite summary'. In a sense, one could say that the ten principles and procedures offer 'generalized' guidelines for qualitative researchers who want to conduct some form of qualitative analysis. I do not propose that the ten principles provide an exhaustive prescription of how to go about the analysis of qualitative data. I do claim, though, that if a researcher adheres to these principles (which, mind you, include the injunction to be creative) and commits no logical or ethical errors, her/his work will qualify as scholarly qualitative data analysis as it is defined today.

Before I become too complacent, however, I must confess that not all types of analysis that I have described (even excluding the extremes) are characterized by these principles and procedures. There is at least one that does not fit: event structure analysis. The main reason is: the organizing system it develops is not a means, but an end. It is the goal of event structure analysis to create a 'model' that represents the logical-chronological laws that 'rule' events of a certain kind or within a certain situation. In this regard, it resembles some of the kinds of research on the 'formal' end of our spectrum, namely discourse analysis and the ethnography of communication, ethnoscience, and structural ethnography.

The recognition of this similarity takes me back to the second method of making a large number of items easier to work with mentally: grouping. One order has already evolved for us. As we just saw, one group of analysis approaches has an entire set of principles and procedures in common (at least the ten I identify above). Another group shares with event structure analysis the creation of models that mirror the structure of the phenomenon under study, such as events, interactions, language usage, or the organization of cultural knowledge. We have yet to name the two groups or 'categories'. Labels always confine; they emphasize one aspect of a category and obscure others. They make distinctions more crass than they are and, therefore, distort. However, without such simplifying labels we would have a hard time communicating. So let us call the one type of analysis **structural** analysis and the other type **interpretational** analysis.

The groups are uneven in size. Structural analysis would include discourse analysis, ethnography of communication, ethnoscience, event structure analysis, and structural ethnography. All other types of qualitative research (except those that have no explicit analysis procedures) fall into the interpretational category. Naturally, some of the research approaches in the interpretational group are borderline cases. Ecological psychology, for instance, is not purely interpretational, but is also structure-oriented, as are phenomenography, ethnographic content analysis, and even transcendental realism. However, this rough division into two groups is merely an intellectual tool for a certain purpose, not a 'result' for which I claim validity.

The interpretational category is rather large. It might be convenient to subdivide further. Indeed, notwithstanding the ten commonalities described above, there is at least one important distinction that can be made within this category. On our chart at the end of the chapter on research types the two center groups are characterized as research whose purpose is to discover regularities and research that is meaning-oriented. You will notice that there is a cluster of research approaches at the very left side of the regularities-seeking group in which the interest is mainly in 'identifying and categorizing elements and establishing their connections'. The purpose of discovering such relationships is to postulate conceptual linkages or, to use a more traditional terminology, to generate plausible hypotheses. Although not strictly seeking generalizations, these research approaches are theory-building in the sense that they aim at stripping away the particulars and arriving at some underlying principle that is likely to apply to similar situations. To distinguish this analysis process from the mere identification of patterns or the discerning of meaning, we will call the two interpretational analysis subtypes 'theory-building' and 'interpretive/descriptive', respectively.

Again, the subgroups are uneven in size, and the labels are somewhat forced, making the boundaries fuzzy. All interpretational types of qualitative analysis are descriptive to a certain extent, and all of them - being scientific work - contribute to theory. The distinction is between the explicit intents of the analysis procedure.

Theory-building analysis is represented mostly in grounded theory construction and the application of transcendental realism. Ethnomethodology, symbolic interactionism, and phenomenography are descriptive, but more theory-oriented than the various ethnographic approaches, naturalistic inquiry, phenomenology, or hermeneutics. The evaluation- and action-oriented types of research have the least interest in theory-building analysis, but add a special emphasis on problem solution.

The grouping of analysis types, then, would roughly proceed along the following lines:

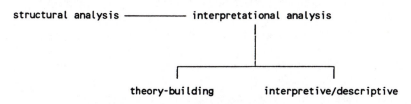

Regardless of the type, all qualitative data analysis processes operate on a conceptual and a concrete level simultaneously. As data are segmented and organized into categories (see commonalities number four and number five above), manual tasks must be performed, although all steps require intellectual involvement. In this book special attention is being paid to the part of structural and interpretational analyses that is amenable to assistance by a computer: the mechanics. Two separate chapters in this book are devoted to the two main groups of analysis. Interpretive/descriptive and theory-building analyses are treated as subtypes in the chapter on interpretational analysis. You can also find additional details about the differences between the two subtypes in the chapter on organizing systems.

References

ALTHEIDE, DAVID L. (1987, Spring) 'Ethnographic content analysis', *Qualitative Sociology*, 10, 1, pp. 65-7.

BARRITT, LOREN; BEEKMAN, TON; BLEEKER, HANS and MULDERIJ, KAREL (1985) *Researching Education Practice*, Grand Forks, ND, University of North Dakota, Center for Teaching and Learning.

BECKER, HOWARD S.; GEER, BLANCHE; HUGHES, E. and STRAUSS, ANSELM L. (1961) *Boys in White: Student Culture in Medical School*, Chicago, Chicago University Press.

BECKER, HOWARD S. and GEER, BLANCHE (1982) 'Participant observation: The analysis of qualitative field data', in BURGESS, ROBERT G. (Ed.) *Field Research: A Sourcebook and Field Manual*, London, George Allen and Unwin.

BLUMER, HERBERT (1969) *Symbolic Interactionism*, Englewood Cliffs, NJ, Prentice Hall.

BOGDAN, ROBERT C. and TAYLOR, STEVEN J. (1975) *Introduction to Qualitative Research Methods: A Phenomenological Approach to the Social Sciences*, New York, John Wiley and Sons.

BOGDAN, ROBERT C. and BIKLEN, SARI K. (1982) *Qualitative Research for Education: An Introduction to Theory and Methods*, Boston, Allyn and Bacon, Inc.

COLAIZZI, PAUL F. (1978) 'Psychological research as the phenomenologist views it', in VALLE, RONALD S. and KING, MARK (Eds.) *Existential-Phenomenological Alternatives for Psychology*, New York, Oxford University Press.

ERICKSON, FREDERICK (1986) 'Qualitative methods in research on teaching', in WITTROCK, MERLIN C. (Ed.) *Handbook of Research on Teaching*, Third edition, New York, Macmillan Publishing Company.

FLORIO-RUANE, SUSAN (1987, Summer) 'Sociolinguistics for educational researchers', *American Educational Research Journal*, 24, 2, pp. 185-97.

GARFINKEL, HAROLD (1967) *Studies in Ethnomethodology*, Englewood Cliffs, NJ, Prentice-Hall.

GEERTZ, CLIFFORD (1973) *The Interpretation of Cultures*, New York, Basic Books.

GIORGI, AMEDEO (1975) 'An application of phenomenological method in psychology' in GIORGI, AMEDEO; FISCHER, CONSTANCE T. AND MURRAY, EDWARD L. (Eds.) *Duquesne Studies in Phenomenological Psychology*, Vol. 2, Pittsburgh, PA, Duquesne University Press.

GLASER, BARNEY G. and STRAUSS, ANSELM L. (1967) *The Discovery of Grounded Theory: Strategies for Qualitative Research*, Chicago, Aldine Publishing Company.

GOETZ, JUDITH P. and LECOMPTE, MARGARET D. (1984) *Ethnography and Qualitative Design in Educational Research*, Orlando, FL, Academic Press.

GUBA, EGON (1978) *Toward a Methodology of Naturalistic Inquiry in Educational Evaluation*, Los Angeles, CA, Center for the Study of Evaluation.

GUBA, EGON and LINCOLN, YVONNA (1981) *Effective Evaluation*, San Francisco, CA, Jossey-Bass Inc.

GUMPERZ, J. J. and HYMES, D. (Eds.) (1972) *Directions in Sociolinguistics: The Ethnography of Communication*, New York, Holt, Rinehart and Winston.

HALFPENNY, PETER (1979) 'The analysis of qualitative data', *Sociological Review*, 27, 4, pp. 799-825.

HAMMERSLEY, MARTYN and ATKINSON, PAUL (1983) *Ethnography: Principles in Practice*, New York, Tavistock Publications.

HEISE, DAVID R. (1988, Spring) 'Computer analysis of cultural structures', *Social Science Computer Review*, 6, 1, pp. 183-97.

HYCNER, RICHARD H. (1985) 'Some guidelines for the phenomenological analysis of interview data', *Human Studies*, 8, pp. 279-303.

JACOB, EVELYN (1987, Spring) 'Qualitative research traditions: A review', *Review of Educational Research*, 57, 1, pp. 1-50.

LAZARSFELD, PAUL F. (1972) *Qualitative Analysis*, Boston, Allyn and Bacon Inc.

LOFLAND, JOHN (1971) *Analyzing Social Settings*, Belmont, CA, Wadsworth Publishing Company.

MARTON, FERENCE (1986, Fall) 'Phenomenography - A research approach to investigating different understandings of reality', *Journal of Thought*, 21, 3, pp. 28-48.

MILES, MATTHEW B. and HUBERMAN, A. MICHAEL (1984) *Qualitative Data Analysis: A Sourcebook of New Methods*, Beverly Hills, CA, Sage Publications.

MILLS, C. WRIGHT (1959) *The Sociological Imagination*, New York, Oxford University Press.

MULKAY, MICHAEL (1985) 'Agreement and disagreement in conversations and letters', *Text*, 5, 3, pp. 201-27.

MURDOCK, G. P. (1971) *Outline of Cultural Materials*, New Haven, CT, Human Relations Area Files.

PACKER, MARTIN J. (1985) 'Hermeneutic inquiry in the study of human conduct', *American Psychologist*, 40, 10, pp. 1081-93.

PATTON, MICHAEL Q. (1980) *Qualitative Evaluation Methods*, Beverly Hills, CA, Sage Publications.

ROGERS, MARY F. (1983) *Sociology, Ethnomethodology, and Experience*, Cambridge, MA, Cambridge University Press.

SPRADLEY, JAMES P. (1979) *The Ethnographic Interview*, New York, Holt, Rinehart and Winston.

SPRADLEY, JAMES P. (1980) *Participant Observation*, New York, Holt, Rinehart and Winston.

STRAUSS, ANSELM L. (1987) *Qualitative Analysis for Social Scientists*, Cambridge, MA, Cambridge University Press.

TAYLOR, STEVEN J. and BOGDAN, ROBERT (1984) *Introduction to Qualitative Research Methods*, New York, John Wiley and Sons.

TESCH, RENATA (1987) 'Emerging themes: The researcher's experience', *Phenomenology + Pedagogy*, 5, 3, pp. 230-41.

TURNER, BARRY A. (1981) 'Some practical aspects of qualitative data analysis: One way of organizing the cognitive process associated with the generation of grounded theory', *Quality and Quantity*, 15, pp. 225-47.

URMSTON PHILIPS, SUSAN (1984) 'The social organization of questions and answers in courtroom discourse: A study of changes of plea in an Arizona court', *Text*, 4, 1-3, pp. 225-48.

VON ECKARTSBERG, ROLF (1978) 'Person perception revisited', in VALLE, RONALD S. and KING, MARK (Eds.) *Existential-Phenomenological Alternatives for Psychology*, New York, Oxford University Press.

WEBER, R. PHILIP (1985) *Basic Content Analysis*, Beverly Hills, CA, Sage Publications.

WERNER, OSWALD and SCHOEPFLE, G. MARK (1987) *Systematic Fieldwork, Vol. 2*, Beverly Hills, CA, Sage Publications.

WERTZ, FREDERICK J. (1985) 'Methods and findings in a phenomenological psychological study of a complex life-event: Being criminally victimized', in GIORGI, AMEDEO (Ed.) *Phenomenology and Psychological Research*, Pittsburgh, PA, Duquesne University Press.

The Mechanics of Structural Qualitative Analysis

Introduction

A list of commonalities in structural qualitative research would probably consist of a single item: an interest in some kind of regularity in the organization of the phenomenon under study. The reason is that the procedures in structural analysis are much more diverse than in interpretational types of research. No one definition can be made to fit, even loosely, all five research approaches in this group: discourse analysis, ethnography of communication, ethnoscience, event structure analysis, and structural ethnography. The major difference between the conceptualization of the analysis procedures in these types of research and in interpretational approaches is this: the interpretational researcher 'overlays' a structure of her/his own making on the data, as a device for rendering the phenomenon under study easier to grasp; while structural analysts assume that the structure is actually inherent or contained in the data and the researcher's job is to uncover it.

The single shared characteristic of the structural group permits us at least to deduce some commonalities, since it holds certain implications. A structure, as we use the term here, is 'the interrelation of parts as dominated by the general character of the whole' (Webster's, 1964, p. 2267). Any analysis, therefore, must discover the parts, and then determine their interrelations. This necessarily produces a two-step process: identification of the parts, and identification of the relationships.

Parts and Relationships

The 'parts' in event structure and other sequence analyses are the smallest dynamic units into which actions or interactions can be divided. In discourse analysis, ethnography of communication, ethnoscience, and structural ethnography the 'parts' are language units, either linguistic units such as words, phrases, sentences, etc., or conversational units such as utterances or speaking turns. Unlike the text segments with which interpretational researchers work, these 'parts' are recognizable elements. They are discrete; one is clearly differentiated from the next. The boundaries of these analysis units are not fuzzy; they rarely overlap.

In event and sequential analyses all data parts are significant; if one item were dismissed, the sequence would no longer be the same. That is the reason why the structural analyst usually works with a small, but typical or otherwise significant data set, for instance brief excerpts of interactions from a conflict situation, or people's verbalizations while they perform a particular intellectual task. The researcher may even deal with a single case, such as one folk story or other piece of cultural material. Where sequence is of no consequence, researchers usually first identify the data parts that are relevant to the analysis. If, for instance, the indigenous knowledge within a cultural subgroup is explored, terms and phrases commonly used in most other cultures reveal little. Instead, 'folk terms' or 'native' terms and phrases must be identified. The terms that are deemed relevant are separated from their context; context matters only in so far as it clarifies the meaning of the part. Next, the bulk of concrete instances must be 'reduced' by stripping away the detail, so that the researcher can concentrate on the 'general'. Many different wordings may express 'gratitude', for example, or an 'invitation' can be worded in various ways. The 'general' is the fact that gratitude is expressed or an invitation is extended.

The main task of the analysis is to discover connections, not only between two parts, but among many. An interpretational researcher may be satisfied to postulate a relationship between two organizing categories or concepts; the structural analyst looks for an entire system of connections. We could, somewhat simplistically, divide the five research approaches listed above into two groups according to the nature of the connections sought. In one group, researchers look mainly for **interactional** structures. Many discourse analysts explore the patterns found in every-day language exchanges. Ethnographers of communication have a similar goal; they want to discover what typically happens, either verbally or non-verbally, between people in certain social situations. The other group is comprised of ethnoscientists, structural ethnographers, and event/sequence analysts (as well as phenomenographers). They are interested in the **logical** or cognitive structures revealed through their data, i.e., which logical rules apply in the way events follow each other or in the way terms are related to each other.

Interactional Structures

Discourse analysts and ethnographers of communication focus on the 'micro' processes of social interaction (Jacob, 1987, p. 18). They attempt to uncover the 'rules' or structures that underlie these interactions. Frederick Erickson (1986) provides an account of the mechanics of handling field notes, videotapes, site documents, and interview transcripts that the researcher has collected as samples of social interactions.

> The researcher may find it useful to make one or two photocopied sets of the whole corpus of field notes . . . Analogous instances of phenomena of interest can be circled in colored ink. . . These may be instances of a whole event or of a constituent episode or phase within an event, or of a transaction between focal individuals. A number of searches through the notes can be made in this fashion, to identify evidence for or against the major assertions the researcher wishes to make, circling instances in different colors of ink, depending on the assertion the instance relates to. At this point some researchers cut up a second copy of the field notes and tape the various instances to large file cards, which then can be sorted further as the analysis proceeds. (Erickson, 1986, p. 149)

The 'major assertions' in this quote are the equivalent of what other researchers would call categories: they provide a system by which to organize the data <Organizing systems>. According to these categories data items are collated that constitute 'analogous instances of the same phenomenon' (*ibid.*, p. 148). The categories are established tentatively at first, and then are revised in the course of the analysis process, which consists of several cycles (Jacob, 1987, p. 21). Individual researchers have employed different techniques to achieve the goal of categorizing their data. All of them use some kind of 'indexing' of the entire data corpus that enables them to group data pieces and to order them. Linkages between/among the data groups or categories are then inferred from that order. This process is similar to interpretational analysis, except that the analysis techniques are more diverse - depending on the nature of the research project - rather than being variations of a basic model. Furthermore, the data come in more natural 'chunks', and the focus is on smaller units of social intercourse.

Logical Structures

The emphasis on uncovering structures that are believed to exist in the data is greatest in this group of research approaches. Ethnoscientists and structural ethnographers explore 'an informant's cultural knowledge' which 'is organized into categories all of which are systematically related to the entire culture' (Spradley, 1979, p. 93). Event sequence analysts 'study structures embedded in cultural texts of varying kinds' (Heise, 1988, p. 183). These researchers deal with distinguishable units, namely 'cultural symbols', most often in the form of 'native terms' (Spradley, 1979), or 'simple events' in narratives (Heise, 1988). These units may not be obvious, and the structural system of which they are parts is even less apparent. The system is viewed as a logical structure, which may be conceptual/semantic (words denote concepts whose meaning is dependent on their similarity with or contrast to certain other concepts), or temporal (events follow other events in a non-random, rule-determined order).

When interpretational analysts seek to discern relationships among the entities they have identified in their data, usually the relationship is one of association, sometimes suggesting a causal link. More often an assertion of co-occurrence is all that is desired for the descriptive purpose of the qualitative researcher, with the nature of the relationship remaining open or even inconsequential. Structural analysts work with a set of relationships whose nature is well established. Their goal is to determine between which ones of the elements one of the several types of possible relationships exists. In language-oriented studies, commonly explored relationships are those of inclusion (a *kind* of), attribution (an *attribute* of), means-end (a *way* to), rational (a *reason* for), function (is *used* for), and also spatial, temporal, and cause-effect relationships (Spradley, 1979, p. 111). The simplest one is the part-whole relationship.

One way in which the language-oriented analyst starts an analysis is to scrutinize language samples and narratives for terms that lend themselves to the gradual discovery of one of these relationship structures. For example, one might look for 'cover terms', which are terms that are used for more than one thing. For example, we can use 'research' as such a cover term. Once a list of such terms is accumulated, the researcher systematically elicits from 'informants' the subordinate terms that are included under the chosen term. 'What different kinds of research are there?' or 'Is content analysis a kind of research?' are the types of questions through which data are collected. The researcher might also ask what the components or 'parts' of research are, or how research differs from journalism or evaluation. The result is a collection of definitions expressed in terms of these semantic relationships. Most lend themselves well to graphic representation, especially those that can be expressed as taxonomies. Taxonomies are usually depicted as inverted tree-type diagrams. Our graph at the end of the chapter on different types of qualitative research is an example of such an inverted tree diagram (although the 'tree', in this case, lays on its side).

The mechanics of arriving at such a structure are by no means standardized. Most researchers collect their data by filling out scores of work sheets, and later sort multitudes of cards on which important terms are recorded (Spradley, 1979). Some techniques are described by Werner and Schoepfle (1987, vol. 2, chapter 1). They consider their data to be a 'data base' consisting of 'ethnographic records'. For the data to be selectively retrievable, they must be 'indexed'. The indexing process entails '1) highlighting all key words and phrases, and 2) inserting new titles, key words or phrases that [the researcher] deems necessary to the project goals' (*ibid.*, p. 49). Categories for indexing may be adapted from established ethnographic classification schemes, such as Murdock's (1971) Outline of Cultural Materials. The indexed items are sorted and stored on cards, or in loose-leave binders. Edge-punched cards provide the convenience of being multiply classifiable. These are large cards that hold the data in the center, while a row of numbered holes around all four edges provides a means for indicating the 'categories' to which the data piece is relevant. If a piece of data falls into category 17, for instance, the connection of hole 17 to the rim of the card is punched out. With the cards in random order, a knitting needle passed through hole 17 will pull out all cards but those whose hole 17 has been punched. These remain and constitute the set with which the researcher intends to work at this time.

Electronic Data Handling

Werner and Schoepfle (1987, vol. 2) suggest that the search and indexing functions of word processors, multi-window editing, and the special concordance and indexing programs that were often developed first for mainframe computers, can make the researcher's work more efficient. Today a profusion of programs for the personal computer exists that could be useful for manipulating data. They are variously called text data base managers, indexers, text retrievers, concordance programs, note takers, personal information managers, etc. Unfortunately, their names do not distinguish them neatly. Each program consists of a different configuration of text handling functions, and a program's name is not necessarily indicative of its main operation. So many of these programs exist, that an entire book could be compiled with descriptions of each, and a listing of the differences among them. Therefore, we will deal here with categories of programs instead of single software packages. Basically, the programs fall into two categories: text data base managers, and text retrievers. These two categories are described in detail in separate chapters <Text retrievers> <Data base managers>, but they are introduced briefly below.

With a few exceptions, the programs in these categories are 'general purpose' programs, i.e., they were not developed specifically for academic research. Their producers hoped that they would find a large range of applications. Therefore, when a researcher works with one of these programs, s/he must adapt it to her/his particular purpose. There are, however, a few software packages that have been developed specifically for the scholar. The two packages most useful for structural analysis are TAP, a text analysis program, and ETHNO, a program that elicits statements about items and their logical connections from the user, and creates from them tree-diagram graphic representations. Both are described in detail in separate chapters.

For a first orientation on the nature of text data base managers and of text retrievers, as well as the two academic programs, you may read the sections below. If you want more detailed information, it will not hurt to skip them and go directly to the appropriate chapters.

Text Data Base Managers

Structured or semi-structured text data base managers allow researchers who are interested in interactional structures to 'format' the data base into 'fields' that are useful for entering the natural units of their data, for instance, individual utterances or actions. Each set of data would be considered one 'record' by the data base manager. The subdivisions within the record, i.e., the individual data units, can then be coded with 'key words' and retrieved across all records of the data base. They do not search for 'patterns' in the sequence of the occurrence of codes. They merely enable the researcher to find particular subunits of her/his data records quickly.

Unstructured or 'free-form' data base managers will search for any term in the data base and pull out and display any record that contains that term, highlighting the term itself. This is a valuable function for researchers who are interested in language use for the development of logical structures and wish to study the usage of a word in its natural context. Data base managers are superior to word processors in their search capabilities, since they are designed to search *across* many records (not merely through one of them), and they do so with great speed. Some advanced word processors can also search across records, but they are slower, and usually they display only the name of the document containing the word or phrase, not the document itself, thus necessitating a second step (document retrieval).

Text Retrievers

I have placed under the heading 'text retrievers' all programs that are designed to operate on individual words and phrases, not 'fields' of data. (Their second distinction from data base managers is that text retrievers 'import' data to work on; they don't act like mini-word processors which allow the user to enter text directly.) Text retrievers make lists of the occurrence of all words in a document, or of specified words, count how often the words appear, create indices (alphabetic lists with information about each word's location in a document), and often also provide concordances (lists of words, plus a specified number of the words that surround them in the document). All of these functions are potentially useful to qualitative researchers who are interested in language.

Electronically created key-word-in-context concordances permit the researcher to comb through large numbers of samples of natural language (provided they are made available to a computer) and extract instances of a word's occurrence. The various meanings of the word can then be inferred from these uses. Although it may seem to the lay person that simple word occurrence lists might not have much to offer, they are especially valuable where documents are compared, such as language usage samples from one culture or subculture with those from another. Words that are consistently used more frequently in one of these cultures may be indicators of a certain cultural 'theme'. If, for instance, a concept was referred to much more often by urban dwellers than by rural dweller, the notion that it represents a more central concern in the urban subculture would warrant further study.

Text Analysis Package (TAP)

TAP is especially well suited to the discovery of interactional patterns. It imports text (in ASCII form) from a word processor and permits the user to divide the text into segments according to the natural structure of the document or any other criterion s/he wishes to apply. Each segment can be coded with up to four separate codes. These codes, which can be either numeric or mnemonic, designate categories into which the researcher expects to order the segments.

Codes can be attached to segments by typing them into designated places in the text's margin, or they can be entered electronically. For instance, the program, given the names of the speakers in a transcribed conversation, can use them to code each of the segments produced by each speaker. Another code can be added by the user to indicate the nature of what was said. Later, the program can be asked to search through all documents for instances in which certain types of utterances are followed or preceded by a particular other type of utterance. The researcher can even make up sequences to search for to discover whether they indeed occur in the data. The program also searches for co-occurrences of codes within the same segment, which allows for the exploration of the relationship between the type of speaker and the type of utterance. This is useful when one goal of the research project is to find out whether, for instance, male speakers use certain modes of communication more frequently than do female speakers, or whether teachers have a typical way of communicating with students, or professionals with clients. TAP provides frequency distribution tables for all code words used in either a single document, a specified set of documents, or all documents.

Since TAP is a designated analysis program, it is reviewed also in the chapter on the basic structures and functions of MS-DOS programs for qualitative analysis.

ETHNO

ETHNO does not assist in the analysis process. Instead, it creates data displays and enables the researcher to examine and correct the logical appropriateness of the connections depicted in the display. ETHNO constructs the displays on its own, based on responses elicited from the user. The displays are always inverted-tree diagrams and represent logical structures. These may be taxonomies or any of the other relationship modes that ethnoscientists and structural ethnographers explore, or they may be 'event grammars'. Event grammars are not displayed directly, since they constitute an abstract set of rules about the order in which events can logically happen. However, displays can be constructed that depict the order of events that actually did happen in a particular real situation or in a story, and then each concrete event can be replaced by the class of event of which it is an instance.

Event grammars are the most sophisticated set of relationships for which ETHNO can be used. It can, of course, also handle very simple relationships, such as a 'part of' structure (things or concepts are 'part of' another thing or concept). The program elicits its input, i.e., the user is expected to provide information for which s/he is prompted. That information must be gleaned from the data, if the structure is to be a research result. Two types of information are elicited: the names of the elements of the structure (names of things, events, concepts) and the way in which each element relates to those elements already entered. If, for instance, you entered "sentence" just now, and previously you had entered "phrase" and "story", the program may ask "Is sentence a part of a phrase?" Upon your response, it will proceed to ask "Is sentence a part of a story?" The prompt 'a part of' is one the researcher has specified to be used for this particular set of relationships. A number of such prompts are provided by the program; others can be created by the user.

For more information on TAP and ETHNO see the respective chapters.

References

ERICKSON, FREDERICK (1986) 'Qualitative methods in research on teaching', in WITTROCK, MERLIN C. (Ed.) *Handbook of Research on Teaching*, Third edition, New York, Macmillan Publishing Company.

HEISE, DAVID R. (1988, Spring) 'Computer analysis of cultural structures', *Social Science Computer Review*, 6, 1, pp. 183-97.

JACOB, EVELYN (1987, Spring) 'Qualitative research traditions: A review', *Review of Educational Research*, 57, 1, pp. 1-50.

MURDOCK, G. P. (1971) *Outline of Cultural Materials*, New Haven, CT, Human Relations Area Files.

SPRADLEY, JAMES P. (1979) *The Ethnographic Interview*, New York, Holt, Rinehart and Winston.

Webster's Third New International Dictionary (1964) Springfield, MA, G. and C. Merriam Company.

WERNER, OSWALD and SCHOEPFLE, G. MARK (1987) *Systematic Fieldwork, Vol. 2*, Beverly Hills, CA, Sage Publications.

The Mechanics of Interpretational Qualitative Analysis

Introduction

Interpretational qualitative analysis is not mechanistic, as you will know if you have read the chapter on the various types of qualitative analysis. How, then, can we talk about the 'mechanics' of qualitative analysis? The answer has to do with a difference in meaning between the words mechanic and mechanistic. The word 'mechanistic' means 'mechanically determined', whereas 'mechanic' is defined as 'of or relating to hand work or manual skill' (Webster's, 1964, p. 1400/01). Every researcher who has conducted a qualitative analysis project will tell you how s/he became involved in a lot of 'hand work'. Indeed, to some it may seem that there was more handiwork than anything else.

Qualitative analysis, while obviously a demanding intellectual task, is done in almost constant interaction with the data. The data are not some esoteric entity; they consist of pieces of paper with a lot of words on them. Two of the commonalities in interpretational analysis are that the 'data are segmented' (point 4 in the chapter on analysis types), and 'the data segments are categorized according to an organizing system' (point 5). This has to happen in some concrete way.

Before we go into the details of the mechanics, however, let us review the purpose of interpretational qualitative analysis, so we will not lose the larger perspective. According to the dictionary, analysis is 'a detailed examination of anything complex made in order to understand its nature or to determine its essential features' (Webster's, 1964, p. 77). No methodologist could say it better. If we want to become more specific, i.e., relate the term specifically to qualitative data, we could adopt Bogdan and Taylor's definition: '"Data analysis" refers to a process which entails an effort to formally identify themes and to construct hypotheses (ideas) as they are suggested by data and an attempt to demonstrate support for those themes and hypotheses. By hypotheses we mean nothing more than propositional

statements . . .' (1975, p. 79). The differentiation between inter-
pretive/descriptive and theory-building analysis <Types of analysis> is not
prominent in this definition, but is discernible in the distinction between
'themes' and 'hypotheses'.

Obviously, analysis is a complex process. At least two different
operations play a role in that process: First, there is the 'detailed examination' or the 'identification of themes', and then there is the 'determination
of its essential features' or 'understanding' or 'construction of propositional
statements'. Some methodologists, accordingly, prefer to think of two
separate phases: data organizing and data interpretation. For a better
understanding of the process, it helps to distinguish these two notions
theoretically, although in practice they are intellectually intertwined and
sometimes happen simultaneously. One way of thinking about the distinction is to see data organizing as the preparation for data interpretation;
without organizing the data in some way, interpretation is just about
impossible. Both operations together are often referred to as 'analysis'.

Researchers as a group, however, rarely adopt a unified terminology,
and therefore it should not surprise us that some of them reserve the term
'analysis' for what we have called 'data organizing'. To these researchers,
'interpretation' is what follows the analysis of the data and includes seeing
the data in the light of existing concepts and theories. This is closer to the
way in which quantitative researchers think about their processes since, in
their case, data organizing (usually called: 'statistical analysis') and data
interpretation are, indeed, two separate operations. As a rule, however,
qualitative research methods books include under 'analysis' a discussion of
both, rarely making a distinction between the two.

Whether you take the term 'qualitative data analysis' in its broader
or its narrower sense, organizing the data involves some concrete, manual
activities (unless your analysis is purely 'reflective'). As a rule, you must
somehow divide the text into segments, and then you must sort these
segments into groups. The question is: How is this done? This question
neatly reveals the dual nature of qualitative data handling, i.e., the way
mechanical and intellectual tasks are intertwined. The question can be
interpreted as 'How do I go about it?', but also as 'How do I know where
to make the divisions, and what groups to construct, and which segments to
put where?' The answers to both versions of the question are equally
important for the analysis of qualitative data.

As noted earlier, data 'segmenting' and 'categorizing' are the features
that interpretational types of analysis have in common. When concentrating
on description, the categories are used to discover the commonalities across
cases, or the constituents of a phenomenon. When theory-building is the
purpose of the project, relationships between/among the categories are
postulated. Although one could conclude that descriptive/interpretive
analysis can be turned into theory-building analysis by simply adding another

phase to the analysis process, such a conclusion would be misleading in most cases. In real life, many qualitative research projects do not clearly belong to the one or the other group. For instance, a researcher who mainly provides description may venture a few propositions about connections among some of the entities of the analysis. As a rule, however, a researcher who sets out to construct theoretical notions will think of her/his categories somewhat differently than the researcher who mostly wants to make use of categories as a temporary organizing device.

The existing literature on qualitative analysis does not make clear distinctions between the procedures used for descriptive/interpretive and theory-building analysis processes. As each author describes her/his method, s/he does not set it apart from other methods, much less pointing out the differences, or even clearly labelling the purpose of the analysis. As a result, a novice qualitative researcher often finds descriptions of methods bewildering. Worse, many researchers read only certain authors and remain quite ignorant of analysis purposes and procedures different from the ones their favorite methodological writers describe. This state of affairs is the result of an outdated belief that there exists only one qualitative method. We have reached a new stage in the development of qualitative research. The plurality of ways has been recognized. Now, therefore, it is necessary to discern what the several ways are, and how they are to be distinguished. In the remainder of this chapter, you have the opportunity to find out about basic distinctions in conceptualizations and procedures. First, the concepts of 'de-contextualization' and 're-contextualization' will be explained and illustrated within the process of **descriptive/interpretative** analysis. Next, we will turn to **theory-building** analysis, and finally, we will describe the difference between physical (manual) and electronic data handling.

De-contextualizing and Re-contextualizing in Descriptive/Interpretive Analysis

My favorite way of thinking about segmenting and categorizing involves the concepts of 'de-contextualization' and 're-contextualization'. (I first heard the two terms used by John Seidel, the creator of The Ethnograph, a software package described in this book.) These words are cumbersome, and I don't usually like convoluted terminology; but I have not been able to find simpler words that illustrate the process more aptly.

Segmenting

Your data usually don't come as one amorphous mass. There are field notes from different sites, or interviews with different people, or records of different origin or from different periods of time. Thus, they are naturally partitioned into sets or individual documents. Furthermore, each statement, i.e., each sentence or paragraph within a document, is embedded in the context of that document.

As we have repeatedly noted, qualitative researchers identify in their data documents smaller parts, which they may call segments, items, incidents, meaning units, or analysis units. My definition of such a unit is: a segment of text that is comprehensible by itself and contains one idea, episode, or piece of information. I will give some concrete examples of meaning units. The following illustration comes from a faculty interview about using computer networking in an external degree graduate school:

Researcher: How often do you log in on the electronic network?

Respondent: Well, I know I am supposed to log on every night to check my mail, but I find it a chore and often forget. To be honest, I guess I average about once a week. They're always after me to be more prompt.

Researcher: What kinds of things do you communicate about on the network?

Respondent: That's the problem. I don't have anything I want to communicate. I'm much more comfortable with the mail, and I don't really know why that isn't good enough. I will admit that my students do use the system a lot, and they want to negotiate their assessment contracts and ask questions about their dissertations and even submit their assessment examinations on the system. But I type so slowly and painfully I just can't spend the time doing that.

Researcher: Don't you compose your messages on your word processor and then send them by uploading on line?

Respondent: No. I don't have a word processor. I have a secretary. But she's not available at night when I have to use the network. Anyway, I'm opposed to computers for serious writing. They force you into a narrowly logical and intellectually sterile writing style, and you can't use your imagination, and they are really inhuman machines.

Researcher: So you consider the electronic network more of a burden than a benefit?

Respondent: Yeah.

Researcher: Since you only rarely have face-to-face contact with some of your students, wouldn't the network allow you to get to know these students better?

Respondent: I suppose so. At least, that's what the computer aficionados all say. Perhaps I'm just old fashioned. I like to know people from personal contact, not on the other end of a wire. Of course, I'll admit that the people who have been conducting their student work on the network for some time really think they have developed highly personal relationships with their students. And of course they also point to examples that indicate students have been more direct and honest, and more ready to engage in meaningful debate, than they ever were in class. But I tend to discount these stories, because after all, those are the same people who tried to persuade me that computers are good for real writing, and I know that's not true.

The first relevant segment could be:

How often do you log in on the electronic network?
Well, I know I am supposed to log on every night to check my mail, but I find it a chore and often forget. To be honest, I guess I average about once a week.

This portion of the text is comprehensible by itself. It is just large enough to have meaning. The researcher's question might even be omitted, but its inclusion makes the meaning of the segment unmistakably clear. On the other hand, the following does not make sense by itself:

They're always after me to be more prompt.

If the researcher is interested in the content expressed in this sentence, the entire previous segment must be added, or we won't know what this statement is about. You might have noticed that even so we make a number of automatic assumptions, because we know in what context and for what purpose the interview was conducted. In the first instance, we assume that 'mail' refers to 'electronic mail', and in the second instance we assume that 'they' means whoever is in charge of the electronic network, probably someone from 'the administration'. Relating segments to the 'whole' in terms of the entire study, as well as the entire data document, makes these kinds of assumptions more trustworthy.

Here is another example of a meaningful segment:

I will admit that my students <u>do</u> use the system a lot, and they want to negotiate their assessment contracts and ask questions about their dissertations and even submit their assessment examinations on the system.

And another that is not meaningful:

I suppose so. At least, that's what the computer aficionados all say. Perhaps I'm just old fashioned.

The question 'How do I know where to make divisions?', therefore, can be answered partly by saying: Text segments must be carved out of their context in such a way that they retain meaning, even when they are encountered outside of their context. The other part of the answer is: Unless you are doing a kind of analysis where every utterance or statement matters, carve out of the data only those segments that have a potential relationship to the purpose of your study. Naturally, the segments can have any size, up to several pages. The above examples demonstrate the minimum size. For some studies, units that encompass entire episodes or someone's explanation may be more appropriate, and for still other purposes, the researcher may want to use both large segments and shorter ones embedded in them.

The first task, then, is to 'de-contextualize', i.e., to separate relevant portions of data from their context. In graphic form one could picture the process like this:

De-contextualization:

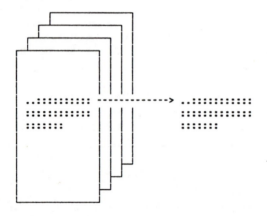

As you have guessed, the 'boxes' symbolize sheets of paper with text. Some of the text, represented by dots, has been taken out of its context or 'de-contextualized'.

Developing an organizing system

Ference Marton, a phenomenographer <Education> who works with 'thinking aloud' protocols, notes that 'each quote has two contexts, . . . first the interview from which it was taken, and second, the 'pool of meanings' to which it belongs' (1986, p. 43). What is this 'pool of meanings'? This question is closely related to our earlier question: 'How do I know what groups to construct?' The answer is much more complicated than how to define meaning units. Constructing groups into which to sort segments is the same as devising an organizing system. The creation of such a system has several stages, and it can be refined to a science - quite literally. There is more to say about it than will fit into this chapter. If you are interested, read the chapter on organizing systems. It explains what such

systems are about, and it also provides explicit advice for researchers who have never developed an organizing scheme before.

I will furnish only a brief review of the matter here. There are two basic avenues for establishing an organizing system: 1) It can be created from prior material, such as the theoretical framework adopted and/or the research questions that guide the investigation; or 2) it can be constructed from the data themselves. As we have noted, interpretive qualitative researchers rarely use the first option. In many cases, the two methods are combined. However, there are certain types of research that explicitly avoid entertaining any prior notions about how the data should be organized, so that the researcher will not confuse what s/he sees in the data with what s/he expects to find.

To give an example for the first approach, let us again use the research project about a recently implemented electronic network connecting adult students of a non-residential graduate program with their faculty. If one of the researcher's interests were to find out how well that network functioned, then 'frequency of use', 'reasons for use', and 'reasons for non-use' could be categories established in advance by thinking about the project. If, one of her/his interests were in identifying types of users, then 'attitudes toward computers' and 'nature of usage' might be useful categories that one would think of before launching the analysis process.

In an open exploratory study, on the other hand, the researcher would, in the process of carefully reading the data, 'start to notice certain features and patterns in the data, and then begin to identify and 'tag' those features and patterns' (Seidel, 1988, p. 7-7). This 'noticing' could happen either before or after relevant text segments are determined, depending on the researcher's working style. One common way of 'marking' these features is to write brief descriptions in the margin next to the pertinent portion of text. For the development of an organizing system, it is important that these descriptions are identifications of the *topic*, not abbreviations of the *content*. The topic is what is talked or written *about*. The content is the substance of the message. For instance, the statement 'Electronic mail is faster than mail, but does not require, as the telephone does, that the other person be available at the same moment' is about the topic 'advantages of an electronic network'. Its content has to do with a comparison between mail and telephone.

A section of data in which 'topics' have been noticed may look like this:

frequency of use	Researcher: How often do you log in on the electronic network?
	Respondent: Well, I know I am supposed to log on every night to check my mail, but I find it a chore and often forget. To be honest, I guess I average
reason for use	about once a week. They're always after me to be

119

more prompt.

Researcher: What kinds of things do you communicate about on the network?

attitude toward mail

perception of student use

reason for non-use

Respondent: That's the problem. I don't have anything I want to communicate. I'm much more comfortable with the mail, and I don't really know why that isn't good enough. I will admit that my students do use the system a lot, and they want to negotiate their assessment contracts and ask questions about their dissertations and even submit their assessment examinations on the system.
But I type so slowly and painfully, I just can't spend the time doing that.

Researcher: Don't you compose your messages on your word processor and then send them by uploading on line?

attitude toward computers

Respondent: No. I don't have a word processor. I have a secretary. But she's not available at night when I have to use the network. Anyway, I'm opposed to computers for serious writing. They force you into a narrowly logical and intellectually sterile writing style, and you can't use your imagination, and they are really inhuman machines.

attitude toward network

Researcher: So you consider the electronic network more of a burden than a benefit?

Respondent: Yeah.

Researcher: Since you only rarely have face-to-face contact with some of your students, wouldn't the network allow you to get to know these students better?

reason for non-use

perception of other faculty's experience

attitude toward computers

Respondent: I suppose so. At least, that's what the computer aficionados all say. Perhaps I'm just old fashioned. I like to know people from personal contact, not on the other end of a wire.
Of course, I'll admit that the people who have been conducting their student work on the network for some time really think they have developed highly personal relationships with their students. And of course they also point to examples that indicate students have been more direct and honest, and more ready to engage in meaningful debate, than they ever were in class. But I tend to discount these stories, because after all, those are the same people who tried to persuade me that computers are good for real writing, and I know that's not true.

After examining the data in this way, the researcher could review all documents, list the 'topics' found in them, and eliminate redundancies:

attitude toward computers	perception of student use
attitude toward mail	perception of other faculty's experience
attitude toward network	reason for use
frequency of use	reasons for non-use

The list above is the beginning of an organizing system. When there are large amounts of data, researchers usually work with a few documents first, then make a list and try out the topics on the list on additional documents. The tentative system becomes refined as the analysis process continues. It is a process with at least two rounds, if not more <Organizing systems>. Usually, categorization systems that emerge from the data themselves start out as quite elaborate lists and require some paring down to the most relevant set of categories. Conversely, a-priori systems usually need some fleshing out. When the researcher finally is satisfied with her/his system for organizing the data, the system is applied to the entire data corpus.

Sorting data (coding)

The better the fit of the organizing system, the easier it is to know where to 'put' each relevant segment of data. In fact, difficulty in sorting the data probably signifies a need to further improve the organizing system. The first step of sorting consists of tagging text segments with information about the category of the organizing system into which it belongs (or several categories if the segment is relevant to more than one). Many researchers call this process 'coding'.

In most cases, 'codes' are simply abbreviations of the labels for the categories. The category 'frequency of use', for instance, could become "frq-use", the category 'attitude toward the network' could become "at-netw". Codes of this type are called mnemonic, since they help us to remember what the actual name of the category is. Some researchers assign numbers to the categories instead of mnemonic codes, and attach the appropriate number to a text segment. Most, however, prefer letter abbreviations. A typical coded section of data may look like this:

```
at-netw   ┌ Resr:  So you consider the electronic network more of a burden
          │        than a benefit?
          │
          └ Resp:  Yeah.

            Resr:  Since you only rarely have face-to-face contact with
                   some of your students, wouldn't the network allow you
                   to get to know these students better?
```

(continued on next page)

```
              Resp:  I suppose so.  At least, that's what the computer
reas no-    ┌        aficionados all say.  Perhaps I'm just old fashioned.
use         │        I like to know people from personal contact, not on the
            └        other end of a wire.
perc oth-   ┌        Of course, I'll admit that the people who have been
fac         │        conducting their student work on the network for some
            │        time really think they have developed highly personal
            │        personal relationships with their students.  And of
            │        course they also point to examples that indicate
            │        students have been more direct and honest, and more
            │        ready to engage in meaningful debate, than they ever
at-comp     ├──      were in class.  But I tend to discount these stories,
            │        because after all, those are the same people who tried
            │        to persuade me that computers are good for real writing,
            └        and I know that's not true.
```

After data are coded, they still are not ready for interpretation. Everything that belongs in one category must be assembled in one place, so that the researcher can read in a continuous fashion about everyone's attitude toward the electronic network, for instance. This assembling is what I call 're-contextualization'. A category is topical, i.e., it deals with one concept, representing one 'pool of meanings'. Our sample organizing system contains the concept 'attitudes toward the electronic network'. This concept forms the new 'context' of a segment. The segment is settled in the context of its topic, in the neighborhood of all other segments of the data corpus that deal with the same topic.

Our graphic representation now looks like this:

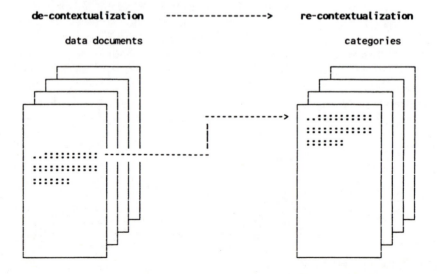

122

The process would continue by transferring the next segment that is relevant to the category context:

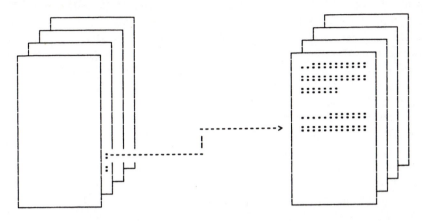

and so on.

As all graphical representations, the ones above have a number of faults. First, they seem to imply that the segment is actually removed from the original data document, which no analyst in her/his right mind would ever do. Rather, it is copied. Second, they imply that the researcher goes through all data documents in search of segments coded a certain way and copies them, one after the other, over to the categories. This sequence is but one way of doing it; most analysts will do it the other way around. They extract all relevant segments from one data document at a time, coding them into the categories as they go along. Thirdly, the drawings depict categories as a linear set. In many cases, categories form a structure, the simplest being subordination (categories have subcategories, which in turn may have further categories, and so on) <Organizing systems>.

De-contextualizing and Re-contextualizing in Theory-Building Analysis

The de-contextualizing and re-contextualizing process in theory-building analysis is similar to that in descriptive/interpretive analysis. The same basic notions of segmenting and coding apply. The organizing system, however, plays a somewhat different role, and the re-contextualization process is conceptualized differently.

Organizing Systems

In theory-building research, categories are viewed not only as intellectual tools for organizing data segments, but as eventual research results. (The distinction between the two is explained in the chapter on organizing systems.) The researcher tries to refine the categories and to sharpen their boundaries, since s/he is interested in developing 'concepts'. The distinction made in the previous section between the specific content of a data segment and the *general topic* referred to in the segment becomes a distinction between specific content and *abstract concept*. The categories are not viewed as containers for data pieces that are about the same topic. They are seen as potential mental constructs. As such, the establishment of a concept is, in itself, a scholarly achievement.

Concepts rarely can be discerned immediately and directly in the data. Therefore, the development of a classification system proceeds slowly, beginning with the development of a tentative organizing system, which is gradually turned into a firmer and firmer structure. In practice, the researcher goes through several rounds of de-contextualization and re-contextualization, until s/he is satisfied that a good fit between the data and the organizing system has been found. The next task is to explore whether connections exist between some of the concepts that have been defined.

Exploring Connections

A simple example of a connection between concepts is the (fictitious) proposition that younger people are more likely to use computers for networking with others than older people. A more abstract example is that computer phobia is based on a combination of low self-esteem and insufficient knowledge about computers.

The difference between the two examples is important. In the second case, the concepts are genuine abstractions; computer phobia and self esteem are psychological constructs that we cannot observe in the same way in which we can count how many people are using a particular electronic network. Someone has postulated that these constructs correspond to some psychological reality, and most of us would not argue with the proposition. However, what counts as evidence for the constructs would be a matter of agreement among us about how the phenomenon manifests itself or how it can be measured. On the other hand, the age of a person can be established easily and definitely. In fact, most people would not think of age and other such phenomena as concepts, but as measurable 'socio-demographic variables' in the quantitative research sense. For the sake of simplicity, we will not make a distinction between socio-demographic variables and genuine concepts in the following exposition. All will be seen as represented by an analysis 'category'.

When a researcher wishes to hypothesize relationships of the kind listed in our examples, s/he is likely to apply codes to segments according to a somewhat different principle than if she were to search for commonal-

The entire process has to be done twice if the research is predominantly exploratory and an organizing system still needs to be developed. It is done once with data that are merely segmented, but not coded. Cut-out segments are shuffled around like cards, being sorted and resorted into tentative groups. Then, when the researcher is satisfied with the organizing scheme, the cutting-and-pasting is done again with data that are coded.

I know of fellow researchers who employ basically the same process, but instead of cutting-and-pasting they excerpt each relevant segment on a 3" by 5" card and then sort the cards. This has advantages; the same cards can be used, first to develop the categories, then to store the data segments according to the categories by simply stacking them in a box with index cards, one index card for each category. When the researcher works with the data cards, however, it is important to mark the category on the card as well, in case one forgets from behind which index master card in the stack the particular excerpt came.

One disadvantage of working with 3" by 5" cards is the excerpting. Poor typists like me, for instance, tend to do anything to avoid additional typewriter hours. Many researchers do not actually copy the data verbatim; they summarize the relevant segments. This is quite acceptable for some kinds of research, where the actual wording does not matter much. It does not work for phenomenological types of research where the way things are expressed constitutes 'data' in itself, or in language-oriented research.

The result of the cut-up-and-put-in-folders method usually is a box of file folders, each holding everything that is relevant to one category (the folder embodies the new 'context' for all the segments in it). Sometimes a researcher will divide the folder content into subcategories, or combine two skinny, related files. When I still worked in this fashion, I usually wrote up the content of each folder independently before relating it to the larger picture, and I pasted illustrative 'quotable material' on the outside of the folder with scotch tape. This way quotes were easy to find when it was time for writing the research report.

The File-Card System (Bogdan and Biklen, 1982, p. 169). This is a more abstract method. It creates a 'secondary' set of data, something like a reference set. The preparatory task is the numbering of each data document, and each line of the data, page by page. Any line can then be represented by three numbers: the data document number, the page number, and the line number.

The researcher codes the data by going through them with a 3" by 5" card in hand. Either s/he writes the category name on top of the card, or s/he uses colored cards, each color representing a major category. As s/he encounters a relevant segment, s/he selects a category-designated card and writes the three source information numbers on it, followed by the number of the line on which the segment ends. One card can hold several 'segments' in this way.

The result of this process, is a set of 'pointers'. The cards point to the material relevant for the category; but the material itself is not on the cards. The researcher has to look it up in the original data. This is a scheme that has time-saving features, especially at the beginning of the process, but, needless to say, it does not lend itself at all to the development of an organizing system. This procedure assumes that the categories already exist.

Progressive people have sometimes in the past used a data retrieval system for text material that involved cards with holes around the edges that could be punched out. (Bogdan and Biklen list this as the third approach, 1982, p. 170.) These cards came as large as 5" by 8", and the data were often typed directly onto them. Each hole in the margin had a small number or letter next to it and could be designated as the representation of one category. That particular hole was punched out toward the rim, while all the other ones were left intact. Then the cards could be stacked in containers in any order. If you passed a device that resembled a knitting needle with a handle through the stack at the location of a certain hole and lifted it up, only those cards whose holes were punched out at that place would be left behind. They contained the material that was relevant to the category you were interested in at the moment.

With this system, it was easy to sort data segments into more than one category; the analyst just punched out the additional holes as well. The problem with this system was that its advantages could be realized only when the data were broken up into segments already at the time of recording. (One could, of course, paste snippets from plain paper copies onto the cards, but then file folders would do just as well - except for multiple coding - and would cost less.) I have used such a system, not for qualitative analysis, but for my growing collection of journal and book references. The stacks were in alphabetical order according to author, and the holes represented subject matter or issues to which the article or book was relevant.

So much for the truly 'manual' procedures in qualitative data processing. It is time to see what a computer could do.

Electronic Data Handling

When I learned to operate my earliest word processing program, one of the first tasks I performed with it was the transcription of data. One of my first thoughts was: How can my work with these data be made easier with this marvelous machine that finally doesn't make typing a torture any more? The computer had all kinds of unexpected capabilities. It could 'highlight' portions of text, even extract them from their original place, and copy them to some other place. It could print out as many copies as I wanted of an entire document or portions of it, and all that without ever touching the original. I would never get my fingers and clothes messy with glue and colored pens again!

Within a couple of weeks I had invented a method of marking the beginnings and ends of data segments by inserting unusual characters (such as a double and a triple slash) in the text. I still worked with a paper copy that I marked up and kept beside the computer, and I decided on preliminary categories from there. Each category was represented by a two-letter code that I inserted right after the beginning-of-segment marker. Now all I had to do was let the computer search for "//AB", and I was taken to the beginning of my first segment relevant to "AB". Once the cursor was there, I activated the highlighting feature and let the machine search for the end-of-segment marker. That was how far the highlighting would go. A few more keystrokes, and the 'block' was transferred to my 'second' document, the one in which I collected all segments relevant to category "AB". What a breeze!

Although a tremendous improvement on my previous methods, the procedure was not perfect. I sometimes forgot, for instance, to type the source information after each segment in my second document. The source information, in general, became a source of irritation. It was cumbersome to type it so often. Even when I graduated to 'macros' (a feature that allows you to have a string of keystrokes carried out automatically while you hit only a couple of keys) and had the computer do most of the typing, I still had to insert the page number since it would not remain the same for each segment. (I often found myself switching back to the original document because I had forgotten to look at its page number.) Also, sometimes it was difficult to remember which macro typed which document name, since there were so many of them.

If you cannot picture all of this, do not worry; it is not important. The main point I want to get across is that word processors are not the perfect instruments for processing qualitative data. They still require too much dull and repetitive labor, leave room for error, and the coded documents with all their markers and abbreviations in the text look dreadful. I began to envision what, given the computer's capacity to handle text, a perfect program for processing qualitative data would be able to do.

As data base managers began to accommodate larger character strings and later almost unlimited amounts of text, I also experimented with them. Just like the information retrieval cards described near the end of the previous section, most data base managers require that the segments are delimited beforehand. It is difficult if not impossible to 'play' with segments or to develop an organizing system. However, in many qualitative studies the data are gathered by various means. Some could be quite structured, such as open-ended questionnaires or interviews with a predetermined 'schedule'. If the organizing system either already exists or is being developed from other data sources, the responses to each question constitute natural meaning units that can be entered directly into a data base manager. One or several codes can be attached to each of these natural segments, and the data base manager will search for the segments that are coded the same and collate them in one place.

There are also 'free-form' text data base managers that allow the researcher to enter an entire data document without structure. Code words can be embedded in the text, and the program will search for them easily, and point to them in their context. The researcher must then decide at the retrieval stage what the boundaries of the segments are, and delete the rest of the material. At best, a free-form data base manager will attach to the word a specified number of preceding or succeeding lines of text, which creates segments that do not necessarily constitute a meaning unit.

Data base managers may be more useful for structural analysis than interpretational analysis <Data base managers>. In general, however, they are designed to collect and store information that is to be looked up over and over. The goal of a programmer who designs a data base manager is to enable the user to easily add information at any time and to allow the user to find exactly what s/he needs as fast as possible, whenever s/he needs it. Data base managers are not designed for a one-time analysis. They are result-oriented, not process-oriented. This means that they emphasize fast, accurate, and sophisticated retrieval, not de-contextualization and re-contextualization.

The 'perfect' programs for de-contextualization and re-contextualization are those that have been specifically created to imitate and surpass the manual procedures described earlier. They invite the researcher to mark segments and code them in preliminary fashion as often as necessary while developing a coding system, or to attach the codes permanently for final analysis. Assigning several codes to one segment is accomplished as easily as attaching to each extracted segment the appropriate source information. The latter happens automatically, so that the researcher does not need to waste time or mental energy on such mundane a task. The programs produce versions of the original data documents with marked and coded segments, and they also print out new documents in which all segments relevant to one category have been brought together - by the computer, not by the researcher.

Such programs have existed already for half a dozen years at the time of this writing. Some were created for mainframe computers first, then were rewritten for the personal computer. Others were designed from the beginning for the personal computer. As the capacity of these 'micros' is increasing, most new programs are now created with the intention of making them available to fellow researchers who own a personal computer. One of the most sophisticated of the analysis programs is QUALOG, which is still a mainframe program (Shelly, 1984), and therefore accessible only to researchers whose university purchases the software.

I call these programs text analysis software, qualitative analysis software, or simply 'analysis programs', although they do not actually 'analyze' text. 'Text processing' might be a better choice, but could be confused with word processing; 'text organizers' might be confused with outline makers, and 'data processing' with data base managers or statistical programs.

Some of the analysis programs that were developed for the process of de- and re-contextualization, i.e., for descriptive/interpretive types of analysis, have begun to incorporate features that are usable for theory-building types of analysis as well. One way of doing so is to indicate or retrieve segments that have been coded with one or more codes simultaneously, so that the researcher can explore whether there is a connection between the categories. Another method comes closer to the process depicted above, where entire documents are 'sorted'. The researcher attaches socio-demographic or other identifying variables to each data document, then instructs the computer to collate all material for a specific category sorted according to the nature of the documents (for instance separated into responses from female participants vs. male participants). QUALOG, and some newer programs for the personal computer, have been designed to explore connections not only between socio-demographic variables and codes, but between any code and any other code.

The chapter on the structure and functions of qualitative analysis programs describes in detail how analysis programs work.

Before leaving this section, however, a few words are needed about a type of software that often is described in ways that make the programs sound similar to text analysis programs. Variously called indexers, concordance programs, or text retrievers, they are basically oriented toward individual words, not text segments. Their strength lies in finding strings of characters within large amounts of amorphous information, spanning many files (there is no crisp distinction between a free-form data base manager and a text retriever). As a rule, their retrieval consists of pointing to certain documents among many that contain the searched-for information, and then calling up those documents with the searched-for term highlighted in some way. I know of three at this time that afford the retrieval of user-defined text segments rather than merely segments consisting of a specified number of lines or words around the code word or 'key'-word: ZyINDEX, WordCruncher, and Text Collector. However, these programs do not automatically collate the segments in a new document after coding, i.e., they do not re-contextualize (segments have to be added to a new document one by one). These programs are described in more detail in the chapter on text retrievers.

References

BOGDAN, ROBERT C. and TAYLOR, STEVEN J. (1975) *Introduction to Qualitative Research Methods: A Phenomenological Approach to the Social Sciences*, New York, John Wiley and Sons.

BOGDAN, ROBERT C. and BIKLEN, SARI K. (1982) *Qualitative Research for Education: An Introduction to Theory and Methods*, Boston, Allyn and Bacon, Inc.

LOFLAND, JOHN (1971) *Analyzing Social Settings*, Belmont, CA, Wadsworth Publishing Company.

MARTON, FERENCE (1986, Fall) 'Phenomenography - A research approach to investigating different understandings of reality', *Journal of Thought*, 21, 3, pp. 28-48.

SEIDEL, JOHN (1988) *THE ETHNOGRAPH: A User's Guide*, Littleton, CO, Qualis Research Associates.

SHELLY, ANNE (1984) 'Using logic programming to facilitate qualitative data analysis', paper presented at the annual meeting of the American Educational Research Association, New Orleans.

Webster's Third New International Dictionary (1964) Springfield, MA, G. and C. Merriam Company.

Organizing Systems and How to Develop Them

The Nature of Classification

When you move into a new house you almost automatically design your system for organizing your belongings. Shoes, forks, and postage stamps don't go in the same drawer, not only because that would hardly be hygienic, but because they don't belong together. Their natures are different; they fall into the categories of clothing, kitchen ware, and desk supplies, respectively.

Many tasks in our daily lives include aspects of organizing. We hardly notice that we work with categories of objects almost constantly, since we take them so much for granted. It would be very difficult to go shopping, for instance, if stores did not specialize in categories of objects, or department stores had no 'departments'. Where would we buy something to read or something to sooth our cough, if we didn't know about the categories 'books' and 'medicine'? One of the first intellectual/perceptual successes of babies consists of their mastery of the task of sorting things according to shapes or colors. They are learning to compare, and to notice similarities and differences.

The most remarkable achievement of all, however, is language. Words are abstractions. As the child learns a language, s/he learns to group things together according to features they have in common, but that are rarely articulated. Calling a tree a tree, whether it's a young apricot or an old oak, or a Christmas tree, is a matter of forming categories or classes of things in our mind and sorting real objects into them.

Much has been written about how we master our world by dividing it into groups of things, be they material objects or abstract concepts. (Bear with me, it will eventually become clear what all this has to do with qualitative analysis.) Categorizing or classification (the terms will be used interchangeably here), is a way of knowing; we have to be cognizant of the attributes of things to be able to group them. In fact, in the early days science was considered largely a way of developing classification systems.

For some scholarly fields classification is still a major objective. Botanical classifications schemes and the periodic table of elements are well-known examples of classification schemes that are the result of enormous research efforts. Darwin would never have been able to develop his monumental theory without classification.

While the periodic table is an example of a classification system that is so seamless that the properties of elements not yet discovered could be deduced from the rules of the system, not all things on earth can be classified neatly. In fact, as a rule, classification has its problems. Even if you consider simple material objects, such as chairs, the matter can become complicated. For instance, to decide which objects fall into the class of 'chair' we need criteria by which to assess them. Usually, such criteria are called the 'properties' of a category. The first property that comes to mind when I think of the class 'chair' is that it is 'something to sit on'. But that is not yet good enough, since I can sit on a bench as well, or a stool, a sofa, or even a fallen log. To rule out the log, I can decide that the next property is: 'must have legs'. The property to rule out sofas would be that the object may have only one seat, and to rule out stools that it must have a backrest. That leaves stuffed chairs as remaining within the category. Not everyone thinks of stuffed chairs as chairs, however. Other languages, such as German and French, have special words for them that are entirely different names. But what about that garden lounger that has legs, only one seat, a declinable back rest, and looks like a cot, which is a subcategory of bed?

If clear categorization becomes difficult in such a simple case, imagine categorizing sea creatures, or research types, or mental disorders. On the one hand, it is obvious that categorization is a helpful, probably essential conceptual tool; on the other hand, it seems artificial in many, perhaps most cases. To avoid forcing categorization, we will have to allow for borderline cases, or concede that categories might overlap.

Although useful notions, overlap and borderline existence have not advanced our reflection about categories as much as another invention that is fairly modern in humankind's thinking: fuzzy categories. The image of categories with clear perimeters is replaced with that of fuzzily bounded categories. Of course, there are some category schemes that naturally have discrete boundaries (such as the dichotomy of being pregnant or not pregnant), but for most objects or concepts categorization is not an either/or question, but a matter of degree. Thus, the entire idea of categorization as a mental overlay on our world becomes more comfortable when we can think of it as stretchable and soft.

People who have given a lot of thought to classification have provided us with some helpful notions that make it easier to contemplate fuzzy boundaries. One of these is 'membership' in a category. Any given object or concept can be a member of a category to a certain degree. If you were a mathematician, you would try to express this degree in numbers (which is exactly what is done in a branch of mathematics called fuzzy set theory). A garden lounger may have a membership of .6 in the category or 'set' called 'chair', and a membership of .3 in the set called 'bed'. The numeral 1 would signify a perfect fit for the category, the numeral 0 an absolute misfit, i.e., the item would have none of the properties that are the criteria for membership in the category (Horvarth *et al.*, 1980). (Interestingly, fuzzy set theory builds on the same logic notions developed by Mr. Boole that are used in text retrieval software <Text retrievers>.)

A second helpful notion is that of the prototype. The prototype, in the context of classification, is the ideal type. It has a 1.0 degree of membership in the class, possessing all the properties necessary for belonging in the category to the fullest extent. For many classificatory systems, the real-object equivalent of the prototype does not exist. The prototype is merely a mental construct with which real objects or existing concepts can be compared to ascertain their degree of membership (Rosch, 1978).

If we had formerly envisioned a classification system as resembling this graphic representation,

A	B	C
D	E	F

a fuzzy set system with prototypes would look more like this:

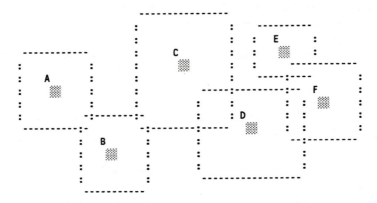

Each box in the two drawings represents a category. The categories in the second are not clearly distinguished from each other, but overlap, sometimes with more than one other category. Their boundaries are not crisp, but fuzzy. Rather than defining categories by properties (an item is judged as belonging to the category if it exhibits the properties that characterize the category), they are defined by a prototype, an idealized 'core' that represents the category, and which the items in the category resemble to a certain degree.

Categorization in Qualitative Research

All but the most impressionistically working qualitative researchers use categorization when analyzing their data. Some of them are very clear about doing so, and others are hardly aware of the process. A few phenomenologists resist the idea. Yet phenomenologists look for 'commonalities' in the themes they have identified in their data. It would be quite impossible to do so, if the themes that are by nature comparable would not get grouped together. The researcher works with one group of themes at a time. If the themes are grouped, they can be said to be 'in a category'. Perhaps some qualitative researchers' resistance stems largely from visualizing categorization systems in the old fashion as rigid, exclusive 'boxes' in which themes cannot belong to another group as well, or cannot fit only somewhat, but must fit totally.

The term many researchers use to describe the nature of the analysis process is 'data reduction', rather than data grouping or categorization. The two notions are similar. 'Reduction' indicates a higher level of abstraction, where one piece of data, such as a segment from an interview, stands for other similar pieces of data. The selected segment serves as a representative of other segments of the same nature, i.e., it represents a 'class' of data. Thus, classification or categorization are inherent in the concept of data reduction. However, the term can be misunderstood. 'Reduction' sounds as if it signifies a decrease in the amount of material with which the researcher works.

Some novice analysts picture the process of data reduction as one of gradually carving down a large mountain of raw data to a few characteristic rocks. That notion is, unhappily, misleading. The first step in the analysis process is re-arrangement or re-organization of the data. Quite opposite to reduction, this step is likely to increase the amount of material to be handled. Increase happens wherever data segments have relevance to more than one category and are placed in several categories for interpretation. Of course, there is always material in the original data that is irrelevant to the research purpose, does not become assigned to a category, and therefore reduces the data mass. However, I have witnessed many cases in which the re-contextualized data printouts from the computer <Interpretational analysis> ended up being a higher paper stack than the one of the original field notes or interview transcriptions. That is why I prefer the words data condensation, or data distillation as a description of the eventual outcome of a qualitative analysis. These words do not imply that the body of data has merely become smaller. Data condensation or distillation is a result brought about by interpretation. Data don't become manageable in the analysis process because there is less to deal with; they become manageable because they are organized. Having a stack of organized data means that the researcher can look at individual collections of data pieces that are relatively homogeneous, rather than having to deal with all data at all times.

Classification systems can be either the result of an analysis, or they can be a tool. In keeping with the notion of fuzzy boundaries, they can also be something in between, or both in the same study. In the social sciences, classification results may take the form of typologies, such as a typology of personalities, or taxonomies, such as a taxonomy of language-in-use, or other conceptual arrangements, such as a circumplex model of interpersonal behaviors (a classification where items are placed in circular fashion in positions around quadrants of a coordinate scale, Wiggins 1982). Such constructions are usually created during an extended research effort; the outcome of small individual research projects is often a simple list of categories and a description of their characteristics.

By and large, in structural types of analysis the establishment of categories is an important outcome; in interpretive/descriptive analysis, categories are used as an organizing tool; and in theory-building analysis, categories start out as tools and become part of the outcome.

Among the studies whose analysis is structure-oriented, the linguistic types are particularly geared toward the construction of classification systems. Such systems become a research goal, because they mirror the natural classification structure inherent in language of the culture being explored. The researcher sets out to discern a mental structure that s/he assumes exists, and describes it as a system of categories, subcategories, and perhaps sub-subcategories. The system is developed entirely from the data; the researcher does not start out with preconceptions about the existence or nature of certain categories.

The more 'meaning oriented' the analysis, the more classification serves as a data management tool. When a classification system functions as a tool I will call it from now on an 'organizing system' or 'organizing scheme'. This term expresses more aptly that the categories are not 'classes' for their own sake and are not perceived as rigid 'boxes', but that the system exists for the purpose of bringing order to a collection of material that is not naturally arranged in a way amenable to analysis. Furthermore, the term 'system' reminds us that classes are not necessarily of a linear nature, as files in a drawer would be. In the paragraph above, it was mentioned that categories may have sub-categories. Except in very simple organizing schemes, not all categories are of the same mental order. They may be connected in clusters, i.e., categories may form thematically related groups, or they may be thematically subordinated to each other (perhaps forming a hierarchy), or they may be connected in an irregular network. When organizing systems serve as data management tools, there is no requirement that such structure be 'valid'; arranging one's categories is merely a convenience to provide an overview over an otherwise unwieldy number of individual categories. The example below represents a small part of an organizing system that was developed for a phenomenological study of lesbian women:

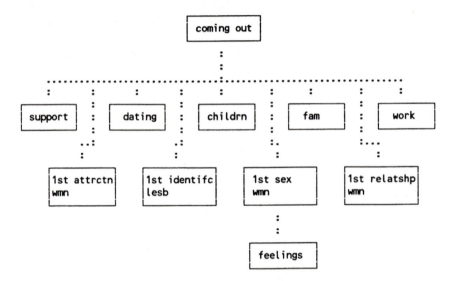

Often such an organizing system is not only helpful for the management of the data, but can also lend structure to the research report.

In theory-building analysis, the categories are even more likely to be arranged in non-linear form. Here, however, the nature of the structure must be carefully generated, since the connections between categories are likely to be just as important as the categories themselves. Grounded theory is a type of qualitative research through which the distinction between categorization as an organizing tool and as a research outcome, or actually the transformation from the one to the other, can be illustrated most aptly. The specific purpose of grounded theory is to arrive at abstract categories that constitute concepts which facilitate our understanding of a phenomenon, and that may have specific relationships to each other (which then are considered 'theories'). One such concept developed by Glaser and Strauss themselves (1967) is 'social loss', a concept that refers to the degree to which nurses perceived the deaths of patients as not merely individual tragedies. his concept was developed after a long process of creating tentative categories, and then constantly comparing the incidents sorted into each category, consequently modifying, expanding, integrating, articulating, confirming, and refining them. Relationships among categories were suggested, and then the data were searched for confirming and disconfirming evidence for these relationships. In the course of the operation, a preliminary organizing system turned into a solid conceptual classification scheme.

It is important for researchers to be mindful of the distinction between organizing as data management and organizing as a research result. Occasionally, novices ask: How do I know when my organizing scheme is complete? Perfectionists have the tendency to polish their systems for organizing data almost as thoroughly as if they were creating a final classification system. While a classification system that represents the outcome of research should be as representative of reality as possible and useful for the advancement of further reflection and understanding about the phenomenon under study, an organizing system that serves as a tool for data management must be as useful as possible for facilitating interpretation, and nothing more than that. Since no claims are made about its correspondence to reality, the refining process can be kept to a level where the organizing system makes meaningful grouping of data pieces possible. The system does not have to be perfect; indeed, two researchers might well develop somewhat different organizing schemes for the same data but, gradually freeing themselves from them in the process of interpretation, arrive at similar descriptions of the phenomenon.

How to Develop an Organizing System

Another question I have often heard researchers ask is: How does one develop such an organizing system in the first place? It is not enough to know what purpose this conceptual tool is to serve. When there is nothing but a mountain of data, and no organizing system anywhere in sight, how and where do I start?

In interpretational analysis, there are at least four sources from which the beginnings of an organizing system can be derived:

a. the research question and sub-questions
b. the research instrument(s)
c. concepts or categories used by other authors in previous related studies
d. the data themselves.

Obviously, all four can be combined. Depending on the nature of the study, the degree to which the first three are fruitful will differ. The research question might be largely exploratory, providing only the most comprehensive, and therefore rather useless concepts. On the other hand, the sub-questions may be geared specifically toward certain aspects of the phenomenon under study (or you, the researcher could begin thinking about aspects), and those could become tentative major categories. If the study involves an instrument for data collection, such as a questionnaire or interview schedule, the questions often provide handy categories. Adopting concepts other researchers have developed appears to be safe (because someone already has applied serious thinking to them and found them workable), but could become dangerous if you believe it is time to break out of a familiar, and perhaps confining, mold. Ideas don't have to be accepted just because they are printed in a respectable journal or book. You might have to explain why you are disregarding them, but you are not obligated to use them unless they are conducive to your purposes.

Since most qualitative research is inductive, or if none of the first three are available to you, the data themselves remain the most suitable and the richest source for the development of an organizing system. In the following we will assume that the data are the only source. One way of deriving an organizing system will be described, and as is customary in the description of qualitative methods, I will point out posthaste that it is not the only way in which such system can be created. It is a way to start if you don't have any idea at all. If you do have ideas, some of the details in the description might stimulate you to flesh out or refine your own process. And, of course, if sources other than your data are available, and it makes sense to use them, you can easily integrate them.

Steps for Developing an Organizing System for Unstructured Qualitative Data:

1. First, get a sense of the whole. Begin with the first data document that becomes available to you (the first transcription of an unstructured interview, for instance). Read it carefully, and read also all others as they come in. This step provides you with necessary background information; you don't need to make an effort to memorize, but you should jot down ideas *about* the data as they come to your mind. This information will reside in the back of your mind and aid in your understanding of individual pieces of data. Go to step two when you have accumulated about one fifth to one fourth of your data, at least 3 sets.

2. Pick any data document to start with; the most interesting one, or the shortest, or the one on top of the pile. As you read it, pay attention to switches or transitions from one topic to the next. Be sure to make a distinction between content and topic. Note the topic, not the *content*! When you look at a piece of data, ask yourself 'What is this *about*?' Don't pay any attention yet to *what* is said, i.e., to the

substance of the statements; you will deal with the substance at some later stage. During this first reading, do not feel any compulsion to capture everything. When you have identified a topic, write it in the margin of the document (work with a copy, not your original).

3. When you have completed this step for three to five sets of your data, make a list of all topics, one column per data document, placing all columns on the same sheet. Continuous computer printouts are especially useful for this purpose. Compare all the topics. Draw lines between columns to connect similar topics. If that becomes confusing, use different pen colors. If you run into a topic description whose meaning you no longer recognize, go back to the original document, find the topic and make sure you understand it correctly. On a separate piece of paper, cluster together similar topics, i.e., those connected by your lines. Choose the best fitting name for the cluster of topics from among your labels, or invent a new one that captures the substance even better. Now make a new list that contains two or three columns: The first column holds the major topics that were constructed from clusters of comparable ones. The second holds unique topics that seem important to the research topic/purpose in spite of the rarity of their occurrence. A third column may hold the left-overs.

4. Go back to your data. Make new copies of the documents you already worked with, and use the list of topics in the first column (and perhaps also those in the second) as a preliminary organizing system. One way of applying the system is to abbreviate the topics as 'codes', and write the codes next to the appropriate segments of text <Interpretational analysis>. This process fulfills two purposes: a) it will show you how well your topic descriptions correspond to what you find in the data, and b) you might discover new topics, if it turns out certain important segments cannot be coded at all with your preliminary system. You must decide whether they are relevant for your research. If they are, make a list of them. Don't forget to keep notes on the ideas that come to mind about anything that has to do with your data. (In the lingo of the profession, such notes are called 'researcher memos'.) Since by now probably some additional data documents have been transcribed, work with a couple of data documents that were not included in the first round of coding. This is a good opportunity to try out your preliminary organizing system on them.

5. When you are done, you are ready to refine your organizing system. Find the most descriptive wording for your 'topics' (which have begun to turn into categories). Place the topics that you remember as

occurring in all or most of your data documents in one list, then make a list of unique topics that are important in terms of your research purpose, and perhaps also a list of those that are less important. Now look at your topics from a new angle: Are some topics closer in content to certain topics than to others? Are some of them subcategories of others? Try to relate your topics (but don't force connections). If you find relations, try to capture them as a 'map', i.e., write each on a big sheet of paper and draw lines between them (see the example earlier in this chapter). Such mapping and grouping helps you to remember your codes. Later, when you begin serious coding and notice a segment of your data that is relevant, you must remember what categories are available in your system. Unless you are blessed with a very good memory, you won't remember your codes if you have more than about forty of them. Researchers often wonder how many categories one should have. That depends, of course, on the purpose of the research project and the nature of the data. In general, your sift is probably too coarse if you have only ten or twenty codes for a large data set. Twenty-five to fifty can be manipulated with a little effort; after that it becomes difficult to remember the entire range of your categories. I have seen more than fifty used only for very special analysis needs. In any case, if your categories exist not merely as a list, but have some kind of shape or order, it is easier to apply your organizing system.

6.   Make a final decision on the abbreviation for each category name and alphabetize these codes (your word processor should be able to do that) to make sure you have not inadvertently created duplicates that mean different things (for instance, the abbreviation "COM" standing for 'depth of commitment', but also for 'ease of communication' in a study on interpersonal relationships). Add the abbreviations to your original list or map, and begin the first complete coding session on the entire body of available data. Remember that categories have fuzzy boundaries, and if a segment is too rich in content to fit in just one category, put it into two or three. Don't allow yourself to be paralysed because you cannot make decisions about where things go. As long as you code relevant sections of text in some sensible way at all, they will be noticed later on, and you can always recode (especially if you use a computer program to manage your data).

7.   When you have finished coding, assemble the data material belonging into each category in one place, and perform a preliminary analysis. (Again, this is easier to do with a computer than manually.) Very simply described, this means that you will look at the collection of material in one category at a time. This is the time when you must

pay attention to the actual content. Identify and summarize the content for each category. Then look specifically for a) commonalities in content, b) uniquenesses in content, c) confusions and contradictions in content, and d) missing information with regard to your research question/topic. When doing this analysis, it is helpful to keep a note nearby that defines your research purpose or lists your research questions, so you are always reminded of what is central to your project, and which data to discard. Not everything is relevant! Note that this is not yet the stage at which you look for disconfirming evidence, since you are still *taking stock.* You can now take a closer look to decide how useful your organizing system is. Are the categories relatively homogenous, or do they contain too much diverse content? Are they too narrow or do they overlap too much with others? Remember that this is only an organizing system; make it as useful as you can without being perfectionistic. If it turns out that many changes are needed in your organizing system, decide whether or not all data need to be recoded using the new system.

8.   If necessary, recode your existing data. Use the results of the analysis to guide you in the next round of data collection. Then apply a similar process of organizing system development for the next set of data that cover new aspects of your research topic. As you do your analysis, and if this is relevant to your project, ask yourself whether some categories can be crystallized into concepts of the kind that are considered research outcomes (see the earlier section of this chapter). When your organizing and interpreting process is completed, your organizing system is likely to help you structure the flow of your research report. However, exercise caution. A strict adherence to the organizing system in your writing will probably not do justice to your study, since the system does not contain any clue about the intellectual importance of your findings, which is the main criterion to which you must pay attention when presenting your results.

References

GLASER, BARNEY G. AND STRAUSS, ANSELM L. (1967) *The Discovery of Grounded Theory: Strategies for Qualitative Research*, Chicago, Aldine Publishing Company.

HORVARTH, MICHAEL J.; KASS, CORRINE E. and FERRELL, WILLIAM R. (1980) 'An example of the use of fuzzy set concepts in modeling learning disability', *American Educational Research Journal*, 17, 3, pp, 309-24.

ROSCH, ELEANOR (1978) 'Principles of categorization', in ROSCH, E. and LLOYD, B. B. (Eds.) *Cognition and Categorization*, Hillsdale, NJ, Lawrence Erlbaum Associates.

WIGGINS, JERRY S. (1982) 'Circumplex models of interpersonal behavior in clinical psychology', in KENDALL, PHILLIP C. and BUTCHER, JAMES N. (Eds.) *Handbook of Research Methods in Clinical Psychology*, New York, John Wiley and Sons.

Qualitative Analysis Programs (MS-DOS): Basic Structures and Functions

Introduction

Qualitative analysis programs are software packages developed explicitly for the purpose of interpretative analysis using data that consists of narrative text. (Some programs are capable of including drawings or other non-text materials as well.) These packages are created by researchers in the social sciences, occasionally in cooperation with a computer scientist who handles the programming details. As a rule, each program grew out of the individual scholar's own analysis needs. Thus, the programs differ from each other along many dimensions. The main difference exists between programs designed for descriptive/interpretive analysis and those designed for theory-building. (This distinction is explained at the end of the chapter on analysis types.) This difference is one of degree; it is not absolute. Other differences have to do with the degree to which a program is language-oriented, to which it prepares data for additional quantitative analysis, or to which it provides special handling of structured data, such as those gathered when using a fixed interview schedule or an open-ended questionnaire. Naturally, work-habits and style also enter into the design of a program and determine the appearance of the screen, the manner of user-interaction, and procedural details, such as the process of code entering or modification of the coding (organizing) system.

At the time of this writing, the qualitative analysis packages developed for the personal computer and available to the general user were mainly descriptive/interpretive analysis programs. Although some begin to facilitate theory-building, they are not specifically designed to do so. Two programs for mainframe computers, QUALOG and NUDIST, have been created for theory-building. The principles used in QUALOG were recently incorporated in AQUAD, a program for the personal computer. PC versions of NUDIST (both for IBM and compatibles, and for the Macintosh) are in preparation. AQUAD and NUDIST are briefly described at the end of this chapter.

The bulk of this chapter is devoted to a general overview of the features of descriptive/interpretive analysis programs. Each of the packages on which the overview is based also has its own chapter in this book. All programs have been used widely, and some have been improved several times since their inception. But many researchers are still doing their data management by hand, and either are not aware that these programs exist, or are apprehensive of them.

One reason why people may be reluctant to use a computer rather than scissors, glue, index cards and multi-colored pens, is that these simple tools are immediately available, whereas a computer program is something whose operation one has to learn. Especially the very early programs required that an entire command structure be memorized. Whenever you wanted to do something, you first needed to press a certain combination of keys that readied the machine for the particular task. So you had to learn an entire set of key combinations for each program. All this was changed, however, when the 'menu' was invented.

Menus are lists of choices for program users. Each choice on the list refers to a task the program can perform. Usually, each task is abbreviated as a single letter. The user can either place the cursor on the task or type the letter, and the computer complies by offering the appropriate next step. Menus either take up the entire screen, or they are 'pull-down' menus. Pull-down menus are often employed when the program is operated from one basic menu, which is spread out in a line across the top of the screen, and each menu choice, in turn, has another set of options. When the cursor is placed on one of the words on the top line, the associated menu 'pulls down', i.e., appears as a list underneath the word. Still another design is used with the Macintosh computer: instead of words, symbols or 'icons' are painted along the rim of the screen, and the cursor is place on one of them with the 'mouse', and clicked.

All of the qualitative analysis programs that run on IBMs and IBM-compatibles use regular full-screen menus. Having menus means that there are no commands to learn; so there is nothing to memorize. That is not the same, however, as saying there is nothing to learn at all. Each program first has to be *understood*. How does it go about the business of reorganizing data? All text analysis programs for descriptive/interpretive research execute the same main functions, and they also have in common a quite similar structure. However, since each programmer developed his software according to his own perception of how a qualitative researcher would approach the task, each has his own working style and prefers a certain terminology. As a rule, the user's manual is written by the programmer himself; therefore, the manuals also remain within that framework. Consequently, it is sometimes not easy to discern the main Gestalt of the program among all the details about which the manual informs. Understanding any of the programs will be quite a bit easier if we first look at the functions they all perform, and at the programs' basic structure.

Before we do that, however, it might be helpful to explain program installation. When you acquire a new program, it usually comes with instructions about how to install it. Why can't we just plug the program disk into our disk drive and run it (especially since it sometimes runs just fine if we try that)? Here is the answer:

For any program to function properly, certain options within your operating system have to be set a particular way. Sometimes you are lucky, and a new software package needs the options set just the way they are configured already in your computer. Other programs will not work without modifying the settings. The new program disk usually has a small sub-program on it that makes these modifications for you. The user manual tells you how to activate the installation routine. This way you don't have to know much about the operating system of your computer. In a typical case, the installation program changes your **autoexec.bat** file and the **config.sys** file, two small programs that are part of your computer's operating system. Installing adds lines to these programs that affect the operating environment. These changes ready your computer to run the new program. They are permanent, i.e., once you have run a program's install routine on your computer, you can from now on just load the software (from your floppy or hard disk) without 'installing' it again.

The Structure of Analysis Software

When researchers work on re-organizing their data, they follow a logical sequence in their data manipulation: first certain things are done, then others, and still others come later. The analysis programs give you the *opportunity* to proceed in exactly that sequence, but they themselves as programs are not structured that way. They are structured in modules. This means that for each task there is a separate module that executes it. One way in which the 'architecture' of a program could be composed looks somewhat like the drawing on the next page.

The center module is not a sub-program, like the others, but a menu, i.e., a list of the available procedures. In a program like this you always return to the main menu in order to get to the other modules, which are the actual working parts of the program. There is no way to get from one task directly to the next, bypassing the center menu. Some programmers call the center menu the 'procedure' menu, since it lists all the procedures the program can perform. Within each module there are usually additional menus that list the sub-tasks of each procedure, and from which you select the proper one.

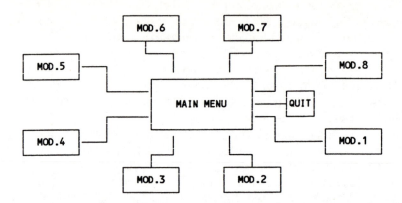

Even when the program structure is a bit different from this model, the main point to understand is that you can't usually get from just anywhere (performing one task) to anywhere else (performing another task) in a program. You usually have to return to some menu and indicate your choice of next task there. This structure implies one more thing: You can't expect an analysis program to guide you through the process. You must decide at any given time what you need to do next, depending on where you are in the course of your work, and then choose the computer procedure (module) that lets you take that next step.

The descriptions of individual programs in this book each will contain a diagram like the one above to make it easy for you to visualize the basic lay-out of the program. If you don't care for maps, just ignore them.

By now you might have started to wonder how you would know each time which is the 'proper' choice to make from all those menus. It's easy once you are aware of the basic functions an analysis program performs and those that are merely auxiliary.

Analysis Software Functions

Analysis programs for descriptive/interpretive analysis perform only *two basic functions*: they allow you to attach codes to segments of text, and they will, according to your instructions, search through your data for the segments that were coded a certain way, and assemble them. All the other operations the software performs are auxiliary functions. Some of these go beyond the basics of plain coding and searching/assembling, and are useful for making your analysis more sophisticated. We will call them '**enhancements**'. The other two types, however, have to do with getting ready for the main functions, i.e., they are '**preparatory**', and with performing those jobs that are necessary in a computer environment, the computer '**housekeeping**' functions. Below is a list of them; just skim it:

A. **Main functions**

    Attaching codes to segments of text

    Searching for text segments according to codes and assembling them

B. **Enhancement functions**

    Searching for multiple codes (segments to which more than one code was attached)

    Searching for a particular sequence of codes (for segments that follow each other in a certain order)

    Searching selectively (through only a specified group of data documents)

    Counting the frequency of the occurrence or co-occurrence of codes in the data

C. **Preparatory functions**

    Importing files (picking up documents that have been created by a word processor)

    Numbering the lines of the data text

    Printing out paper copies of the data with line numbers attached

D. **Housekeeping functions**

    Retrieving files (data documents)

    Saving files

    Changing the directory (switching from one disk drive to another)

    Printing (entire documents, individually retrieved segments, or all segments retrieved in a search for one code or all codes)

All analysis programs perform the main functions and the housekeeping functions. They *differ* in the kind of enhancements they provide and the preparatory tasks they require. Let's look at each type of functions separately.

A   The main functions

You might want to skip the later sections of this chapter, but you should carefully read this one. It will save you a lot of time subsequently, when you read about a particular program, since the many options of the menu will not confuse you. Just single out the basic functions, and it will be much easier to understand the program. You will also find out about some variations on the basic theme, and that might help you to decide which program is the right one for your purposes.

a   Attaching codes to segments of text

Since analysis programs expect that the researcher works with text segments as 'meaning units', not as language parts, they don't predetermine what constitutes a segment. They provide, instead, means by which you can designate the boundaries of a segment. There is one proviso, though. Most of the programs currently available do not recognize the beginning and ending of a sentence. (TEXTBASE ALPHA and HyperQual are the exceptions.) Their smallest working unit is the line. This means you cannot make your meaning unit run from the beginning of sentence A through the end of sentence G, for example. You can only make it go from the line on which sentence A begins to the line on which sentence G ends. Unless the beginning or ending of a sentence coincides with the beginning or ending of a line, (a condition that happens when the meaning unit is exactly a paragraph, a not uncommon occurrence), the program will start the segment in the middle of a sentence and end it likewise. The consequence is that later, when you look at extracted segments, you have to disregard the first few words as well as the last ones, and read only the complete sentences. Although this sounds as if it could become annoying, it actually turns out to be no problem. Most researchers get used to it so quickly they hardly notice it any more once they have worked with the program a little while.

There are two possible ways in which to code data text:

1.   directly on the screen while the data text is showing (TEXTBASE ALPHA, TAP, HyperQual)

2.   in a two-step procedure, using a paper printout of the text (QUAL-PRO, The Ethnograph).

Coding itself involves two operations: the beginning and the end of a text segment must be indicated, and the appropriate code word must be attached to the segment, i.e., the researcher must decide in which category of her/his organizing system the segment belongs. For coding right on the screen, programmers have invented various ways of telling the computer where the text boundaries are. Inserting the code word at the beginning of the segment and then indicating the end of the segment with a particular keyboard symbol or a special key stroke combination are the most efficient ways oOf performing the task. The code name is inserted either in the text itself or in the margin.

When the program does not provide for on-screen coding, the text usually is line-numbered. This means that the program consecutively attaches numbers to each line of the data text. They serve as location indicators. The researcher works with a paper copy of her/his data in which these numbers are printed out. S/he uses whatever method s/he feels comfortable with for identifying segment boundaries and assigning codes. (A common method is to indicate segments with square brackets.) In a second step, the boundary line numbers and the associated codes are entered into the computer, either as a simple list, or into pre-structured on-screen forms.

All programs permit the user to attach more than one code to a segment, since often a segment is relevant to more than one category. Segment boundaries may overlap (the exception is TAP), i.e., a new segment can begin in the middle of another. This is especially useful in open-ended interviews, where people sometimes slide from one topic into the next without a clear demarcation. In this case, the transitional sentences can be included in the first segment, as well as in the second, so potentially important context is not lost. Sometimes smaller parts of a large meaning unit are relevant to a category different from the large one as a whole. They are 'nested' in it. Programs that provide for overlap usually also provide for nesting.

Since in most qualitative studies the organizing system is being developed during the process of analysis, the first coding of the data is tentative. The organizing scheme is still being tried out. Therefore, analysis programs must provide an easy way of redoing or modifying the coding. Of course, the researcher can always discard the entire first round of coding (delete the files that hold the coding information) and start all over again with a fresh copy of the data document. But usually there are some parts that you want to leave the way they are. Since the bulk of the work the researcher has to do on the computer consists of marking segment boundaries and adding code names, you want to save as much of your previous coding as possible. The programs let you change, delete, or add individual codings, and some even allow you to delete a certain code 'globally' (throughout an entire data document), or replace a code with another one.

b   Searching for text segments according to codes and assembling them

Identifying the boundaries of text segments and coding them de-contextual-izes the segments, since they are now carved out from their place in the original data. The next step is their re-contextualization, which means bringing together all segments with the same code. In computer terms, re-contextualization is accomplished through the searching, sorting, and assembling functions of qualitative analysis programs.

In actuality, the programs never 'cut up' the original data document. In fact, they don't ever touch the data. They simply store the information you provided about segment boundaries and associated codes in separate 'files' that they create. Then, when you ask that all segments with the same code be assembled together, they first go to those files, search for all occurrences of that code, take the boundary descriptions, and apply those descriptions to the original text. They find the lines of text within those specified boundaries and print out a copy of them. As the search continues, the next segment is added, and so forth. The document that is created in this fashion provides the new 'topical' context for the segments. Each segment is now placed within the context of one category of your organizing system. Everything in your data that speaks to the same theme or covers the same aspect of your research project is collated for easy comparison.

The newly created document, i.e., the one that is the *result* of a 'search', is temporary. It is not automatically stored as a new file. All programs let you print it out on paper, however, and with most you get the option to 'print to disk'. This latter is a way of saving the document in ASCII, i.e., in a form that is accessible to other programs, as for instance your word processor. In your word processor you can then re-arrange the order of the segments, or you can use one copy of it to 'throw out' everything except those passages that you think you might want to quote.

You may ask: What order are the segments in when they come out of the computer? How does the computer 'sort' them? The answer is easy: The segments are searched for and displayed in exactly the sequence you specify. When you choose the module in the program that lets you search for coded segments, you are prompted to tell the computer two things: 1, for which codes do you want it to perform a search? and 2, in which data files do you want it to look for segments? The sequence in which you respond is the sequence the program uses for 'output'. In some programs you get the option to enter the codes randomly, but have them searched for and printed out in alphabetic order.

One of the most frustrating chores in the manual re-organizing of text data used to be the attachment of source information to every single segment that was extracted. Whether any given segment was taken from file A or from file B often makes a great difference in interpretation. Even when it doesn't, it just isn't acceptable for a responsible researcher to work with data segments whose origins s/he doesn't know. Certainly all segments that s/he intends to use as quotes must have reference information (although in the final report fictitious names are used, of course). Sometimes you might need to go back to the original location of a segment because you did not include enough context and need to check again on the environment from which it came. In the past, the reference information was added painstakingly by hand. It was easy to forget one or make a mistake. Even when word processors are used for cutting and pasting segments, the same problem arises; the reference information, i.e., its source of origin, must still be typed in for each segment. This is one small aspect of the analysis process where computer programs have made a huge difference. With an analysis program you don't need to worry about source information at all.

All analysis programs automatically attach information about the origin of any segment when it is extracted. The least they do is provide the name of the file from which it came. The programs that number the text lines of the original data document don't begin a new number with each page; they number all lines of the data document consecutively. Therefore, they have a perfect way of pinpointing exactly the location of a segment in that document: they print the line numbers out together with the text of the segment. If you have made a printout of your data document after the program has attached the line numbers, all you do is find the same line numbers that are attached to the segment in the original data document. If a segment runs from line 234 to line 256, for instance, you know to look for it on page 5 of the document printout (since there are approximately fifty lines to a page) and down about thirty lines. Voila, on line #234 the segment begins! This is such a handy feature that I recommend you use the line numbering feature of your word processor (if it has one) if you work with an analysis program that does not number lines.

While the capability to find a segment again in the original data is a must, you won't want to have to do that very often. If you knew more about the context than just the file name and the location within the file, you might never have to actually use that option during analysis. There is one program that allows you to do more than attach reference information to a segment. You can embed in the original data 'comments' when the conceptual context changes, that will then be added to any segment that follows that comment when it is extracted, acting almost like a heading for the segment <The Ethnograph>. If you are working with interview transcriptions, the program will also add the name of the speaker.

B   Enhancement functions

Coding and retrieving/assembling coded segments are the core of any analysis program. Although the way these functions are carried out differs somewhat across programs, you have a basic understanding of an analysis program if you are clear about these two main functions. The programs perform a lot of additional tasks, but they are embellishments of these two functions. Let's first look at some 'enhancements' of the basic functions. It is here where the differences among programs matter most: Your particular research project may need to use a special function that only one program provides. In that case it is important that you find that particular program. If you don't care to read this entire section, just find the headings that are relevant to your research.

a   Searching for multiple codes

A multiple code search is a search for co-occurring codes. Some researchers picture such a search as the discovery of the intersection of two or more categories, since you can specify that the computer find segments that have been assigned simultaneously to two or more categories. They have been coded with more than one code. This is a useful feature when you have a hunch that a certain category might be related to some other one. If you are doing a study on divorced fathers, for instance, you might have a category on 'child visits' (in which you gather everything that has to do with the fathers' visits with their children) and a category on 'relationship with ex-wife'. In reading through the printout of "visits" (the code you used for the father's visits), you may realize that the relationship to the father's ex-wife is often mentioned in the context of "visits" (the printout will show you whether a given segment is also coded "relat-ex-wife"). So you ask the computer to find every instance in which segments were coded simultaneously with "visits" and "relat-ex-wife". If it only finds a couple, your hunch could be wrong (although it is not proved to be so). If it finds many instances of co-occurring coding, your hunch was probably correct. You can now pore over the printout to discover what the connection between the two might be.

If a program offers multiple-code searches, it usually allows you to combine more than just two codes in a search. It even might give you the option to exclude a certain code if it is found in connection with others. For instance, you might search for "visits" combined with "relat-ex-wife", but don't want those instances where the segment was also coded "past relationship". (These kinds of combinations/exclusions are called 'Boolean', after a mathematician who invented an algebra that used 'classes' instead of quantities.)

b   Searching for a particular sequence of codes

A special case of a multiple code search is one where you ask the computer to search for codes that were attached in a particular order. An example for a sequence-oriented search is: You want all instances in which you sorted the segment into the category 'past relationship' first, and then you decided it was also secondarily relevant to 'visits'. You don't want those instances in which you primarily considered the segment relevant to 'visits', and only secondarily to 'past relationship'. One of the programs described here allows you to specify that order <TAP>.

There is still another way of ordering. You might want to look for segments that follow each other in a certain sequence. This feature comes in handy when your analysis is, in fact, concerned with sequences in behavior or in speech. Let's say you have field notes from a classroom observation. You code the behaviors of students, and in the process of analysis you get the hunch that behavior 'X' is usually followed by behavior 'Q', and 'Q' is often followed by 'A'. You can check this out by asking the computer to search for all instances in which a segment was coded "X", followed by a segment coded "Q", followed by a segment coded "A". The results of the search will tell you whether your hunch is correct or not <TAP>. (Whether it is significant, of course, depends on the nature and goal of your study.)

c   *Searching selectively*

Searching selectively means searching through a group of data documents according to the specifications you provide for identifying that group. It is not the same as entering only certain file names when you ask the computer to perform a search. Let's assume you are working with a large number of data documents, perhaps interview transcriptions. You are interested in whether the female interviewees as a group reacted to a certain issue differently from the male interviewees. So you enter the code for the issue, but specify that only transcriptions from female interviewees should be used in this search. Then you do the same for male interviewees, and now you can study the two printouts and compare.

How does the computer distinguish between female and male, or any other properties of the individual data files? Like everything else in the world of the computer: only by being told. In programs with a selective search feature you are invited to add something like a profile to each data file. You decide which characteristics of your respondents might be relevant for a later comparison. This is much like thinking of them in breakdowns or groups: age groups, groups from different geographic locations, ethnic groups, groups with a certain life style or taste, anything that is of potential importance to your study. Then you create a 'template' with a slot for each characteristic, and for each document the program now prompts you to fill in the specific values. These values are 'attached' to the document. It is to this list of values that the computer goes when asked to select only certain documents <The Ethnograph, TEXTBASE ALPHA>.

Both co-occurring code searches and selective searches provide the opportunity for the researcher to begin developing theoretical notions about the data. The co-occurrence of codes refers to coded segments, however. In programs for theory-building analysis (AQUAD, NUDIST), co-occurrence of codes refers to co-occurrence within an entire file. For further explanations about theory-building processes see the program descriptions at the end of this chapter and the appropriate section in the chapter on the mechanics of interpretational analysis.

d   Counting the frequency of the occurrence of codes

Making a computer count something is easy. Therefore you will find that all of the programs count how often any given code was used by you to categorize segments. It might be important for your study to find out whether theme "Y" was mentioned frequently, infrequently, or not at all. The code frequency count takes care of that in a jiffy.

The difference among programs in counting has to do mainly with multiple code searches. Some programs that perform multiple-code searches count co-occurrences of codes <TAP>, most do not. The latter merely print out all instances of co-occurrence and leave the counting to you. A further degree of sophistication is the display of frequencies. They can be organized in frequency tables, even with percentages <TAP>. The percentages are calculated in terms of how often a code occurs in relation to the occurrence of all other codes. You can't perform statistical significance tests on these numbers, but they can serve as indicators of relatively greater concern with the matter called "Abcd", for instance, or relatively higher awareness of or pre-occupation with an issue or observation.

The special features listed above are the main enhancements incorporated in the programs described in this book. Others are available or theoretically possible and are no doubt being considered by programmers. The individual program descriptions provide more detail.

C   Preparatory functions

You may skip this section, since the individual program descriptions will tell you how you must prepare your data documents to get them processed by the respective program. This section provides reading, however, if you either are a novice computer user or you want to compare the programs.

a   Importing files

As a rule (and unlike text data base managers), analysis programs are not equipped to let you enter your data directly into the program. (There are exceptions: QUALPRO.) Word processors are much more efficient for that purpose and provide many convenient features that would only make the analysis program unwieldy if it tried to duplicate them. Therefore, all programs let you import files. Importing means: moving into one program documents that have been created by another program.

This is not as easy as it sounds. Each word processor has its own way of embedding formatting information (such as indents, page breaks, underlines, etc.), and these idiosyncracies usually result in an unintelligible mess when the document is processed by another program as is. The solution is a kind of document Esperanto, a simplified 'language' or type of text reproduction that strips a text of embedded formatting characters. It is called ASCII (which, as you have no reason to remember, stands for American Standard Code for Information Interchange). ASCII text is a form of text that is free of all but the most basic formatting symbols. Most word processors have a facility that converts their documents into ASCII. Some analysis programs also include small facilities on the program disk that do conversions. At any rate, if your document appears to have lost its integrity when you look at it from within the analysis program, it is not the fault of the analysis program. The likely cause is an improper ASCII conversion.

In addition to ASCII conversion, some of the analysis programs require that the margins are set a certain way when the document is still in the word processor, and before ASCII conversion. The reason is that these programs create screen images or printouts of your documents that include the analysis codes or other information in the margins. If the margins weren't wide enough, there would be no room for the codes. Actually, the programs selfishly always provide enough room for the codes, even when you don't make the margins wide enough. If they have to cut somewhere, they simply slice off the sides of your document. You would not want to work with a text segment in which the last ten characters or so of each line are missing.

b   Numbering the lines of the data text

In those analysis programs that find data segments by line numbers, the task that must be performed before anything else can be done, is the consecutive numbering of the lines of each data document. This either happens automatically upon import of the document into the analysis program, or a special program module on the menu takes care of it quickly.

Once the lines are numbered, the coding information gets attached to the numbers, not to the text itself. This means that you shouldn't change the data text after numbering, at least not in such a way that the lines no longer contain the same words. If you do, the segment running from line 100 to 110 might now not include the end of the last sentence you were interested in. The computer still works with the same coding instructions with total disregard of the content of the lines. Therefore, a change in text usually means recoding. Since coding is the most time-consuming part of data management, it is best to make sure the data are exactly correct when you import them into the analysis program.

c   Printing out paper copies of the data

One of the main differences among programs is the mode in which codes are attached. You either see the document directly on the screen and type the codes right onto the screen as well <TAP, TEXTBASE ALPHA, HyperQual>, or you work first with a paper copy. These two ways of handling the coding process are not merely peculiarities of the programs, but reflect the work style of the programmer. Some researchers prefer to pore at leisure over the data when deciding what is relevant and in which way. Their eyes wander long distances to take in the 'feel' of the data at any given place. Others are quite comfortable with the twenty-five lines the computer screen displays. (Of course, even the program that allows direct screen-coding will make a paper copy and allow you to work with that first, then on the screen.)

The paper copy on which the coding is to be done consists of your data document, formatted for the respective analysis program, and with numbers printed next to each line. You may draw square brackets to indicate the boundaries of the meaning units, and write the code(s) in the margin. This is the method most programmers suggest. You can do it, of course, any way you like, as long as it is clear which line numbers go with which code. Line numbers for the segments and code names are entered into the computer in the next phase of the process.

Entering line numbers and code words from a prepared paper copy is a dull task. At the same time it must be done conscientiously, since a wrong code word means the segment is lost for the analysis. (If the name is wrong, the segment will be assembled with others to which it does not belong; if the code name is misspelled, the segment will never show up at all, since you are not aware of the error and will not ask the computer to search for the misspelled code.) Unless you are a stickler for details, it might be of advantage to employ a good secretary or data entry person. The computer operation takes only a few minutes to learn.

D   Housekeeping functions

This section is mostly for novice computer users.

a   Retrieving files (data documents)

The above described array of tasks is manifold enough to clutter an analysis program's menus. But there are still more tasks a program must perform, and these simply because the computer demands them. They are familiar to you through the word processor. Before you can work on a document (or 'file'), here as there, you must call up a copy of it to the screen.

Actually, this is not quite correct; you call the document copy up into the computer's RAM, the Random Access Memory that functions as the current work space for the computer. The document does not necessarily appear on the screen at the same time. It only does so when the programmer wants you to see what you are working on. Sometimes a program merely needs to know which document to retrieve, then holds it in memory while you decide what you want to do with it. So don't be surprised if in some cases after 'retrieval' of a file the screen looks just like it did before. The file is now 'active', which means the operations you want to perform in one of the program's modules will be carried out on that particular document (for instance, the attaching of codes). The document does not have to be visible to be worked on. Usually it remains active until you save it again, and sometimes it is automatically saved when you begin working on another file.

b   Saving files

As in your word processor, any new work done must be saved. 'New work' in analysis programs usually means new files that are created by the program as you code, and that are automatically associated with the active document file. You don't need to know the names of these associated files; they will always be retrieved by the program automatically when you tell it you want to work with a particular document.

Usually, you must take the proper steps to save new work. The programs nicely remind you to do so before you exit. One of them <The Ethnograph>, saves everything automatically the moment it is created. Although that results in slight delays at certain times in the program operation, the advantages far outweigh the inconvenience. Imagine, if you will, that you have entered segment boundaries and code names for a twenty-page document, and as you are getting to the last few segments your screen suddenly goes blank because your cat got entangled in the electric cords and pulled out the plug! You could lose hours and hours of work.

c   Changing the directory

One frequent source of bewilderment for users of analysis programs is the message "file not found", or a similar notice. You know that the file whose name you just typed must be there, but the computer is 'stupid' enough not to find it! Usually, the problem is that the file is not on the disk the program is looking at. You need to insert another disk, or you must tell the computer to look on a different disk drive. In order to tell which of these two actions is needed, you must look at the names of the files that are on the disk in question. Usually, you can do that without exiting the program and returning to the DOS prompt (exception: TAP). It is a good idea, however, once you have decided on which disk you want to keep particular data documents, to make a printout of each disk directory, i.e., the list of file names on that disk. Being able to spell the names of your files correctly is one thing the computer stubbornly expects of you.

When a computer program is loaded, the computer usually considers 'active' the disk drive from which it was called up. Unless you tell the computer otherwise, it will look at the disk in that drive or on that subdirectory when asked to retrieve a file. As a rule, analysis programs are set up differently when using two floppy disks: The convention is to put the program disk in drive A, and the data disk in drive B. If you want any other arrangement, for instance if you keep your data in a special subdirectory of your hard disk, you must tell the program so. This can either be done for long-term use (you 'set up' the program accordingly), or just for the moment. Switching from one disk drive or subdirectory to another is called 'changing the directory'.

d   Printing

Analysis programs would not do you any good unless they provided you with hard copies of your re-contextualized data. All programs are set up to connect directly with your printer, and you usually don't even have to set your printer a certain way. The programs contain instructions to the printer and print the coded version of your data document and the collection of data segments that are the result of a search, as well as individual segments.

To understand the menus, you need to know that in computer language 'printing' is a generic term for 'placing text somewhere'. The text can be sent to your printer, but it can also be sent to your screen (remember, it doesn't always arrive there automatically), or to your disk. The latter is not just a different phrase for saving a file. If something is 'printed to disk', it is simultaneously converted into ASCII. An ASCII file can be picked up by your word processor (unless you have an ancient version of a word processor) and reformatted or otherwise manipulated. Since you eventually will write up your research, this means that you never have to type any part of your data (as quotes, for example) over again.

The preceding major section of this chapter, describing the functions of current qualitative analysis programs, follows a specific outline. This same structure is used in the chapters that describe the individual software packages. This way, you can easily compare the programs, for instance, by reading all sections on the basic functions consecutively, or all sections on the enhancements.

Individual Programs

Programs for Descriptive/Interpretive Analysis

In this book five qualitative analysis programs are described in detail, four for IBM and IBM-compatible computers (**TAP, QUALPRO, The Ethnograph, TEXTBASE ALPHA**), and one for the Macintosh (**HyperQual**). These are by no means the only programs that have been invented. They are the ones I am most familiar with, and the ones that currently seem to be the most widely used. I have deliberately excluded text analysis programs for mainframe computers, since they are accessible only to a few people. One additional microcomputer package is known to me with which I have not worked; it is called GATOR. Following is a brief description of it. After that, two programs for theory-building research are introduced.

GATOR (for IBM and IBM-compatibles) was created by Richard Giordano, Jonathan R. Cole, and Harriett Zuckerman at Columbia University. The program works with text that is coded in a word processor. The code (or 'key-word') is inserted in the text immediately in front of the segment. It is made recognizable as a code to GATOR by enclosing it in angle brackets. The boundaries of the segment are marked by enclosing the segment in square brackets. Smaller segments can be nested within larger ones. In that case the code word, in angle brackets, is preceded by a symbol (or 'marker') of one's own choice, which is inserted again immediately after the end of the segment with which it is associated. The codes and segment boundaries can be modified (edited), and new ones can be added in the word processor.

When the coded word processing document is imported into GATOR, the program creates a new file by extracting the code names and their associated segments, along with some additional information. After this, it works much like a data base manager: it searches for code words and retrieves the associated text as a 'report'. GATOR is also capable of searching for specific words and word combinations in the actual data text. Code searches can be selective, i.e., they can be specified for files that represent certain socio-demographic or other variables. These variables are stored in the data base for each data file. When they are numeric, they can provide a link to statistical packages like SAS or SPSS.

Programs for Theory-building

AQUAD (Auswertung **qua**litativer **D**aten) was developed in Germany by Günter Huber, and is based on the American mainframe program QUA-LOG (Shelly and Sibert, 1985). In this program, files (data documents) are considered characterized by their codes. Rather than resembling a heading or a topic descriptor, a category developed for AQUAD already encapsu-lates the substance of statements made (in an interview, for example), i.e., what *kind* of opinion, emphasis, incident, characterization, etc. is reported. If a group of people were asked individually about their attitude toward the promotion policies of their organization, and the group as a whole expressed three distinguishable attitudes, then each type of attitude would get its own code; the researcher would not classify them under the one heading 'attitudes toward promotion'. (For an explanation of coding for theory-building analysis see the chapter on organizing systems.) This principle of 'file-coding' enables the researcher to translate co-occurrence of codes in one document into relationships such as: attitude "A" is always present where people are in situation "B", or behavior "X" is usually connected to personal characteristic "Z".

In AQUAD, which attaches numbers to the lines of the data text, coding can be done either in the text directly on the screen, or by making a list. The list is constructed by entering the numbers of the first and last lines of the segment and then the associated code name. When working with the text on the screen, the margin accepts a start symbol (^) to the right of the line where the segment begins, then the code name, a dash, and the number of the segment's last line. Codes and segment boundaries can be modified best in the code list, where the common word processing functions are available for editing.

Searching for all segments with the same code and assembling them is the simplest data manipulation in AQUAD. The program's emphasis is on the co-occurrence of codes. It offers the researcher the opportunity to formulate her/his own logical conditions about potential relationships and to have the program locate all instances in which these conditions are fulfilled in the data. It even counts all instances in which these particular connections among the specified codes do not exist. Several such hypothe-sis-exploring statements are already furnished with the program, for instance about the co-occurrence of two or three codes within ten text lines, searches for codes in Boolean combinations <Text retrievers>, the chronological sequence of certain codes, etc. Since socio-demographic data or other types of identifiers can also be attached to a data document as an ordinary code, this 'selection' code can be inserted in a logical statement and thus its connection to other codes be explored. At the time of this writing an English screen version of AQUAD was available, but not yet an English user's manual.

NUDIST (Non-numerical unstructured data indexing, searching, and theory-building) has been created by Tom and Lyn Richards at La Trobe University in Australia. It was not yet available for the personal computer at the time of this writing. Both IBM and Macintosh versions are in preparation. The program has advanced from the simple assembly of coded segments to the development of sophisticated organizing systems (called 'indexing system' by NUDIST) that become the main conceptual tool for the researcher's analytic work. Indexing systems are conceived in the form of inverted tree structures (much like the example provided in the chapter on organizing systems) that have no limits to their size and intricacy. While programs for descriptive/interpretive analysis create lists of the codes and their associated segments in a separate file, NUDIST supplies an entire separate database for the categories, their place in the tree-structure, and the information about the associated segments of text (called the 'index database').

Although the researcher must begin the coding of her/his data text with a rudimentary organizing system in mind, this 'indexing' system is gradually built up as s/he works with her/his data. The system is shown on the screen as an inverted tree diagram, and can be added to and modified at any time. A refined organizing system can be viewed as one of the results of an analysis effort (see the chapter on organizing systems).

Like AQUAD, NUDIST works with line numbers to identify the boundaries of segments. When searching for data pieces that are coded ('flagged' in NUDIST) with a certain code, the program can return either the text itself or the location of the text only, expressed as line numbers. This facility allows the researcher to number (by hand) material that is not electronically available, enter line numbers and codes into the computer, and use NUDIST's search functions to indicate the positions of all pieces of data that are 'flagged' the same way. The data pieces can then be located and inspected in the hard-copy material. Moreover, the program's theory-building facilities can be used on such non-electronic material as well.

The main theory-building function of NUDIST is the search for co-occurring or overlapping coding within data segments or within entire files (the places where categories 'intersect'), plus the corresponding search for counter-evidence. Unlike other programs, NUDIST saves the results of such searches. They may be treated as new categories, allowing progressive exploration and testing of emerging theory. These search results, and the memos that can be attached to them and to individual files, let the researcher create an entire database *about* the original data, which in turn can be organized and analyzed.

HyperResearch was the tentative name at the time of this writing for a theory-building program for the Macintosh, developed at Boston College by Sharlene Hesse-Biber, Paul Dupuis, and Scott Kinder. Like HyperQual <HyperQual>, it builds on the HyperCard program provided for these computers. Files are viewed as characterized by the codes attached to segments contained in them, and the program then works with Boolean operators (see the chapter on text retrievers) to find co-occurrences of codes and counter-evidence. The text of coded segments can be assembled together, but the main result of a HyperResearch search is a list of the files in which the specified condition is met (files are assigned numbers, and the results are reported by the program as a list of file numbers).

References

HESSE-BIBER, SHARLENE; DUPIUS, PAUL and KINDER, SCOTT (1989) 'HyperResearch: A computer program for the analysis of qualitative data using the Macintosh', paper presented at the annual meeting of the American Sociological Association, San Francisco.

HUBER, GÜNTER L. (1989) *AQUAD: Manual zur computerunterstützten Auswertung qualitativer Daten,* Bericht Nr. 25, Institut für Erziehungswissenschaften I, Universität Tübingen.

RICHARDS, THOMAS J. (1987) *User Manual for NUDIST: A Text Analysis Program for the Social Sciences,* Replee P/L, Melbourne, Australia.

SHELLY, ANNE and SIBERT, ERNEST (1985) *The QUALOG User's Manual,* Syracuse, NY, Syracuse University, School of Computer and Information Science.

How to Deal With a Computer

Introduction

This chapter is for readers who feel apprehensive about computers or suspicious of them. There are good reasons to have those feelings. Computers can be maddeningly demanding and confusing. But there is a way to get them under control.

In 1974 Ted Nelson wrote *Computer Lib/Dream Machines*, a book that has become a classic in computer literature. In it he said, 'One of the commonest and most destructive myths about computers is the idea that they "only deal with numbers". This is TOTALLY FALSE. Not only is it a ghastly misunderstanding . . . it is a damned lie.' He continues,

> Computers are COMPLETELY GENERAL, with no fixed purpose or style of operation. In spite of this, the strange myth has evolved that computers are somehow "mathematical". Actually, von Neumann, who got the general idea about as soon as anyone (1940's), called the computer THE ALL PURPOSE MACHINE.
>
> (Indeed, the first backer of computers after World War II was a maker of multi-light signs. It is an interesting possibility that if he had not been killed in an airplane crash, computers would have been seen first as text-handling and picture-taking machines, and only later developed for mathematics and business) . . . COMPUTERS HAVE NO NATURE AND NO CHARACTER, save what has been put into them by whoever is creating the program for a particular purpose. (Nelson, 1974, p. 10)

The Myth

Many qualitative researchers have told me they fear that computers may be harmful to qualitative investigation. Their reasons for this conviction are, of course, personal, but I believe they probably derive from a myth. These researchers expect the 'all purpose machine' to have a purpose and nature of its own. They believe this purpose is antithetical to intuition, insensitive to nuance and meaning, and resistant to non-numerical information. But the 'all purpose machine', mistakenly called a 'computer', has no innate purposes or characteristics. It is a 'nothing' machine, awaiting instructions from programmers who tell it not only what to *do*, but what to *become*.

Maybe it is the name that causes these concerns. If we had called them the 'all purpose machines' or the 'symbol handling machines' instead of christening them with the math-sounding 'computers', we might not misrepresent them so often in our minds. There is no doubt that our perceptions can make us misread our own experiences. One researcher once told me about his new word processor. 'I felt like a boob for the first six weeks. I felt stupid because I was stupid about getting the computer to work right. And the handbooks were written in a jargon I could not understand, which also made me feel stupid. I feared the computer would master me, rather than my mastering it. I was fearing to be controlled by this wholly rational/technical world. I was feeling frustrated and insecure instead of empowered and encouraged.'

Where do these frustrations come from? Probably from misguided expectations. Our expectations around computers have been influenced by many factors. For one, there is history. When computer people were only a special few with exclusive access to the 'computer lab', ordinary people never saw the great machines. The insiders, as usual, wanted to keep the outsiders out, and, as usual, they created a language and a culture that helped to keep the gates closed. Early computers were large, delicate machines that had to be housed in special environments. They were so dreadfully expensive their owners would let them be run only by highly trained technicians. This turned the information department managers into machine/knowledge protectors. They were generally not inclined to give up the power and privilege their special know-how gave them. Computer time was a scarce resource; there were many more needs for computer services than were available. The people who wanted information processed had to persuade the specialists to schedule their queries. Furthermore, the clerks who handled the cards and papers produced by early computers were also at the mercy of the computer priesthood and did not understand their mysterious machines. Since they didn't understand them and couldn't control them, the clerks blamed the errors on the computers. When your electric bill said you owed $2,000 instead of $20, the standard response was, 'It was the computer'. There seemed to be little anyone could do.

And then there came the talented youngsters who miraculously broke into the inner sanctum and outsmarted the experts. Obviously, they were geniuses; not your average neighbor's kid. They were bespectacled and sat up all night in the green glow of the computer screen, their brains churning. They were weird. The movies had a great time showing them to us as nerds and hackers.

All this reinforced the sense among computer illiterati, which was most of us, that we were powerless before the computer. That was the baggage we carried along with the Apples and IBM PCs as we started buying them for our homes and offices. Our trepidation was fortified by the new and bizarre language we encountered in the computer manuals. Even today, too many computer manuals are written in the jargon of those early times.

When an otherwise extraordinarily successful professor says, 'I felt stupid', the machine must have prompted insecurities developed long before the computer arrived on her/his desk. S/he understands and feels powerful within her/his field and with the rest of our complicated university culture, from the procedures at the research library to the functioning of the academic senate. But the computer culture is different. It is alien and threatening.

In the common myth, the computer culture is beyond the intellectual reach of ordinary people. Computers deal with symbols most of us do not understand, and therefore we consider the machine to be not only smart, but smarter than we are. There certainly are aspects of this device that are highly technical and complex. Yet, on another level, the computer is a simple machine. As a user, for instance, you don't need to understand *how* it works to make it work, and even to feel in charge. Many people who have no idea how a carburetor works drive their cars with great confidence. Similarly, it is no big deal to climb into the 'driver's seat' of your computer and learn how to steer it. Here are some basic pieces of knowledge that will help you get there.

Basic Facts

1. **You cannot destroy or hurt the computer by anything you do on the keyboard.** You might not be able to achieve what you want, or the screen may display unintelligible messages, but the worst that can happen when you work with your keyboard (unless, of course, you spill your coffee on it), is that the keyboard 'locks up'. That means, no matter what key you hit, nothing happens. The usual reason for this unhappy state of affairs is that the computer, which is extremely literal, has received conflicting messages that it can't carry out simultaneously. When the computer locks up, just switch it off and start again. You may lose whatever you had been typing, but no damage has been done to the computer itself.

Hitting keys randomly - a desperate measure we often resort to - will not fix the computer once it is locked up, nor is it exactly the best way of getting the computer to cooperate. In the normal course of events, you will type information into the computer or give it one-key or two-key commands. If your software is good (we will come back to this topic), that is all the computer will ever ask of you, and unless you made a mistake, it will not disappoint you.

2. **Computers are helpless without instructions.** In computer language these instructions are called **programs.** There are two basic kinds of programs:

a. **Programs that tell the computer how to function as a computer** (how to find the disk drives, how to transfer something from a disk to the screen, how to display things on the screen, etc.). These programs are usually called Disk Operating Systems (DOS), and only a few varieties exist. A normal personal computer works with one operating system, and the software you run on your computer must be compatible with that operating system. IBM computers and computers that are 'compatible' with IBM computers are made to run with IBM-DOS or MS-DOS, Apple computers run with AppleDOS. These programs are usually provided when you buy the computer, and they are on a disk that is either called a DOS disk, or a boot disk. You must 'boot up' a computer every time you switch it on. 'Booting' comes from 'pulling yourself up by the bootstraps'. The initial activities with the operating system turn the computer from a useless collection of oddly manufactured metal, glass and sand into a machine with functions. If yours is a hard disk, the boot program may be installed on the hard disk and the computer set up in such a way that it goes directly to the hard disk when it is switched on and boots itself up. So, if you have never heard of DOS or booting, then you probably got a hard disk with the computer, and someone set it up to do the booting by itself.

A DOS program does quite a bit more than booting up the computer. It can provide a list of the items on the disk, soft or hard. It can transfer (copy) disks or the files on them to other disks, it can rename files, and so on. However, Disk Operating Systems were created prior to the invention of the term 'user-friendly', and dealing with DOS involves learning. Therefore, programs have been developed that duplicate the DOS functions in a user-friendly and more powerful way (such as PCTools). Today, DOS no longer need play a big role in a computer user's life. But it is DOS that makes your computer behave like one before you load a program, and after you have exited one. (DOS puts the "A>", "B>", and "C>" on your screen, for instance, to tell you which disk drive is active.)

b. **Programs that make the computer perform specific services** for you (such as word processing, calculating, accounting, drawing, time managing, keeping and tracking information, and all kinds of astounding things). As you well know, there are thousands of these programs. They are generally called software (technically, DOS programs are software, too), or application programs (DOS is specifically *not* an application program). More about application programs later.

3. **There are two places where the instructions** (and the electronic products you create with their help, such as word processing documents) **can reside**: they can be **on a disk**, soft or hard (the latter is inside the computer in most cases), **or 'in memory'**. You could compare these with the drawers and the top of a desk. The disks correspond to the drawers, the memory to the desktop. (There is one important difference: just because something is 'in memory' doesn't mean you can see it on the screen. Only what the program you are working with instructs the computer to place on the screen is visible to you. In other words, your screen acts somewhat like a 'window' to your desktop.) The memory is the working surface, so to speak. It is the famous RAM, that goes with numbers like '256K' or '640K'. The bigger this number, the larger your working surface, i.e., the more you can keep simultaneously 'active' (although, as I said, not necessarily visible) at any given time.

The advantage of having a separate 'working surface' memory is that you never need to touch the original content of the 'drawers'. Every time you 'load' something from a disk into memory you are in actuality copying it. Then you work with that copy. When you work with a word processor, for instance, a copy of the word processor resides in the memory, and so does the document you are creating. Unless you torture the disk, the original program and all documents already saved will remain safe and sound. The disadvantage, or better the danger in having a separate working surface lies in the fact that the computer treats it as temporary. The moment the computer is shut off, the working surface is cleared out (as if you had a janitor who instantly feeds everything you leave on top of your desk into a shredder). That's the most common way to lose newly created work. As you know, the computer is sometimes shut off not entirely on purpose, as for instance by a power failure. Therefore, number one rule when working with a computer is to 'save' one's new work at regular intervals. This means replacing the original on the disk with the new version from the working surface. I myself long ago decided that I can't bear the agony of a possible loss of my cumbersomely typed creations, and will refuse to work with a word processor that does not periodically save my current working document automatically, nicely creating a special 'back-up file' for it.

4. **DOS programs** have been around for a long time and **are almost never the cause of any trouble**, because they are long since 'debugged' (unless they are a version new to the market), which means that they have

no flaws. If you ever have reason to get mad at your computer, it's probably not the computer or its operating system that are at fault. The problem is likely to be with the software (or with the software's user manual, if it makes it difficult for you to understand what you are supposed to do).

Whenever you do anything at all with your computer (except listing the content of your disks or other DOS procedures), you must use a program. Each program is nothing more, and nothing less, than the reflection of the mind of the person (or persons) who created it. The moment you call up a program you are beginning an interaction with another mind (or group of minds). Any word processing program, for example, is how some programmers imagined you might want to handle the construction of documents. You are responding to a collection of decisions made by a single person or, more likely, a small group of people about the best way to readjust text on the screen, the best way to insert or correct text, the 'most intuitive' way to search for and replace information, the most effective way to find and fix spelling errors, and so forth. Different word processing programs are collections of different sets of decisions, reflecting the personal choices of a different group of programmers. If you don't like the way your word processor numbers pages, for example, it is not the computer that displeases you, it is the judgments and decisions of that group of people programmers who decided how your word processing program was to number pages.

The fact that some person or persons are responsible for 'what the computer does' means that everything from the conceptualization of the comprehensive task of word processing, for example, down to every detail, such as the design of the screen, the way you are asked to select a command, or the writing in the manual is a matter of human choice. If you have problems with the program (or the manual), you and the computer programmer have different work styles or thinking habits, or the program (or manual) is not well conceived for anyone.

Appropriate Expectations

Since the intent of programmers is to provide you with useful tools, you have a right to expect that your computer will please you. The computer is supposed to do exactly what you want, and do it in a way that is easy for you and efficient. Fortunately, we live in an age where programmers compete with each other, and that gives the consumer power. This power was recognized a few years back when the 'user-friendly' slogan arrived on the scene. In the early days, when application programs were developed the procedures were usually determined by the internal logic of the programming language, and the rules of efficiency. If it did what it was supposed to do, a program was fine, whether or not ordinary human beings could understand how to make it perform. Thankfully, we have come a long way since. Users are 'talking back' in the interaction. They demand 'user support' from the software companies, and manuals have become much easier to comprehend ever since programmers realized that to sell software they must tune in to the reader rather then ask the reader to learn their 'culture'.

The conclusion from all this is: Most of the time when you say, in anger or frustration, 'The computer . . .', you are actually referring to 'The software . . .', which means, in turn, 'Whoever produced the software . . . '. No one has the right to frustrate you or make you feel stupid. You can refuse to be treated that way. Before you purchase a program, read some reviews or ask people who have worked with it. You are perfectly justified in demanding a 'user-friendly' program, and should expect to be provided with well organized and helpful instructions in the manual.

Much more important, however, than following a few pieces of practical advice, is to adjust one's attitude. Expectations are powerful. What you expect to get is what you get, by and large, because what you expect determines in large measure what you perceive. If you expect your new computer to be controlling and anti-intuitive, that's the way it will be for you forever, unless, persisting until you become genuinely familiar with the way it operates, your expectations are amended by your experiences. If computers make you insecure, it is not because of their nature, it is because you anticipate computer behavior and resistance that will frustrate and demean you. The computer, the 'all purpose machine', will do its best to oblige.

Ted Nelson taught us long ago that 'Computer Lib' is a matter of conforming our beliefs about the machines to their functions. It probably helps to 'anthropomorphize' our personal computers. We tend to do that anyway, to think of them as having intentions and purposes. More than any other symbol of our high technology, with the exception of the automobile, the computer has become 'alive' for us. We develop relationships to our computers. We hate them or love them, and sometimes become convinced that our computers have minds of their own. But we must be careful to impute the proper character to our computers. In our new myth, we could design our expectations to fit the computer's actual functions, rather than the imaginary ones that have misled us. The first step is to recognize and accept the fact that the 'minds' of our computers are really the minds of their programmers. People often act as if they were trying to comply with the expectations of their computers; if something goes wrong, they feel somehow at fault, as if they have failed the computer. It is always the other way around: the minds whose programs we are using have let us down. They have sought to imagine what we would want and need in our applications, and have missed.

Recognizing the power of expectations is liberating. We can create a set of expectations that empower us in relation to these machines. We can decide to approach computers, for example, as engaging puzzles, as useful tools, as All Purpose Machines. We can understand that the machine is NOTHING until someone tells it what to be.

Changing our expectations about our computers and their functions can help put us truly in control of them. To be sure, you are not going to get away without expending any effort at all. There are still facts about working with a computer you must know and understand. But those facts don't require a technical genius. Most of them are simple, just like the ones explained above. They won't take months to learn, since the basics of computer literacy are few. All of the text analysis programs described in this book are menu-driven and require no or very little learning of 'commands' (special key combinations that instruct the computer to perform a certain task). They do require that you understand them conceptually. Sometimes that is another reason why the computer at first seems mysterious to us. We don't know what it is 'up to'. Again, this is an artifact of programming. To accomplish a certain job, the programmer has to break down the process into many small steps (many more than you will ever become aware of just by running the program). The sequences in which these steps are then carried out must make sense, but there are many options for organizing them. Each programmer has her/his own way of deciding what works best. Therefore, two programs that perform exactly the same functions can have quite different 'architectures'. The program will also have its own style of 'talking' to you on the screen; the programmer uses her/his own language when designing the screens. The language is the vocabulary the programer is accustomed to in her/his work. A psychologist will use terms that are different from those of a sociologist or a linguist, not to mention personal preferences.

The lesson to learn is that you should not expect to sit down with a new program for academic work and immediately understand everything it says to you. Some software producers provide 'tutorials' with their programs that guide you key-stroke by key-stroke through all the functions the program can perform. But many people get impatient with them. They don't want to spend hours working with other people's material; they want to begin doing something with their own data. I am one of these people. Tutorials, especially the ones that take up 101 pages in the manual, terrify me. Faced with such lengthy exercises I ask, 'Can't someone just show me how this goes?' I want to be able to play with the program, to begin doing some small but basic tasks with outcomes I can use. I don't want to sit there as I used to do in my high school Latin class, mechanically following instructions and memorizing details. If you feel the same way, try to find someone who has worked with the program already and can introduce you to its use. There often are 'hands-on' training workshops available, even for such relatively low-use programs as the text analysis software described in this book (the people from whom you buy the program are likely to know about them). Or there are introductions written specifically for first-time users. After you read the brief program descriptions in this book, for instance, you should be able to feel 'in charge' the moment you begin working with one of them.

The moral of the story is: our expectations must be well balanced. There is no reason to be mystified by the computer or to feel helpless. On the other hand, one should not expect to get away with no investment in time or no mental struggle whatsoever. Computers are 'all-purpose-machines' for sure. They will expedite and simplify much of our work. But don't forget that you want to use them for *intellectual* work, and that rarely comes easy.

References

NELSON, THEODOR H. (1974) *Dream Machines (The Flip Side of Computer Lib)*, South Bend, IN, Theodor Nelson.

How to Read the Descriptions of Text Analysis Programs

Text analysis programs have a limited market and, therefore, have not attracted the attention of software reviewers who write for computer journals. No introductions or reviews are available elsewhere, and it is not likely that they will be. That is one reason why the programs are described here in detail.

Each description of the software packages in this book follows the same outline used in the chapter on the basic structure and functions of MS-DOS text analysis programs. The main intent is to show how each one tackles the tasks of de-contextualizing and re-contextualizing, and what enhancement functions it offers. In addition, you will be introduced briefly to each program in general. The introduction and the section on underlying concepts each programmer incorporated are meant to give you the flavor of the program and help you understand why the program is set up the way it is.

Since you are not likely to have the program in your computer and therefore cannot play with the keys nor look at the screens, the descriptions will seem rather lifeless. It's much like reading about a strange country without actually travelling there; after a while it gets boring. If you fear this might happen to you, don't read each chapter from beginning to end. There are two reasons to read these chapters in the first place:

1. to discover which program best suits the research projects you usually conduct, or are currently engaged in.
2. to learn which program is most congruent with your work style.

The best way to go about these tasks is to proceed in the following manner:

Step 1:   Read the chapter sections on the enhancement functions performed. This is where the major differences among the programs are found. If a program does not have the capabilities you'd like to use for your research, pay no further attention to it.

Step 2:   Read the introductions and perhaps the 'underlying concepts' sections on each program you still are considering. This will give you a better idea of the character or 'feel' of the programs. Some descriptions may sound more appealing to you than others; some programs might fit your style of thinking and working more closely than others.

Step 3:   Once you have narrowed your choices, read the entire chapter on the programs still in the running. Look at the screen reproductions, and especially the way the results of the re-contextualization are displayed (in the sections on searching/assembling coded segments). Decide which one you would be most comfortable working with. Visualize your own data there and imagine which one would be most helpful for your interpretation.

Step 4:   Browse through the other descriptions briefly, even those that you don't expect to serve your research purpose. You might discover that some program will let you perform operations quite likely to enrich your analysis, in ways you would never have thought of.

Here are a few rules of thumb (but don't let them influence you too strongly). All text analysis software packages described here are reliable, smooth, and user-friendly programs that are worth owning. If you are doing a fairly basic qualitative research project that requires no special treatment, consider QUALPRO. If you are phenomenologically oriented, planning to do intensive in-depth work on your data, both QUALPRO and The Ethnograph are well suited. The Ethnograph is also useful for the beginnings of theory-building. If your data are a bit more structured, or if you are interested in linguistic aspects of your data, TAP might be the one to pay attention to. (Look at text retrievers, too, if you are a linguist.) TEXTBASE ALPHA is similar to TAP in this respect, and even lends itself to studies in which the same data are to be analyzed quantitatively as well as qualitatively. It also is similar to The Ethnograph, but let's you code right on the screen. For theory-building, TEXTBASE ALPHA let's you connect socio-demographic variables to categories, but not categories with each other (which The Ethnograph does to a certain degree) <Types of analysis>.

Special programs for theory-building research were just beginning to become available in the US at the time of this writing. Three of these, AQUAD, NUDIST, and HyperResearch, are described briefly at the end of the chapter on the major functions of qualitative analysis programs.

Incidently, once you have acquired one of the described programs, you can use the brief description in this book as an introductory guide. The 8glossary will help you understand the manual and menus. Best of all, when the first menu appears on your computer's screen, the program will not be a complete stranger from whom you don't know what to expect.

Text Retrievers

Introduction

Text retrievers retrieve words and phrases, not chunks of text. In the general computer literature, the term 'text' is often used to distinguish narrative material from 'data', which could be numbers, names, addresses, or other bits of information. Text retrievers do operate on narrative material, but it would be more accurate to call them 'word retrievers'. Unlike data base managers, they focus on individual words and phrases (known in computer talk as 'strings'). This characteristic also distinguishes text retrievers from qualitative analysis programs, which are meant to deal with meaningful segments of text <Qualitative analysis programs>.

Text retrievers do not constitute a homogenous group, as word processors and data base managers do. Some are simple utility programs in the sense that they help users find information in files whose names are no longer remembered. Others work more like text data base managers with special search facilities, and one even claims to 'automatically discover the underlying structure of textbase resources' (IZE). The programs I review in this chapter were selected because their capabilities render them potentially useful to qualitative researchers. They come from two subcategories of text retrievers: search programs and content analysis programs.

In principle, search programs are set up to find individual words and phrases in text (across many files), while content analysis programs perform the basic function of taking inventories of the words contained in a text. In practice, actual software packages incorporate many operations; some to such degree that the two categories begin to overlap. A search program may create an 'index' for each text document in which it stores the various locations of all the different (unique) words in the documents (many programs do so in order to speed up the actual search). Such an index is not very different from the 'inventory' that a content analysis program produces. Conversely, a content analysis program may allow the user to specify individual words for which to indicate the location, an operation which practically amounts to a search.

Among text retrievers are programs that can accomplish the following tasks:

making lists of all words used in one or more documents;

counting the frequency of each word's occurrence, or the frequency of specified words;

comparing the word lists (vocabularies) of different documents;

locating specified words in one or several documents;

constructing indexes (word lists providing the locations of each word in a document);

counting the frequency of 'categories' (groups of synonyms) in one or more documents;

extracting specific words from a text, together with the words preceding and succeeding each occurrence (key-word-in-context concordances);

extracting specific words from a text together with the sentences or paragraphs in which each occurs;

extracting specific words from text together with user-selected context (cut-and-paste).

Not surprisingly, some of these features are exactly right for traditional **content analysis**, while others come in handy for language-oriented research such as **ethnoscience** and **structural ethnography**. (These programs also include features that have relieved scholars who perform literary analyses of some of their more mundane and time-consuming chores.) Even researchers who normally deal with interpretational analysis, in which they handle meaningful chunks of text rather than words, could find some of these programs' options helpful. For instance, a researcher may notice that a certain concept is alluded to in her/his data. As a validity check s/he could create a list of synonyms and phrases that capture that concept, and explore whether, and how frequently, it was directly addressed by the participants in her/his research. Or a researcher might remember that somewhere in her/his field notes or literature excerpts s/he referred to a topic whose relevance was not clear at the time, but now it has become of special interest, and s/he needs a fast search program to locate the reference in one of her/his many files.

Let us take a look at search programs and content analysis programs as software packages first before paying more detailed attention to the functions they perform. A better understanding of their nature will be of advantage when individual programs are mentioned later in this chapter.

Search Programs

Search programs owe their existence to the proliferation of electronically stored materials on every computer user's desk. Who has not, now and then, tried unsuccessfully to recall the file name under which s/he has saved a certain document? The advent of hard disks with their enormous storage capacities especially contributed to many computer user's private information explosion. Good word processors can search for a specific term in all files of a directory, but hard disk directories are so large that a word processor's relatively simple techniques often take more time than the impatient user is willing to commit.

Search programs take pride in being extremely fast. I am not sure how some of them achieve that feat, but many of them do it with the help of 'indexing'. That has certain implications for the user. When working with a search program that requires indexing, files that are not yet indexed cannot be searched. As a rule, indexing involves no more than indicating to the search program which file to index. The process will be accomplished rather quickly, usually upon a single command or menu choice.

When a search program indexes a file it automatically creates a new file containing information about the location(s) of all unique words used in the file. Then, when it performs a search, the program consults the index instead of searching through the file itself. To understand why that makes a difference, try to picture an alphabetic column of words as opposed to the long lines of text, in which words repeat (the word 'text' has already been used in this chapter twenty-three times!). Since few people have an interest in locating words like 'and', 'but', or 'he', it would make a search even faster if the program were to ignore such words. That is exactly what many search programs do. They contain a list of ignore-words, also called 'noise words', 'connecting words', 'stop words', or even 'boring words', which don't become part of an index, thus keeping it as short as possible. What many users don't like about indexing is that it creates additional files that take up extra storage space on the disk.

Search programs that work without indexing are **GOfer**, **Golden Retriever**, and **The Text Collector**, as well as **Text Analyzer** (for Apple computers). **Memory Lane** makes indexing optional, while **Concordance**, **SearchExpress**, and **ZyINDEX** require indexing. **IZE** indexes key-words, which are attached to the documents or marked in the text by the user (similar to the way key-words are handled in data base managers <Data base managers>).

Indexing is not the only preparation that some search programs require. Except for Concordance and IZE, search programs do not allow text to be entered directly into the program from the keyboard. All search programs work with text files created elsewhere, usually on word processors. Since word processors are by no means standardized in the way they embed invisible formatting instructions in their documents, some search programs require that files be stripped of everything except the actual text characters and carriage returns (margin and indents become regular spaces). This process is called ASCII conversion. ASCII stands for American Standard Code for Information Interchange and is a simplified standardized text format. The conversion is usually done with the word processor, not in the search program.

GOfer, Golden Retriever, Memory Lane, The Text Collector, and ZyINDEX do not require ASCII conversion, although The Text Collector's output sometimes is sprinkled with unintelligibles and run-togethers if the input file is not in ASCII. Concordance not only requires ASCII, but the files must undergo further conversion within the program. SearchExpress and IZE accept input directly from a number of popular word processors.

The core of a search program is the so-called 'search request' or 'query'. A query consists of the instructions to the program, defining what to look for and in which file(s). The most basic query, of course, specifies one word or phrase. According to the user's needs, searches can be either expanded (finding more 'matches') or narrowed down (finding fewer 'matches'). To expand, the query would operate with a truncated word or 'wild cards'. A common use of truncation is the provision of the word's root only, with the stipulation that all words containing that root be considered matches. "Operat", for instance, would stand for the words operate, operated, operating, operation, operations, operator, and operators. 'Wild card' searches involve using a wild card symbol to take the place of any character. The symbol ? usually stands for one character ("wom?n" would yield both woman and women), the symbol * for none to many characters ("*man" would retrieve man, woman, but also ottoman, doberman, Andaman, superman, ombudsman, and so forth).

An effective way to narrow a search is to set conditions. For instance, one could specify that another word must be in the same document or, conversely, may not be in the same document. Queries use certain 'operators' to set these conditions. 'AND' usually serves the first purpose, 'OR' the second. (These operators and a couple of others are often referred to as Boolean, after a nineteenth-century logician.) One can become even more exclusive by using operators like 'NEAR', 'NEARBY' or 'WITHIN' to define how close the secondary word must be to the search term. The technical term for such queries is proximity searches. Almost all search programs make Boolean operators available (exception: Golden Retriever).

A relatively new kind of query is the phonetic search, also called 'sound-alike', 'recognition', or 'fuzzy' search. The user enters a search word whose spelling comes as close to the word s/he wants as s/he can remember. The program then uses a set of algorithms (for substituting consonants with similar-sounding ones) to dig up all words that make good candidates. Phonetic searches are available in GOfer, IZE, SearchExpress, The Text Collector, and ZyINDEX.

The output of a search program usually consists of a list of files in which the search word was encountered. In addition to the file name, some programs also record the frequency of the word's occurrence in each file. Selecting one of the listed files usually calls up the actual text of that file, with the search word highlighted. A couple of programs (GOfer, The Text Collector) present the portions of the file in which the word occurs immediately when they list the file names.

While GOfer and Golden Retriever are quite simple and straightforward searchers, Concordance, Memory Lane, The Text Collector, and ZyINDEX are substantial programs with a multitude of functions (more about these later in this chapter). Text Analyzer, the program for Apple computers, is actually more similar to an analysis program <Qualitative analysis programs> than a search program, but lacks the ability to attach codes to user-determined segments of text, which is the distinguishing characteristic of those programs.

IZE and SearchExpress go beyond searching by attempting to be organizers. When the user asks IZE, for instance, to retrieve all files containing a certain key-word (key-words are attached to documents by the user), and then to organize these files, the program registers all key-words in each file that was retrieved. It then compares them with all key-words in all other files also retrieved and determines which key-words the files have in common. The more key-words are shared by two or more documents, the more closely 'related' they are. If you had asked for files with the key-word "research", for example, IZE would look at all key-words in each of the files retrieved. If it had originally found ten files, and eight of these also contained the key-word "qualitative", it would present that fact in a hierarchical 'outline', in which it actually types the name of the common key-word (for which you had not asked directly). If five of the files also contained the key-word "analysis", this term would be added to the outline on another level, and so forth. This is a way of suggesting thematic relationships among certain documents. It is what IZE means by 'discovering the underlying structure of textbase resources' (their advertisement). SearchExpress uses the word comparison of documents to suggest a similarity in document content.

Content Analysis Programs

Content analysis programs have an interesting history. Well before word processors were common, the first content analysis program existed (1963), and was the subject of an entire book (Stone et al., 1966). The program was called **The General Inquirer** and ran on a large mainframe computer. Its main feature was the development and application of a content analysis dictionary. 'Content analysis dictionaries consist of category names, the definitions or rules for assigning words to categories, and the actual assignment of specific words' (Weber, 1985, p. 25). A category is comparable to a list of word idioms and synonyms, but goes beyond that insofar as the words and phrases in the category are meant to cover all important aspects of the concept represented by that category. The computer then applies the rules to the words it encounters in a document and sorts them into the appropriate category.

The General Inquirer did not become a microcomputer program. A promising package for the personal computer did not arrive until about twenty years later. Developed at BYU, it was first called BYU Concordance. Unlike The General Inquirer, it was originally designed for literary analysis, not traditional content analysis. Its main function was retrieval, but retrieval of a different kind from that offered by programs like Golden Retriever or Memory Lane. Instead of listing file names, BYU Concordance produced 'citations', i.e., specifications about the location of search word(s). Similar to GOfer and The Text Collector, the portions of the text in which the search word appears were called up to the screen together with the citation.

BYU Concordance did quite a bit more than provide references (as it calls its search results). It created indices and key-word-in-context lists, and was capable of handling several foreign languages, including Hebrew. Today, the former BYU Concordance is improved and marketed by The Electronic Text Corporation as a general text analysis tool under the name **WordCruncher**.

WordCruncher is a complex program for which all documents must be pre-indexed. A series of much simpler, but effective content analysis programs were developed by David Garson at North Carolina State University. Each of the programs is meant to do a specific content analysis job: **Word Match, KWIC Text Index,** and **Content Analysis**. The latter is one of the few text retrieval programs I know of that runs on Apple computers.

One other program that can be run on Apples comes from Germany. It is called **TEXTPACK**, and is also available for IBMs. TEXTPACK was originally created to help analyze open-ended questions in surveys. As more and more functions were added, the 1972 program grew into a full-fledged specialized content analysis package.

All content analysis programs work on material created somewhere else. Therefore, they face the same problems as search programs: the conversion of extraneous documents into a format they can read. Since content analysis programs expect to be used for the analysis of standard works of literature and of material downloaded from electronic information services, all of them accept standard ASCII files. The currently available content analysis programs cannot handle any other formats.

Like search programs, some content analysis programs require preliminary work before they can function. In this case, the documents must be subdivided into smaller units. Consider that the index of a book works because it provides you with the number(s) of the page(s) on which the word can be found. Clean ASCII documents like the ones most content analysis programs work with, consist of a continuous stream of words without permanent page numbers. Therefore, if a program is to produce an index, some way must be found to specify the location of each word in the document, or its 'reference'.

Content analysis programs customarily use the metaphor of a book to construct location parameters. The entire file is called a 'book', which is then further divided into pages and paragraphs or sentences. The terminology can be changed by the user or, as in Word Match and KWIC TEXT INDEX, everything below the book level is simply called a 'chunk'. Where each 'page' or 'chunk' begins and ends can be determined by the user and communicated to the program through the insertion of a marker such as ¦ or *^*. A text can be automatically subdivided. In that case the program orients itself on formatting conventions like two carriage returns for paragraphs and a period with two spaces for sentences. The parts of the document are then successively numbered (done automatically by the program), and it is these numbers that are given in an index instead of the traditional page numbers. TEXTPACK and WordCruncher both provide these automatic 'reformatting' options.

Operations

a   Making lists of all different (unique) words in one or more documents

A list of the 'vocabulary' used in transcriptions of natural language samples can be helpful in the early exploratory phases of language-oriented ethnographic studies and for traditional content analysts.

Creating word lists is the basic 'inventory-taking' function. The computer prepares a list of all words in a document, omits the duplicates, sorts the list alphabetically, and prints it out in a long column. Since researchers usually are not interested in words that are mere grammatical connectors or otherwise very ordinary ('noise words') the programs usually provide an 'ignore file' that contains words to be excluded. Most programs come with a such a file that can be applied by the user as is, or it can be customized.

Word Match is a simple program that prepares a list of all unique words in a document and sorts it alphabetically. The list is not sent to the screen while in Word Match, but to an ASCII file. To read that file, the user can send it to the printer directly from a DOS command, or import it into a word processor and manipulate it there further. The beginning of a list of all words in this chapter looks like this:

```
a              adding
able           addresses
about          advantage
accept         advent
accomplish     all
accurate       allow
achieve        also
across         am
actual         American
added          among  . . . etc.
```

Had I applied the filter of the 'ignore file' furnished with Word Match, the words **a**, **across**, **also**, and **all** would not have been included in the list above.

TEXTPACK and WordCruncher generate a frequency count with their word lists (called 'vocabulary' by TEXTPACK). Similar to Word Match, both these programs enable the researcher to create a 'stop list' with which to keep the inventory free of insignificant words.

A stop word or noise word list is also used by Concordance and ZyINDEX. These search programs can handle many documents at once. They make an alphabetized list of all words (which Concordance calls 'dictionary') for an entire set of documents (called a 'database' by Concordance), not for individual files. Both programs automatically report in the word list the total number of times each word occurs. Concordance also indicates the number of documents in which each words occurs. While in Concordance 'dictionary' is a menu choice, ZyINDEX provides a separate utility, ZyLIST, to convert the index it has created (at the time a document is imported) into the program into user-readable form.

The Text Collector can be made to produce word lists for one or more documents, but must be set up correctly accomplish this task. (TEXTBASE ALPHA, one of the qualitative analysis programs, also produces simple alphabetized word lists.)

b   Counting the frequency of each unique word or of specified words

Content analysts are interested in how frequently a word occurs when they wish to determine which concepts are emphasized in a document. High frequency occurrence of certain words also provides clues to the ethnoscientist who wishes to select clusters of words for detailed lexical/semantic analysis.

As mentioned above, Concordance, TEXTPACK, WordCruncher, and ZyINDEX automatically add a frequency count for each word in their vocabulary lists. WordCruncher provides a small utility that sorts words by decreasing frequency. The output is a cluster of words all of which fall into the same frequency range (for example 'between 39 and 30'), followed by the next highest cluster, and so on.

Word Match's main function is word counts, either for an entire document, or for each of its subdivisions, the individual 'chunks'. Normally, the researcher specifies a word or several words for which to search. The program then produces a table listing the words vertically, the 'chunk' identification numbers horizontally, and the frequency counts in the cells. The table for the first four 'chunks' of this chapter and for ten words looks like this:

Frequency of occurrence of each word in each chunk:

Word	1	2	3	4	TOTAL
accomplish	0	0	0	0	0
accurate	1	0	0	0	1
actual	0	2	0	0	2
addresses	1	0	0	0	1
allow	0	1	0	0	1
among	0	0	0	0	0
amounts	0	1	0	0	1
analysis	2	3	0	0	5
automatically	0	0	0	0	0
base	1	0	0	0	1

According to the above table, most words occur only once per chunk (in this case a chunk equals a paragraph), except for the word analysis, which shows up twice in paragraph 1 and three times in paragraph 2.

If the researcher wants to obtain a frequency count for the entire 'vocabulary' of a document, it is easy to produce a word list with Word Match (see above), and then use that list, without re-typing, as a search specification list for the count.

The Apple-program Content Analysis will produce word frequency counts, but only in conjunction with dictionary category counts (explained under f below). Text Analyzer (also an Apple program) counts the occurrence of words the reader specifies in a 'key-word' list (see below under d).

c   Comparing the word lists (vocabularies) of different documents

When content analysts want to compare concepts in two or more documents, a comparison of the frequencies of the occurrence of certain words allows them to draw tentative conclusions.

Among the content analysis programs, only TEXTPACK and WordCruncher compare the frequency of word occurrences across documents. TEXTPACK works with two documents at a time and calculates the difference for each word included in both vocabularies. WordCruncher can compare several files at a time, but uses only the words from the first document for the comparison.

SearchExpress institutes its own type of document comparison. It concentrates on frequently occurring words only, first for one file, then examines other documents to discover which ones have a similar distribution of frequently used words. The program then retrieves a specified number of files whose text content it considers comparable, based on their word usage.

Text Analyzer works with an entire list of 'key-words', a 'dictionary'. The key-words are the words in the text that are of interest to the researcher. Certain key-words can be selected from the dictionary, and the computer is then instructed to find them in the text (one file at a time) and print them out, together with up to five lines of surrounding text. Text Analyzer can also count the frequency of occurrence of each key-word in the document.

d   Locating specified words in one or several documents

When ethnoscientists and structural ethnographers work with natural language samples, they often notice a term in one of these samples that they consider potentially significant. Search programs allow researchers to explore whether, and in what context, the term occurs in the remaining samples. Content analysts use the context of words to learn about the range of their meaning.

All search programs can locate user-specified words in one or several files. The standard display of the results consists of a list of file names on the screen. The search word appears at least once in each file; the programs usually provide a count of the 'matches' as well. The researcher then may select one of the files and call up a screen-full of context for the word. The search word itself is highlighted within that context. Commonly, a simple command lets the user jump from the first occurrence to the next, and so on. Most search programs offer the option to print out all files in which the word occurs.

The Text Collector displays a user-specified amount of context (paragraph, sentence, etc.) together with the file names after the search is completed. It then provides the option of looking at one context at a time. GOfer also sends context material to the screen (sixteen lines) but not as an entire list, like Text Collector. It pauses after encountering the search word in a document and immediately displays the surrounding text. The user instructs the program to continue the search when s/he is ready (or has sent the material to the printer or another file). Alternatively, GOfer can produce just a list of file names.

Among content analysis programs, only WordCruncher will locate individual words, but it provides its own location specifications rather than file names. WordCruncher includes in its output a small portion of context for the occurrence of each search word.

e   Constructing indexes (word lists with location indicators for each word in a document)

Since search programs' findings appear only on the screen, and since the search word is not highlighted when the files are printed on paper, ethnographers who do language-oriented studies might want a more permanent record of word locations. An index provides such records. With the help of an index, the researcher can easily locate the word on her/his paper copies.

TEXTPACK and WordCruncher generate indexes. TEXTPACK is set up to produce a total index of a file, i.e., it lists all words in a text in alphabetical order together with the numbers that specify its location. (The numbers are those that were automatically assigned to each level of context, for example: book, chapter, sentence.) In WordCruncher, the user selects words to be included in the index. The program prints for each word a set of locations consisting of the abbreviated name of the 'book' in which it occurs, and the number of the section and line in which it can be found.

f   Assigning words in the text to 'categories' (groups of synonyms or related words) in one or more documents

Word 'categories' play an important part in content analysis. When the researcher wishes to explore a particular concept, s/he must find all instances of its occurrence in a text. The concept can be expressed in many different ways. A list of synonyms is a simple example of a category of words. However, a concept may be so broad that mere thesaurus-type synonyms will not capture the entire category. The concept 'economic' for example, could include 'all words that relate to economic, commercial, and industrial matters' (Weber, 1985, p. 28). An entire system of category definitions is called a 'dictionary' by content analysts. 'Content analysis dictionaries consist of category names, the definition of rules for assigning words to categories, and the actual assignment of specific words' (Weber, 1985, p. 25).

Several content analysis programs allow the user to create such a dictionary and apply it to a text. Word Match works with a simple thesaurus file, which is a file into which the user enters groups of words, each group separated from the next by a blank line. The first word of each group is the category name. The program then searches through a document for all occurrences of the words in a group and computes the frequency of occurrence for that group. The resulting display lists the category names and their counts; these counts include the category name itself plus all of its synonyms.

TEXTPACK permits the researcher to create dictionaries of words which share a common meaning. Each set of words is called a category and is assigned a number. The output lists the frequency with which each category occurs in each of the smallest subdivisions of the text. TEXT-PACK will also insert the category numbers directly into the text (called 'coding') and print out a copy of the coded text.

CONTENT ANALYSIS restricts the 'content search dictionary' which can be generated by the user to fifty categories, each category containing up to thirty 'specifier words' (including the actual category name, if desired). The program then searches the text for the specifier words and displays each category, one after the other, as a column of words. A parallel column provides a count for each word, and its percentage of the total word frequency in the document.

In WordCruncher the user can search for 'related words'. For all occurrences of any of the words in the list the 'references' (locations) will be given, but no counts.

g   *Extracting specified words from a text together with the words preceding and succeeding each occurrence (key-word-in-context concordances)*

Both content analysts and language-oriented ethnographers are interested in the manner in which words are used. KWIC (Key-Word-in-Context) lists 'draw attention to the variation and consistency in word meaning and usage. Second, [they] provide systematic information that is helpful in determining whether the meaning of particular words is dependent upon their use in certain phrases or idioms' (Weber, 1985, pp. 46-47).

All specialized content analysis programs produce KWIC concordances. As the name implies, KWIC TEXT INDEX specializes in producing such concordances. It is a very simple program; a concordance of the words 'analysis' for this chapter produced by it looks like this:

```
analysis programs, which are meant  + retrievers from qualitative// :RETR :C#1
analysis programs>////Text retrieve +gments of//text. <Qualitative :RETR :C#1
analysis programs.////In principle, + Search programs and//content :RETR :C#1
```
(continued on next page)

```
analysis programs//perform the basi +ss many files), while content    :RETR  :C#1
analysis program produces.  Convers +e//'inventory' that a content     :RETR  :C#1
analysis program may allow the user +uces.  Conversely, a//content     :RETR  :C#1
analysis, while others come in hand +ight for//traditional content     :RETR  :C#1
analysis in which they handle meani +g with//interpretive kinds of     :RETR  :C#1
analysis programs as//software pack +t search programs and content     :RETR  :C#1
analysis programs////Content analys +ocument content.//////Content     :RETR  :C#1
analysis programs have an interesti + analysis programs////Content     :RETR  :C#1
analysis program existed//(1963), a +ere common, the first content    :RETR  :C#1
analysis dictionary.  'Content anal +and application of a content//    :RETR  :C#1
analysis dictionaries consist of ca +nalysis dictionary.  'Content     :RETR  :C#1
```

The target word (usually called key-word) is first, followed by the characters that succeed it in the document (altogether thirty-five characters). The + in the center indicates the beginning of the preceding characters; to make sense of this list, one has to read the right half of the text first. The column at the very right gives the file name (RETR) and 'chunk' number. (Since I did not divide the file into chunks, the whole file is considered Chunk number one.) Each double slash represents a carriage return in the original document.

Other KWIC concordances place the key-word in the center. WordCruncher, for instance, prints the 'citation' first (a location indicator), then thirty characters of text, the key-word, and then another thirty characters. Thus the key-word forms a column in the center. Alternatively, the researcher may specify that the line be extracted in which the key-word appears. In that case, naturally, the key-words do not form a column; each line must be scrutinized for the key-word. TEXTPACK presents one line of context characters, with the key-word always starting at column 71.

h   Extracting words from a text together with the sentences or paragraphs in which each occurs

In many cases the researcher would rather look at words in the context of their natural language units, such as sentences and paragraphs. This facility is provided by CONTENT ANALYSIS, TEXTPACK, and The Text Collector.

CONTENT ANALYSIS offers the researcher the option to specify that all words to be searched for be printed out together with the sentence in which they appear. This can be done both for simple word searches, as well as category searches (see above, section f). When searching for categories of words, the sentences are printed with the category name (code) inserted into each the sentence.

In both The Text Collector and TEXTPACK, the user must set certain parameters to make searches extract natural language units. The computer has to be told what it is to consider a unit for the purpose of a search. In The Text Collector a special menu lets the researcher select words (i.e., 'no context'), sentences, lines, paragraphs, or text in quotes or in parentheses as the context units.

TEXTPACK calls the output in which the word is presented in its natural language unit a 'Key-Word-out-of-Context' list. The researcher must define, at the outset, subdivisions for each document that TEXTPACK works with. The subdivision may be a sentence or a paragraph, or any other unit. If the paragraph is chosen as the smallest unit, then the program will produce a KWOC list in which the key-words precede, like headings, the paragraphs in which they occur. They are not highlighted in the paragraph itself. If the researcher chose sentences as the smallest units, the printout will be quite similar except it will present for each key-word only the sentence in which it occurs, one sentence after the other (the key-word is not listed separately).

i   Extracting words from text together with user-selected context (cut-and-paste)

Although examining words in a paragraph often provides sufficient context, researchers may sometimes want to see a word in its larger surroundings and then decide how much context is needed to interpret the occurrence properly. Such a feature would be useful even to researchers who are not particularly interested in language, but work with in-depth interviews or other data that don't call for linguistic analysis. Once a concept is considered important to an analysis, the word(s) that connote that concept can be located in all data, then 'cut' out with whatever amount of context is deemed relevant and 'pasted' to an output file in which all text segments found in one search are collected.

(This is not the same as the 'cut-and-paste' that qualitative analysis programs simulate. There are two differences. First, in qualitative analysis programs the researcher works with one data document at a time and marks the relevant passages as s/he reads through the text, designating them for different output files by coding them according to their topics or themes. The computer then does the accumulating of passages from all coded files automatically, creating the appropriate content output files as it finds the text segments. Search programs, on the other hand, provide the researcher with relevant excerpts from many files, creating a single output file with a single type of content. The researcher does the 'sending' of the material to the output file. Secondly, search programs define 'relevance' only in terms of the presence of certain words or phrases. For work with qualitative analysis programs, no specific words or phrases have to occur in the text in order for a text passage to end up in a specific output file.)

Almost all search programs, except Concordance and SearchExpress, provide the cut-and-paste option. Usually, the operation begins when the search is completed, the file names are listed on the screen, and the researcher has selected one file to be displayed. At this point, the user can move the cursor around in that file, highlight text (each program provides special commands for highlighting text), and send the highlighted block to an output file. Another commonly used terminology for this operation is 'mark and save'.

Text Analyzer (Apple) specializes in printing out the words it has found together with up to five surrounding lines. It will also add the name of the file to each chunk of text.

Conclusion

The programs described here vary greatly in capacity, ease of use, and price. For a serious content analyst or student of language, it makes sense to buy a heavy-duty program like Concordance, IZE, WordCruncher, TEXTPACK, ZyIndex, or The Text Collector. All of these programs are designed for use with very large sets of documents that remain relatively stable. Concordance, IZE, WordCruncher, and ZyIndex, however, require a lot of preparatory work and quite a bit of learning before they can be used. The time investment is justified only if the documents that are readied for these programs will be used often or extensively. If that is the case, one of these programs might be just the right tool for a particular research task.

For researchers who only occasionally do a traditional content or linguistic analysis, or who wish to use these techniques as a triangulation measure or validity check on their main analysis, the smaller and cheaper programs will be satisfactory. Researchers can be using KWIC TEXT INDEX or Word Match, for instance, within twenty minutes of reading the fifteen-page manual. Just like the Apple programs Content Analysis and Text Analyzer, these have a low price and are not lavish in screen design; they are also relatively slow. Golden Retriever and GOfer are perfectly good search programs. If you want added convenience, you can install GOfer as a memory-resident program that pops up whenever you need it without forcing you to leave the program you are currently working in. Memory Lane comes as a memory-resident program only. It prefers to index your files before it searches them, which is a bother when files continue to be edited. But since the program automatically updates all files once it has initially indexed them, this is really not a disadvantage.

In general, text retrievers are probably not yet sufficiently appreciated by qualitative researchers, since they either are not well advertised (especially the academic packages), or are advertised so dramatically that they invoke distrust. Rarely are they described in such detail that scholars can form a good image of how useful they could be. The above account provides the minimal information needed to select the appropriate research tool.

References

STONE, PHILLIP J.; DUNPHY, DEXTER C.; SMITH, MARSHALL S. and OGIL-
VIE, DANIEL M. (1966) *The General Inquirer: A Computer Approach
to Content Analysis*, Cambridge, MA, The M.I.T. Press.
WEBER, R. PHILIP (1985) *Basic Content Analysis*, Beverly Hills, CA, Sage
Publications.

Software references

Concordance (MS-DOS)
    Dataflight Software, 10573 West Pico Blvd., Los Angeles, CA 90064,
    (213) 785-0623. Version 4.0: $495.00, Version 3.0: $295.00.
Content Analysis (Apple)
    National Collegiate Clearing House, NCSU Box 8101, Raleigh, NC
    27695, (919) 737-3067. $23.00.
GOfer (MS-DOS)
    Microlytics, 300 Main St., East Rochester, NY, 14445 (716) 377-0130,
    $79.95.
Golden Retriever (MS-DOS)
    S K DATA, Box 413, Burlington, MA 01803 (617) 229-8909, $99.00.
IZE (MS-DOS)
    Persoft Inc., 465 Science Dr., Madison WI 53711, (608) 273-600,
    $445.00.
KWIC Text Index (MS-DOS)
    National Collegiate Clearing House, NCSU Box 8101, Raleigh, NC
    27695, (919) 737-3067. $45.00.
Memory Lane (MS-DOS)
    Group L Corp., 481 Carlisle Dr., Herndon, VA 22070, (703) 471-0030,
    (800) 672-5300, $99.00.
SearchExpress (MS-DOS)
    Executive Technologies, Inc., 2120 16th Ave. S, Birmingham, Alabama,
    35205, (205) 933-5494, $349.00.
Text Analyzer (Apple)
    National Collegiate Clearing House, NCSU Box 8101, Raleigh, NC
    27695, (919) 737-3067. $23.00.
The Text Collector (MS-DOS)
    O'Neill Software, P.O. Box 26111, San Francisco, CA 94126, (415) 398-
    2255, $69.00
TEXTPACK (MS-DOS, Apple)
    ZUMA, Postfach 5969, D-6800 Mannheim 1, West Germany, 621-
    18004, $30.00 (for academic institutions).

WordCruncher (MS-DOS)
> Electronic Text Corporation, 5600 North University Ave., Provo, UT 84604, (801) 226-0616, $299.00.

Word Match (MS-DOS)
> National Collegiate Clearing House, NCSU Box 8101, Raleigh, NC 27695, (919) 737-3067. $45.00.

ZyIndex (MS-DOS)
> ZyLab Corporation, 233 E. Erie St., Chicago, IL 60611, (800) 544-6339, (312) 642-2201, $95.00 (Personal), $295.00 (Professional), $695.00 (Plus).

Data Base Managers

Introduction

Data base managers have one of the longest software histories. They began as simple list makers. First, they simulated the card file, with the added convenience that there was no need to keep it in alphabetic order to find any item in it easily. The computer did not need this human mental crutch to locate things quickly. Furthermore, if someone did want the entire list in alphabetic order, the data base manager would quickly sort all the entries and print them out. Searching and sorting are still the main functions data base managers perform.

The first simple data base managers probably found their most common use as address list keepers and mailing label printers. Unlike paper file cards, which are usually sorted only according to last names, data base managers could quickly sort by cities, zip codes, or any other information that the user found important, such as occupation, or merchandise preference. Once the list was in the data base manager, criteria could be set up, and subgroups of items that met specific criteria could be generated and printed out quickly. One could easily get a list of all persons whose addresses were within a specified zip code range, for instance. The larger the data base became, and the more often different selection criteria needed to be met, the more efficient it became to keep one's lists in a data base manager, not in a Rolodex card file.

Soon people (and software promoters) found all kinds of applications for data base managers. They could keep inventories, track personal information, or organize libraries. As data base managers became more popular, software producers added some calculation capacities (a facility on which spreadsheets are based), stretched the size limits on individual entries, as well as the entire data base, allowed different databases to be connected with each other, and provided means by which the user could customize the data base manager. Today hundreds of data base managers are commercially available, and the most powerful of them can be used to handle the entire record keeping of a large business, service agency, or academic institution.

Data base managers are now so diverse that it is just about impossible to say anything about them as a group that is true for all of them. There will always be a program that is the exception. Some are no longer called data base managers, because they are meant for special applications. Mail mergers, note takers, text retrievers, all are based on the original data base manager notion and are variations or outgrowths of them. In this chapter, we will provide a rudimentary description of the data base manager concept, and familiarize you sufficiently with the terminology and basic principles so you can judge whether your research work would be facilitated by a data base manager.

Basic Principles and Original Structure

The basic functions of data base managers are to store information, to modify (add, update, delete) that information, to sort it, and to search/select/retrieve it. Data are entered directly into the data base manager, although by now most of them also import data from other sources (often rather cumbersomely). The basic data unit is the 'character', i.e., anything, whether numeric or textual, can be stored and retrieved.

In the beginning, all data base managers were structured. This means that they had 'boxes', so to speak, into which the user placed information items. The vocabulary used to describe these boxes is fairly standard: they are called 'fields'. Several fields combine to form a 'record', and several records combine to form the 'data base'. In graphic form, one could visualize a data base manager structure like the illustration on the next page.

The large frame symbolizes the entire data base. It contains, in this case, five records. Each record in this base is divided into six fields. Records are usually the units of information that constitute one entity, such as one address, or one completed questionnaire. Each field contains a part of that entity, the name or the town, the answer to question 1 or 2, etc. Typically, a data base can accommodate a limited number of records, and each record can hold only a limited number of fields. Note that fields have different sizes. However, each record has exactly the same structure; the corresponding fields have the same size in each.

Since data base managers are multi-purpose programs, they don't come with pre-determined numbers of records, fields, or field lengths. The number of records is flexible, so that more can be added any time (up to the limit). The number of fields, however, is usually determined by the user before any data are entered. It is also up to the user to decide how large s/he wants a field to be, although there is a limit to the length of a field.

In the past, field length limitations were tight, since no one expected more than short entries. Using the full length of a field would 'reserve space' for it in the data base that might be needed elsewhere. Therefore, one did not assign more space to a field than the anticipated longest entry would require.

DATA BASE

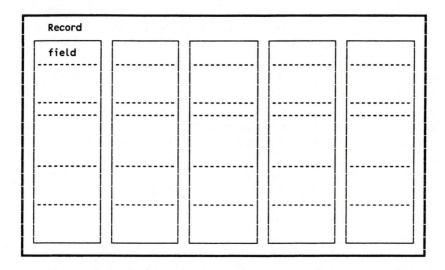

Because these preparatory considerations have to be undertaken first, working with a data base manager usually calls for quite a bit of advanced planning. How many fields are needed, and how long is each to be? The first screen the user sees in a structured data base manager usually is not a blank for information entry, but an invitation to structure the data base, i.e., to create something like a template that the program will use to regulate data entry (the 'layout').

Fields not only need length specifications, but also names. One reason for names is to help the user know what item to enter in what place as the data base becomes larger. The telephone number, for instance would go in a field most likely called "phone num", the answer to question 3 of a questionnaire would go into the field "quest3", and so forth. Another reason for field labels is to facilitate the search for items known to be located in specific fields. The data base itself also needs a name, since more than one can be created within one data base manager. Records, on the other hand, are distinguished by the entries in certain primary fields, usually the first field, in which it is customary to keep the name of the addressee or the questionnaire respondent.

Just as the data entry is 'designed' to a degree, so is the output. The output of a data base manager is usually called a 'report'. It presents the information in the data base in a selective and organized way, in whatever format best fits the user's purposes. To design a report, the user needs to determine which records to include, the order in which they shall be presented, the fields within the record that will form the content of the report, and in what sequence they should appear. In the simple case of a client list, for instance, the report could include all clients who have been inactive for more than three months, in alphabetical order by name, followed by the date of their latest interaction, followed by a description of the nature of their case. A researcher might want a printout of the responses to questions 10 through 20, from respondents in the Eastern States only, in order of increasing zip code. These kinds of specifications have to be communicated to the program, and consequently, data base managers provide facilities with which to design report formats. The reports themselves are customarily columnar, i.e., they list the field the report is to begin with in the first column, the next field in the second column, and so on. Each horizontal row holds information from a different record. Going across a horizontal row the user thus finds pieces of information from one and the same record (or the record as a whole, if it has not been broken down into fields). Since fields traditionally were short, this format used to be quite satisfactory for most purposes.

Program Architecture

Data base managers often come as two distinct programs: the data base, and the report maker. In its simplest form, the most common structure of the software can be visualized somewhat as shown on the next page.

The data entry module assembles the data base, the report maker accesses it to produce customized printouts. Most data base managers allow the user to view the data from within the data entry module. Usually, there is also an edit mode in which the user can modify or delete information in the data base. As a rule, one record at a time is called up to the screen. Some programs boast a 'browse' mode; with its help the entire data base can be reviewed, sometimes as a large table with rows (records) and columns (fields). Naturally, all but the tiniest data bases are too large for the computer monitor's screen. Therefore, the user either scrolls the screen, or the field the user indicates with the cursor gets expanded in a special window or at the top of the screen.

A good data base manager provides for sorting and searching in the data entry module, so that selections appear on the screen and can be scrutinized immediately. For the user, it is quite important to be clear about the difference between searching and sorting. The next section explains how the two functions are distinguished.

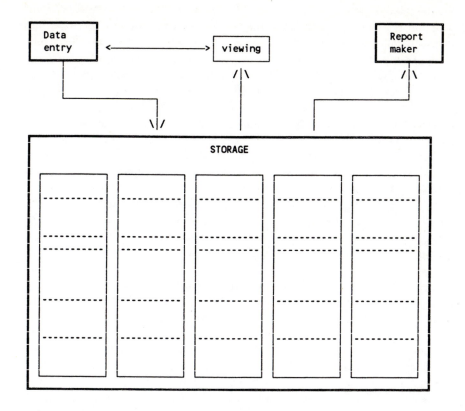

Sorting and Searching

Sorting is done when the user wishes to display the items in a data base in a certain order. Numerical and alphabetical orders are the most common, either ascending (from the lowest to the highest number, or from a to z), or descending (from the highest to the lowest number, or from z to a). The user specifies which field to use for the sorting operation, and how many characters deep the sorting is to go. For instance, for a bibliography it would make most sense to sort according to the first field, the authors' names. In a short list, the first character of the name may suffice. In a very large one, one might have to sort at least four characters deep to have Braithwaite be followed by Brameld, and Brameld by Brent. A good program can sort according to all letters in a field, but it takes a bit longer.

In many cases sorting according to one field will not yet yield a satisfactory outcome. Therefore, most data base managers let the user specify several fields to sort by, in a specified order. A large bibliography might contain works by the same author with different publishing dates.

Consequently, once the first round of sorting has been accomplished, the program is asked to go right on and sort within that ordered list according to ascending dates (most data base managers have special date fields that allow sorting even by day, in spite of the traditional mm/dd/yy entry).

Usually, the entire data base is sorted, but in the report module the user can also request that only certain records be ordered. The sorting is usually temporary, i.e., it is merely a matter of screen display or printing. However, the sorting can also be made permanent, by actually rearranging the data according to a sort. It makes sense, for instance, to keep a bibliography in alphabetic order. The individual records are then actually placed in the data base in that order, and when anything is subsequently searched for, it will be printed out in that order.

The **searching** functions of data base managers are activated by the user when s/he is looking for a specific piece of information in the data base. Let's say you need the reference for the book on interviewing you read a while ago, but the author's name doesn't come to mind. The program can be instructed to search through the 'title' field in your bibliography data base and find everything that has the word 'interview' in it. All records that contain the word in the specified field will be displayed or printed out, and you can pick out the one you had in mind.

There is one problem, however. What if the word in the title was not 'interview' but 'interviewing'? You will not find the reference in your list, because computers are literal creatures. A data base manager would lose its sole reason for existence, however, if you could not find whatever you wanted. Therefore, programmers of data base managers have refined the search procedures to an amazingly intricate degree. Asking for something to be retrieved is called a 'query,' and you would rarely enter just one simple word in a query. You can make 'interview' the root, and retrieve anything in which this string of characters appears (wild card searches), or specify that the word be within a certain number of words from another word (proximity searches), or that another word must also be in the same field entry (Boolean searches), and so forth. (Searches are the special domain of text retrievers, and the various ways in which they can be set up is explained in the chapter on text retrievers.)

In large data base managers searches can take quite a bit of time. There are two ways to expedite them. One is to index the entire data base. This means that, in essence, something like a 'shadow' data base is created. It contains information about the location of the words in the data base. Then, when the user wants to retrieve a word, the program does not search the entire data base, but its index. There it finds the information that points it to the right record(s), and that record is the one it retrieves. Usually, only 'content' words are indexed. Such nondescript words as 'is', 'or', 'they', etc. are 'noise' words and are disregarded. (Again, more on this can be found in the chapter on text retrievers.)

The second way to speed up retrieval is the insertion of key-words. They are like those ingenious electronic devices that let you find your car in a crowded parking lot by making it whistle or flash its lights. A small receiver is installed in the car, and your hand-held device transmits on just the right frequency to trigger the receiver. Key-words 'characterize' records. They are especially useful when the data are not likely to contain the search word itself. The book on interviewing you need could, for instance, have the title *The Research Dialogue*. There is no way to find it, unless your bibliographical data base has a key-word field. In that field you install a 'tag' for your record, or several tags. The tag for *The Research Dialogue* could be "interview", and perhaps you would add also "qualitative research" and "data collection". The data base now looks like the drawing on the next page.

The key-words act like the small receivers in the car; when you search for them, they 'flash', and the relevant records are retrieved immediately. It takes a good bit of planning on the user's part to attach the right key-words to each record, so that they will correspond to the various purposes that might come to her/his mind in the future. A poorly conceived key-word is about as useful as the car finder you left in the car.

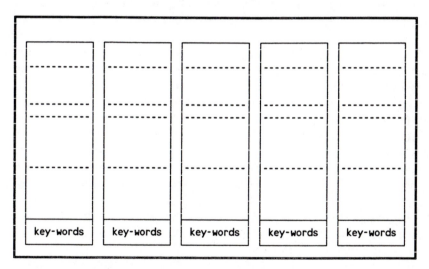

Development of New Features and Types

As data base managers began to compete with each other, programmers added new features or made them more powerful. The improved packages, in turn, were emulated by other programmers, and thus data base managers became more sophisticated and more diverse from generation to generation. The simple first data base managers did not even sort data, or let the user browse through the data base to review it. They just stored information, accepted regular additions, and retrieved data pieces according to the user's specifications. Later, sorting and browsing were added. Next came three important enhancements: calculated fields, variable length fields, and long text fields.

Whenever designing a structured data base, the user is asked not only to specify the name and length of a field, but also its nature: numeric or text (some data base managers have special date or money fields, too). This has to do with sorting and searching; you can't sort in descending numerical order or search for values 'greater than x' in a field if the program is not told that this particular field is to be treated as a mathematical entity. Calculated fields are those on which several kinds of arithmetic operations other than mere sorting functions can be performed. They can be totalled, for instance, or averaged. In the most powerful data base managers the entire set of normal accounting functions can be performed on calculated fields.

The length of a field has been 'variable' for a long time, in the sense that the user could specify each field's lengths. But once that was done, the length was fixed for that particular data base. Let's say, it was set to twenty. This would mean that the field took up the space for twenty characters in each record, whether all twenty were actually filled in or only two. Nowadays, when data base people speak of variable length fields they mean that the field is only as long as the information entered into it. A variable length field can accommodate two or twenty characters without wasting storage space.

Thirdly, long 'text' fields were introduced. While field size limits of only forty or sixty characters were quite common in early data base managers, now many have at least one field that can hold up to 254 characters. That number amounts to about three normal typed lines of text.

Some further enhancements and innovations have resulted in the creation of entire 'classes' of data base managers. The next page provides a graphic overview.

The diagram should not be viewed as a hierarchy (in terms of power), or even a chronology (in terms of development). The locations in the chart merely signify differences in nature.

The first distinction is between structured and unstructured data bases. **Structured data base managers** have been described above. **Unstructured data base managers** simply have done away with fields or feature variable length fields whose name or nature need not be defined beforehand. They allow information of 'unlimited' length to be entered, much like word processors. In the process they have, in fact, become somewhat like word processors. They are used mostly for long text documents; some software reviewers call them 'text-based management systems'.

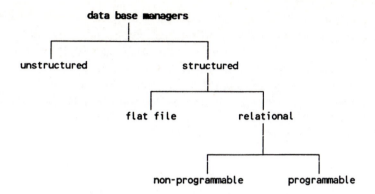

Instead of files, unstructured data base managers have the customary records. Their advantage over word processors is that they search through all records, instead of only the designated document file. Furthermore, their search procedures are usually more sophisticated than those of ordinary word processors. (The boundary between unstructured data base managers and word processors becomes more fluid the more sophisticated the word processor. Some word processors today include data base managers or perform almost all the functions of one.) Instead of columnar out-put, unstructured data base managers produce 'line reports', i.e., they actually print out lines of text. Considering the large and diverse data base manager market, it is not surprising that software packages exist that combine the features of both structured and unstructured managers.

The structured data base managers described earlier were so-called **flat-file data base managers**. This means that every data base is separate. It is just about impossible to exchange data between two data bases, unless they have exactly the same structure (the same number of fields with the same names and lengths). If they had exactly the same structure, there would be hardly any point in having two separate bases. The term 'flat-file' was not common until some clever programmer 'related' two data bases to each other through a common field. These are the **relational data base managers**. Being related means that data in one base can be accessed through a link with the other. If, for instance, you had structured information about a research site in your data base, and someone else, using the same program, also had structured information about the same site, and both of you had a field for names in which you had put the same data, you could make use of each other's data bases.

Programmers of data base managers have always been eager to allow the user to customize procedures, so they would best suit her/his individual purpose. Designing data entry and report formats was a first step. Soon, users were invited to do even more. Data base managers began to provide what amounted to a simple programming language, so that the user could shape the data base manager in any way s/he wanted. This was especially necessary for the first relational data base managers. **Programmable data base managers** have done much to establish the genre's reputation as being difficult to learn. While programming languages were welcomed by professional users who gained the power to create programs for unique applications, not everyone who wanted to use a relational data base manager also wanted to learn how to program. Therefore, **non-programmable data base managers** soon became available that could be customized to a certain degree, but required no actual programming.

Conclusion

This brief description of data base managers does not come close to providing a sense of what these programs can do. They perform enormously complicated feats in business and administrative settings. The most well-known powerful data base manager is probably dBase III (now out in its most recent version, dBase IV). This program is not only widely used, but its programming language is on par with other languages, allowing all kinds of free-standing software to be created in dBase III language. Yet the kind of tasks data base managers tackle are only marginally related to qualitative analysis tasks.

Structured data base managers require that data come in discrete entities. They lend themselves well to studies that use structured question-naires or interview schedules, and where the answers are open (rather than forced-choice), but brief enough to remain within one topic. Each completed questionnaire or interview transcript becomes one record in the data base, and each question becomes one field. Data are entered accordingly. It is easy to create a 'report' that contains all answers to a specified question, since merely one field across the entire data base needs to be printed out. The sorting feature can be used to print out data selectively, such as all answers to question one by people over twenty-five years old (if the data base was set up to include an "age" field).

Since data base managers, structured and unstructured, search for words across files (their 'records'), they can also be useful to researchers who study word usage or other language features. Unless these researchers feel very comfortable working with a familiar data base manager, however, a text retriever might be the more appropriate tool, especially one that is specifically designed for language studies <Text retrievers>.

Unstructured data base managers have only small advantages over word processors for qualitative analysis. While their search features are more sophisticated, the result of a search is usually the pinpointing of a record. The data base manager announces in which record it has found a word, and the word in question is highlighted. There is no easy way to freely segment text, however. While fields in structured data base managers are most appropriate for natural meaning units (and are the entities that are printed out as a result of searching or sorting), unstructured data base managers leave the segmenting of the data to the user at the time the word is found, just as word processors do.

One of the major differences between data base managers and text analysis programs is that data base managers are 'accumulators'. They expect that the information which has been entered is there to stay, being updated and added to periodically. Large longitudinal ethnographic projects might need just such a facility. Most smaller qualitative studies, however, are based on data that are not modified and rarely added to. For them, text analysis programs may often be the better choice. Text analysis programs are not accumulators, but 'processors', facilitating the process of analysis by specifically preparing data for interpretation.

Since data base managers have been available for such a long time, however, many qualitative researchers have made them work for their projects and often found them quite useful. In this manner, some favorites have evolved (Brent et al., 1987, p. 312). Among them are Reflex, a structured data base manager that enables the user to scroll the entire data base across the screen in tabular form; askSam, a text data base manager that can also be made to provide structure and that recently has incorporated hypertext features <How to read this book; HyperQual>; and FYI 3000 Plus, a powerful text data base manager that is part of a word processor/data base manager package by the name of Notabene, designed especially for academic use. Also intended for text manipulation and quite affordable and serviceable are Nutshell and Notebook II.

References

BRENT, EDWARD; SCOTT, JAMES and SPENCER, JOHN (1987) 'The use of computers by qualitative researchers', *Qualitative Sociology*, 10, 3, pp. 309-13.

Software References

askSam
Seaside Software, P.O. Box 1428, Perry, FL 32347, (800) 327-5726, $295.00.
dBase III
Ashton-Tate Corp., 20101 Hamilton Ave., Torrance, CA 90502, (213) 329-8000, $695.00

FYI 3000 Plus
> Software Marketing Associates, 4615 Bee Cave Road, Austin, TX 78746, (512) 327-2882, $395.00

Notabene
> Dragonfly Software, 409 Fulton St., Suite 202, Brooklyn, NY 11201, (718) 624-0127, $495.00

Notebook II
> Pro/Tem Software Inc., 2363 Boulevard Circle, Walnut Creek, CA 94595, $189.00.

ETHNO

Introduction

ETHNO is a program for facilitating the study of structures in qualitative data. Unlike programs for text analysis, it does not deal with raw data as one continuing flow of text. The program creates graphic representations of relationships among entities (diagrams in the form of inverted tree charts). The researcher must enter these entities into the program one at a time.

ETHNO can be used to visualize connections among entities such as concepts or events. A system of connections can be quite simply structured. For instance, a hierarchical organizing system for qualitative data could be depicted with ETHNO, or an outline for a paper, or the semantic structure of a cultural 'domain' (Spradley, 1979, p. 101), i.e., a 'cover term' and its associated set of included terms used by a cultural group. The structure could also be very complex, as it would be for a causal network or for an 'action grammar' ('a set of rules for ordering some kind of element', Heise and Lewis, 1988, p. 114). Narratives that describe events follow such rules in the sense that the events are not happening randomly, but according to conditions that have to be met before any specific event can occur. Folk tales and historical documents could be analyzed to discover what their unique 'grammars' are.

All of ETHNO's drawings are composed of vertical and horizontal lines. The program does not draw arrows, nor does it construct matrices, as spreadsheets do. All names of entities listed in the drawings are abbreviated to three letters. On the next page is an example of an ETHNO chart. (It's not important at the moment what the entities in this chart mean.)

Vertical lines in the drawing represent a connection in which the lower entity is subordinate in some way to the higher entity, or the lower entity follows the higher one chronologically or logically. The horizontal lines complete the vertical lines; the vertical lines simply 'run horizontally' for a while. (These rectangular lines are drawn instead of diagonal ones since otherwise the user would need a special graphics program to run ETHNO.) Gaps around a vertical line mean that the horizontal line bypasses that particular vertical line.

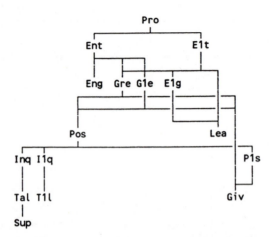

ETHNO comes ready to accept input for two types of conceptual systems: taxonomies and sequential structures. There are three different 'frameworks' for taxonomies, and one for sequences of events. 'Framework' refers to the character of the relationship among the entities, the character of the connecting lines, so to speak. What the lines mean in the illustration above depends on the framework used. For example, the three **taxonomic frameworks** that come with the program are the following:

1. One entity is '*a kind of*' another entity. For instance, A Macintosh is 'a kind of' personal computer. A Compaq is also 'a kind of' computer, but it is not 'a kind of' Macintosh.

   ETHNO calls this framework a 'AKO-framework' (**A K**ind **O**f).

2. One entity is '*a part of*' another entity. For instance, a keyboard is 'a part of' a personal computer. A monitor is also 'a part of' a personal computer, but it is not 'a part of' a key-board.

   This framework is called a 'PART-OF-framework' in ETHNO.

3. A person (social actor) '*generally is*' in a certain role vis-a-vis other persons. For instance, the people who work together for large collaborative research project could be characterized in their role relation vis-a-vis other people in the same project. This would be

212

done according various dimensions, such as whether a person is a professional or support personal, whether s/he works in the field or in the research office, or is involved full-time or part-time. The research director 'generally is' a professional, 'generally is' a full-time employee, and 'generally is' an office worker, planning and overseeing the project and analyzing the data. The interviewer 'generally is' a professional, a part-time person, and a field worker. The secretary 'generally is' a support person, etc.

This framework is called by ETHNO an S-framework (a **S**tatic framework in comparison with those frameworks that deal with the sequence of events, which are dynamic).

One could think of other relationships among entities, such as 'a result of', or 'an attribute of', or 'a way of'. Using a special ETHNO function, you can create your own frameworks to fit your needs. More about this later.

A **sequential structure** requires a more complex framework than taxonomies. The relationship in this framework is one where *one event logically and chronologically follows another event*, i.e., a certain event 'requires' a specific other event in order to happen. A simple example is working with a computer. Running a word processing program, for instance, 'requires' loading it from a disk. If there is no hard disk, loading a program from a disk 'requires' inserting a disk into a disk drive. Thus inserting a disk is a prerequisite for loading a program, which in turn is a prerequisite for running a program.

The above example describes a technical task. When we deal with human social behavior, the options are much richer. Usually, after an action or 'event' has occurred, various alternate actions could follow all of which would make sense in the particular context. In such a dynamic setting, actions could be repeated, or one action could have more than one prerequisite. ETHNO calls the framework for sequential structures a D-framework (for **D**ynamic).

Once a 'framework' is created (ETHNO comes with the four described above), the data are entered as answers to questions posed by the program. This technique is called 'elicitation'. In ETHNO there are two kinds of questions. One type elicits information about one entity at a time, and the other about the relationship between a newly entered entity and the previously entered entities.

A simple example will illustrate the process. Let's assume we are creating a taxonomy of qualitative research approaches. The general 'domain' is elicited first, and we enter: "qualitative research". Next we would enter any piece of data. For instance, our 'data' could come as an alphabetical list like the one in our chapter on basic qualitative research types. Therefore, we enter "action research". The program immediately represents this relationship graphically:

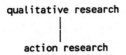

With that relationship established, the program asks: "Next element?" We answer with another piece of data. Since "case study" is next on the list, that's what we enter. Now the program comes back with **"Is** case study **a kind of** action research?" We answer "No", but that is not yet sufficient for a firm conclusion. Both diagrams below could still be possible, because in each "case study" would be a kind of "qualitative research":

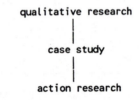

or:

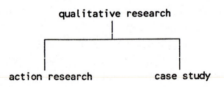

Therefore, ETHNO asks one more question before it can depict the relationship: **"Is** action research **a kind of** case study?" Since the answer is "No", ETHNO draws the lower diagram. For every new entity entered, ETHNO automatically asks all questions necessary to establish the exact relationship to all other entities. Fortunately, the program is 'smart' enough to omit unnecessary questions.

As mentioned above, ETHNO allows you to create 'customized' frameworks. This is achieved by letting you generate your own types of questions (they would replace, in this instance, the question "Is Y a kind of X?").

Program Structure

The program has three basic functions and three enhancement functions. The three basic functions are:

DEFINE A FRAMEWORK
(develop a new frame-
work if the available
frameworks are not
useful for your task)

CREATE A STRUCTURE
(fill in one of
the available frame-
works)

MODIFY A STRUCTURE
(edit or expand a
framework already
filled in)

All three enhancement functions are to be used with sequential structures. When a series of events is entered in the framework, the structure can be tested to see whether it is consistent, i.e., whether the logical structure '. . . explain[s] the sequence of events' (Heise, 1988, p. 9). This function is called 'analyzing a series'.

The event structure can also be used to 'simulate' events, i.e., to see what happens if alternate paths (that are logically and chronologically possible) were chosen at different points in the structure rather than the ones that actually happened according to the raw data. This function is called 'generating a series'.

Thirdly, the structure can be expressed more abstractly, i.e., for every concrete event that was originally entered, the corresponding general class of event can be substituted (for example, instead of "running the word processor" one could say "running a program").

ETHNO, therefore, can be visualized as structured somewhat like this:

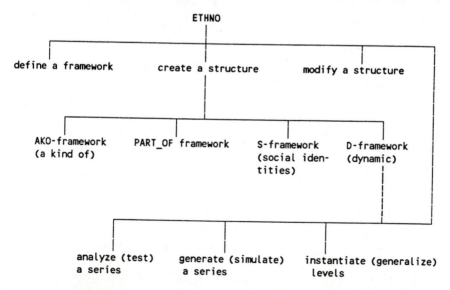

The last row in this chart represents the enhancement functions. Although they are meant for working with event sequences (the **Dynamic**

framework), these functions are not accessed from the D-framework module. Instead, they are accessed directly from the main menu. Of course, they only work if an event structure has been created previously and is now stored, thus being available to be tested, or to be used for simulation, or to be transformed to a more abstract level.

ETHNO opens directly with the **main menu**, which, according to the structure described above, looks like this:

Create a structure   Analyze a series   Generate a series

Modify a structure   Instantiate levels   **Define a framework**

The three basic functions on this menu are bolded here (not in the program). The remaining three are the enhancement functions.

Working with ETHNO's Basic Functions

Filling in a framework ('creating a structure')

Since elicitation is the program's operating principle, working with ETHNO is as easy as answering questions. This means that all intellectually simple operations are simple with ETHNO as well. The more sophisticated and complex the intellectual research tasks become, the more difficult it is to respond to the questions. Constructing a basic taxonomy, for instance, is elementary, as demonstrated by the development of the beginning of a qualitative research classification scheme (in the introduction to the program, above). However, the resulting chart looks different from the one I provided with that example. ETHNO charts are not easy to read. Compare the over-all qualitative research diagram at the end of the chapter on research types, for instance, with the one ETHNO constructed when given the same input (on the next page, and slightly truncated in width to fit into the available space).

Notice the three-character abbreviations. As mentioned earlier, they were produced by ETHNO automatically. The program will print out a list of the terms that underlie the abbreviations in the chart. However, in a large chart it is still bothersome to have to look up everything. The charts are made not so much for gaining an overview as for carefully examining individual pieces by tracing the relationships.

Incidentally, you might notice that the 'entities' in this chart are not presented in the same geographic locations as in the original diagram from our earlier chapter. I entered them in exactly the order in which one would read that earlier diagram, namely from left to right and from top to bottom. ETHNO, however, decides on its own where to place the 'entities' in the chart. As in this case, certain graphic information (namely how structured a type of research is) can get lost when locations are changed.

Types of qualitative research, partial chart:

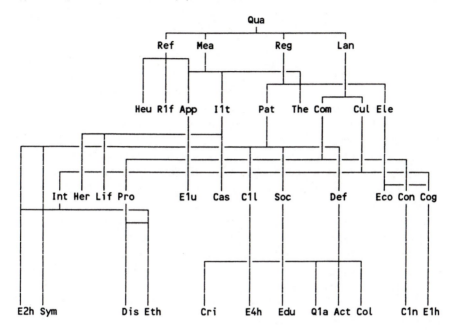

In spite of its size, the above chart is still very straightforward, because it represents a simple taxonomy: terms higher up in the chart are more generic than those further down. Conceptual structures can become more complicated. The ETHNO manual provides an example of a more complex framework: a framework for typologies. According to the program's author, typologies are distinguished from taxonomies by an added dimension: cross-classification. Usually, typologies are presented as grids or matrices that can have two or four, or many more cells, depending on the classification criteria. The drawing below depicts a four-cell typological matrix with four criteria:

DATA COLLECTION	direct contact	indirect contact
obtrusive	interview	questionnaire
unobtrusive	participant observation	diary study

This is how ETHNO would construct the same chart:

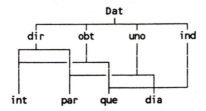

As you can see, ETHNO's diagrams take some getting used to. You can find your way around in the chart by tracing from the bottom items only those lines that lead to an item further up, not to an item on the same level or along a line that bends downward. From int(erview), for example, the first branch leads to the right and up to obt(rusive); don't follow it down to "que". The next branch leads up to dir(ect); don't follow it down to "par". There are no further lines going up from int(erview). Therefore, this diagram conveys that "int" has the two attributes of being an **obtrusive** data collection technique carried out in **direct** contact with the informant.

Sequential structures are depicted in much the same manner, except that the diagrams become even harder to read. The filling in of an event structure framework, however, is still relatively straightforward. ETHNO's question when eliciting information about the sequence of events is "Does Y require X (or a similar event)?", where Y is the most recently entered event and X one of the formerly entered events. The tricky part is the conceptual decision you must make when answering this question. In many complex social situations it isn't that clear whether Y can happen only after X has occurred. In addition, the actual data may merely imply happenings that for ETHNO must be stated explicitly, and 'each event has to be stated in a simple regular way so as to be comprehensible during ETHNO analysis' (Heise, 1988, p. 15).

Making changes ('modifying a structure')

It is not necessary to enter all data for a structure in one session. ETHNO lets you continue where you stopped as if you had never interrupted. This is accomplished by choosing the 'modify function' from the main menu. The same diagram you originally constructed will appear, and the same questions are asked as when you filled in the framework initially. Within this program module you can add entities to the structure, change their names, their relationships (and other properties of sequential structures), or delete them. The manual explains how to carry out the more complicated editing tasks in complex event structures.

Creating a new framework ('defining a framework')

If your project requires the construction of a conceptual structure that is neither a simple taxonomy nor an event structure, you can create that framework with ETHNO. The technique is again elicitation; the program asks questions, and you provide the answers. Giving the right answer, however, requires quite a bit of prior knowledge about the way frameworks operate in ETHNO. The author provides two examples in the manual, one for a typology that accommodates family membership roles, and one for a flow chart that can show the connections among computer program subroutines. Nevertheless, it took a bit of experimenting before I was able to construct my own framework. (Fortunately experimenting is painless: if you goof, you can replace the deficient framework with an improved one by simply using the same name again. The new framework will automatically replace the old framework that is stored under the same name.)

Technical Adequacy

The only 'technical' problem with the program is that the terms used on the screen are not intuitively plausible. Take the menu options, for example. Initially, you don't know whether to choose "create a structure", "analyze a series", "generate a series", or "define a framework" for entering your data. You have to learn what each means. The S- and D-distinctions for frameworks are also peculiar. If S stands for static, why is this the framework meant for 'social identities' or roles which can change, while conceptual taxonomies are, in fact, the 'static' structures? But these might be residues of the program's developmental history and could easily be corrected in future versions.

The vastly more important characteristic of the program is its reliance on elicitation, which makes it truly user-friendly, since all you ever do (in addition to a minimum of menu selection key-strokes) is to type in answers as if you were using a typewriter. Learning to do word processing is much more demanding than learning how to use this program, as far as technical skills are concerned. Furthermore, the program does not ever leave you with no way out: hitting the Esc-key gets you out from almost anywhere, including out of the program altogether. There are a couple of exceptions, but in those cases quick dummy answers and completion of the elicitation sequence gets you to the point from which ESC works again. ETHNO is also forgiving; anytime you don't like what you did, you can start over by pressing the Esc-key instead of typing a file name when asked whether you want to save your work. Large existing diagrams that you don't want to throw out altogether, can easily be changed with the "modify" function. There are also help-screens available that explain clearly and extensively what will happen when certain choices from the screen options are made, or how to perform various tasks at certain points in the process.

Unlike text analysis programs, this 'structural analysis' program does not save its results in ASCII files that can simply be picked up by word processors. This is not surprising since the results are not text, but diagrams. However, ETHNO screens can be accessed by utility programs that provide 'cutting and pasting', with whose help diagrams can be transported into a word processor.

Enhancements

ETHNO is a peculiar program in the sense that it can be used for very simple tasks almost immediately, and yet provides the options for extremely sophisticated procedures that even require a special language to explain them, as well as some technical learning to operate them. The enhancements functions in the program are of this nature. All of them apply to dynamic event structures, where the relationships are much more complex than in static taxonomies or typologies. The ETHNO manual explains them well. They are applicable only to the special case of qualitative sequential analysis, and therefore the following is nothing more than a brief and simplified description of the functions available.

Testing the fit between actual events and the model

When using ETHNO's event structure framework, the diagrams (and consequently the 'model') are drawn according to certain assumptions built into the program. These are quite elementary: 'An event can't happen until its prerequisite events happen. An event depletes material conditions so that prerequisite events have to happen again if the event is to happen again. An event can't be repeated until it has been depleted, [i.e.] until its effects are used up by some other event that requires it' (Heise, 1988, p. 28). Let's use our example about working with a computer to illustrate these three assumptions:

a. An event can't happen until its prerequisite events happen: Running a word processing program can't happen until it has been loaded.

b. An event depletes material conditions so that prerequisite events have to happen again if the event is to happen again: Exiting from a program 'depletes' loading the program. Running and exiting the program requires that the prerequisite loading of the program happens again.

c. An event can't be repeated until it has been depleted, [i.e.] until its effects are used up by some other event that requires it: Loading the program can't be repeated until its effects of running and exiting it have been 'used up'.

You might not have noticed, but we fudged a bit in this example. Twice we referred to two events together (running and exiting) when the 'rule' only spoke of one. These are exactly the types of incidents for which ETHNO provides the function that lets you 'test' whether the 'model' you constructed (by answering ETHNO's questions during elicitation) in fact fits the real situation, i.e., whether 'we now have a grammar of action that accounts for event order' (Heise and Lewis, 1988, p. 9).

The testing function is performed within the "analyze a series" module of the program. When using this function, ETHNO reports where the model constructed from your entries violates one of the above three rules and lists ways in which the events could be ordered such that the rules are not broken. You decide whether your input was indeed erroneous (for instance, not precise or explicit enough) and you should accept one of ETHNO's suggestions for change, or whether the rules must be broken in this case to accommodate reality.

Discovering priorities

One question that might be important in the interpretation of an event sequence model as constructed by ETHNO is: When several events were possible at once (i.e., when their prerequisites exist), which one did actually occur? For instance, both running a program and exiting it are possible once the program is loaded. Which one occurred according to the model? If 'running' occurred, ETHNO would, not unreasonably, consider this a 'priority'. In an actual research situation, such priorities might help to interpret the preferences or values of the actors.

Discovering priorities is a function also contained (and easily run) in ETHNO's "analyze a series" module.

Simulating potentially possible event sequences

Since event sequence models are usually complex enough to contain the prerequisites for several events, as assumed in the priority establishing process above, it is theoretically possible that an event other than the one that actually occurred could have happened. ETHNO provides a way of playing with these possibilities in its "generate a series" module. It lists the options, and when you choose one, it will reconstruct the model (diagram) accordingly and show the next list of options from which to choose. This is helpful not necessarily for theory-building, but for an additional check on the faithfulness of the model. In the process of simulation, ETHNO might provide you with a list of theoretically possible options that practically don't exist. If that happens, you can revise the model so it makes sense.

Transforming to a higher level of abstraction

When entering data from real research projects, the events are concrete. It is possible to think of the actors in the event sequence as representative of a general class of actors, and of their actions as representing general classes of events. ETHNO lets you substitute these general concepts for the concrete entities, creating a parallel model to the one that already exists. The "instantiate levels" module of the program elicits 'abstract' entries to be used in place of the concrete ones. This transformation provides another perspective from which to view the model; it is likely to enrich its interpretation.

Technical Description

ETHNO was created by David Heise; it came out in version 2.0 in 1988. It operates on any IBM and IBM-compatible personal computer with at least 512K of memory.

Price: $35.00. Distributed by National Collegiate Software Clearing House, Duke University Press, 6697 College Station, Durham, NC 27708. Telephone 919/737-2468.

ETHNO Glossary

A glossary is provided in the ETHNO manual's reference section.

References

HEISE, DAVID R. (1988, Spring) 'Computer analysis of cultural structures', *Social Science Computer Review*, 6, 1, pp. 183-97.
HEISE, DAVID R. and LEWIS, ELSA M. (1988) *Introduction to ETHNO*, Raleigh, NC, National Collegiate Software Clearinghouse.
SPRADLEY, JAMES P. (1979) *The Ethnographic Interview*, New York, Holt, Rinehart and Winston.

Text Analysis Package (TAP)

Introduction

TAP is set up to make coding fast. It displays the data text on the screen as you enter codes; therefore, no paper printouts of the data documents are needed for coding. Of course, the program will print out the text if you prefer to work on paper first. The text appears as a broad column, about two thirds of the screen width, on the right side, and you can scroll it up and down. The cursor sits in front of the first line when the screen comes up, then is moved up and down the lines with the arrow keys, as one would expect. It can also be moved into the blank left third of the screen (but not to the right into the data text). As you press the left arrow key the cursor jumps to the left and makes a small box appear into which you are supposed to type your code. Pressing the Enter-key returns the cursor to its place in front of the text, from where it can be moved swiftly to the next coding place.

The programmer of TAP has thought of two additional ways to expedite the attachment of codes. For one, the researcher may assign the ten most frequently used codes to the ten function keys on the keyboard. Then, instead of typing out a code, one simply hits a function key, and the code associated with it appears in the coding box.

The second way to speed up coding is reserved for a special case: the case in which the assignment of codes coincides with the occurrence of a certain term or phrase in the data text. TAP will look for the term/phrase in the data text, find all occurrences, then assign the code specified by the user to the line in which the term appears. This is genuine (and mindless) 'automation', which can come in quite handy. More about it later.

Underlying Concepts

TAP has been created for the researcher with some linguistic interest. In its basic operating configuration (the 'default' mode), it attaches codes to a line of text, not an entire segment. Although it is easy to work in the segment (called 'unit') mode as well, the operation requires an extra step. A symbol must be inserted in front of the line that contains a segment boundary. Since linguistically-oriented researchers are often interested in the spacial relationships of words in a text, there is just as much emphasis on the **detection of co-occurrences of codes** and **occurrences of code patterns** (coded segments that follow each other in a certain order) as there is on the **retrieval of coded text segments**. Frequencies receive more attention than in other text analysis programs; TAP even produces frequency distribution tables.

TAP calls for no preparatory work beyond ASCII conversion: you import a file from your word processor and begin coding it. There is no need to attach numbers to each line or to print out a paper copy. However, these conveniences also have their associated disadvantages. Since codes are attached directly on the screen, only as many can be used as fit on one line in the left margin. This limits the codes to four, i.e., any given segment (or line) can be sorted into up to four categories, but no more. Furthermore, the segments are discrete; the next one can't begin until the preceding one has ended. There is no overlap. Neither can the user carve out a smaller segment within a large one and code it differently than the large one itself.

Since the text lines are not numbered, the coded segments that are extracted are not printed out with line numbers. Therefore, it is more difficult in TAP than most other programs to locate a segment's original place in the data document. If the researcher needs to do so, the best way to find a particular segment is to call up the data document (either in TAP or in a word processor) and search for the text string with which it begins, or any unusual word combination in it.

Unlike other text analysis programs TAP is not totally menu-driven. It also uses 'commands'. Fortunately, there are few, and they are consistent. Commands are either single letters (for instance "S" initiates a search) or combinations of the control key with a letter ("ctrl-S" repeats the search for the same term/phrase). One especially convenient command is "ctrl-K". It gets the user out of most ongoing operations and back to the menu.

Program Structure

TAP has only one main and two small procedure menus (see drawing next page). They are shown in the starred boxes.

The program modules, shown in plain boxes, are called 'subsystems' by TAP. The "default values" module is a very small one through which the user can set the directory in which the data are kept, and make one change in the printer setting (see the section on printing, later in this chapter). The "data retrieval" module is the one that retrieves the coded segments, while the "retrieve file" module loads into the computer's memory the data document on which work is to be done.

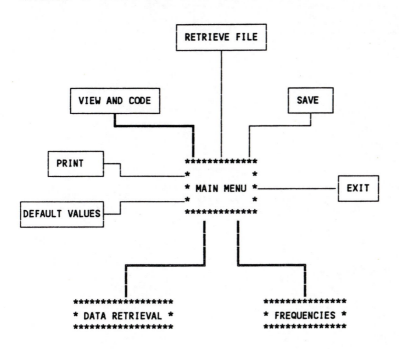

The two small procedure menus are structured as shown on the next page.

"Line Mode" and "Unit Mode" (in the left center box in the next drawing) give the researcher the choice of working with individual lines of text or with text segments. "Text return" refers to the display of coded text segments, while "pattern return" has to do with consecutive segments that are coded in a certain order. The 'table' mentioned in the "frequencies" module is a frequency distribution table. 'Retrieving' a file in this context means adding the codes of another file to the table. A 'TFN file' is the list of files that has been created by retrieving additional files to be used for the frequency distribution table. All this is explained in the appropriate sections below.

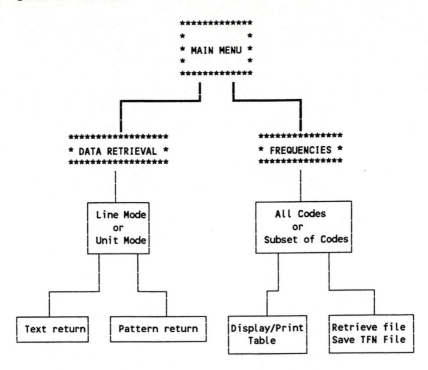

How TAP Works

A   The main functions

a   Coding

As mentioned earlier, TAP makes attaching codes particularly easy and fast. Codes are simply typed into the left margin of the data text that appears on the screen. Before we go into the techniques, however, something needs to be said about marking the beginning and ends of data segments. TAP calls segments 'coding units' or just 'units'. The program 'thinks' of the basic coding unit as one single line. This means, if the researcher did nothing else but type code words into the left margin, these code words would be attached to the one line of text that is opposite them. To identify a segment of text, the user must mark its boundaries. This is usually done after the code is typed. A symbol is inserted just in front of the line where the segment begins. The place in front of the lines is the normal resting position of the cursor (it moves up and down). If the U-key is pressed (for Unit), a + (plus symbol) appears at the cursor location, and that line has now become the segment's start line. There is no special symbol for the end of a coding unit. A segment simply ends where the next + with a code word is encountered. If the segment ends before the next segment starts, one must enter a phony code word at the end of the unit, such as "end". (This creates some problems with the frequency percentages, however. More about it later.) If the researcher changes her/his mind about the beginning or end of a segment, the cursor is placed beneath the existing **+**, the U-key is pressed again, and the **+** disappears. The U-key is a toggle switch; it is used to erase the marking symbol as well as to insert it.

Back to the actual coding. There are three ways of doing it. The researcher may use the basic method, or a variation of it, and there is also an 'automated' feature. As you enter the coding module of the program, the file you retrieved appears on the right side of the screen. The cursor sits in front of the first line. You move it up and down the lines with the arrow keys. When you are at the line on which your first segment begins, move the cursor to the left. As it jumps there, it creates a box in the left margin (the box is called 'field' by TAP). The screen looks like this:

```
********************************************************************************

introduc.tap [this is the file name]   CTRL/K TO QUIT [reminder how to get out


                                TAP is set up to make coding fast.  It dis-
                                plays the data text on the screen as you enter
                                codes; therefore, no paper printouts of the data
   ::::::::                     documents are needed for coding.  Of course, the
   ::::::::                     program will print out the text if you prefer to
                                work on paper first.  The text appears as a broad
                                column, about two thirds of the screen width, on
                                the right side, and you can scroll it up and down.
                                The cursor sits in front of the first line when
                                the screen comes up, then is moved up and down the
                                lines with the arrow keys, as one would expect.
                                It can also be moved into the blank left third
                                of the screen (but not to the right into the data
                                text).  As you press the left arrow key, the
                                cursor jumps to the left and makes a small box
                                . . . etc.
********************************************************************************
```

The box on the left designates the place for the first code word. This is where you are supposed to type it. But wait! There is a little quirk. You must signal to the program that you want to *add* something to your data file. Press the plus key (+ key), and now your input will be accepted. (If you don't press the plus key, nothing at all happens; the computer just plays dumb.) When you have entered the code, the cursor jumps back to its resting place in front of the line. You may play this little game another three times, and each time a new box will be made available. Four is the limit of codes per line. The screen has changed to this:

```
******************************************************************************

introduc.tap                          CTRL/K TO QUIT


                         TAP is set up to make coding fast.  It dis-
                         plays the data text on the screen as you enter
                         codes; therefore, no paper printouts of the data
Abcd   Efgh   Ijkl   Mnop  _documents are needed for coding.  Of course, the
                         program will print out the text if you prefer to
                         work on paper first.  The text appears as a broad
                         column, about two thirds of the screen width, on
                         the right side, and you can scroll it up and down.
                         The cursor sits in front of the first line when
                         the screen comes up, then is moved up and down
                         the lines with the arrow keys, as one would
                         expect.  It can also be moved into the blank left
                         third of the screen (but not to the right into the
                         data text.)  As you press the left arrow key, the
                         cursor jumps to the left and makes a small box
                         . . . etc.
******************************************************************************
```

A variation on this basic method is to let the computer do some of the typing. Whenever you code, a list of function keys sits at the top of the screen (not shown in the previous reproductions of the screen). This is what it looks like:

```
******************************************************************************

introduc.tap              CTRL/K TO QUIT               LINE:   1

   F 1:          F 2:          F 3:          F 4:          F 5:
   F 6:          F 7:          F 8:          F 9:          F10:


                         _TAP is set up to make coding fast.  It dis-
                         plays the data text on the screen as you enter
                         codes; therefore, no paper printouts of the data
                         documents are needed for coding.  Of course, the
                         program will print out the text if you prefer to
                         work on paper first.  The text appears as a broad
                         column, about two thirds of the screen width, on
                         the right side, and you can scroll it up and down.
                         . . .etc.
******************************************************************************
```

When a function key is pressed together with the shift-key, the cursor (normally sitting in front of a line) jumps to the respective function key position on the list above the text, blinking expectantly. The user is supposed to type one of the codes s/he expects to use most. When this is done, the cursor jumps back to where it came from, while the code remains visible at the function key position, so the user is reminded which code was assigned to that function key. All ten function keys can have codes assigned this way. Now, whenever one of these ten codes is needed, the appropriate function key is pressed, and one can watch how the word magically appears. (This is not only time-saving, but error-saving as well.) Since all one needs to do to change an assignment is to shift up to a function key again and type in a new code over the old one, it makes sense to do that whenever a certain code is used frequently.

The third way of attaching code words to text is useful only when it seems that there are certain terms or phrases in the data document that signal the relevance of the surrounding text to a category of the researcher's organizing system. TAP can be asked to search the entire document for that term/phrase (up to fifty characters long, including spaces), told what code word to attach there, and the program will complete the task. There is a problem, however. If your term/phrase happens to be wrapped around to the next line rather than sitting nicely on one line all in one piece, the computer refuses to notice it. This is a genuine flaw, but not fatal. (To be sure you caught all occurrences of your term/phrase, just do a search for the first five characters or so, without coding. The cursor, with great probability, will take you to all places where the wrapping occurred, and you can insert the code by hand.)

Automatic coding presents the user with the question of how to mark the beginnings and ends of the associated segments. The automatic procedure has attached the code only to the one line in which it found the term/phrase. There are two ways to accomplish segmenting. If the researcher is quite sure that a meaningful segment will be within ten lines preceding and succeeding the coded line, and s/he doesn't care much about extracting potentially irrelevant material, nothing needs to be done at the time. Later, when asked for the coded lines to be extracted, it is easy to specify that (up to) ten lines be printed out with the coded line, before and after, and this chunk of text constitutes the 'segment'. If that does not work for a particular project, TAP lets the researcher conduct a search for all occurrences of the particular code word right on the screen. This way, every time the code is encountered, the boundary markers can be placed by hand.

Changing codes is as easy as attaching them in the first place. The technique is exactly the same as the original 'basic procedure'. The researcher locates the code s/he wishes to change by making the program search for it. (TAP will, of course, find all occurrences of that code word.) When the right place is recognized, the cursor is positioned in the code box in the left margin, and the existing code can be edited as one would in a word processor. It can be deleted with a single key stroke, the minus key. There is also a 'global' procedure for deleting a code at every occurrence throughout the document. If the researcher wishes to replace an existing code word with a different one, a global 'search and replace' is activated, and the code specified is changed to the new one wherever it occurs.

b   Sorting/assembling

This activity is the part of TAP that requires LEARNING. On the other hand, if all you desire is the printout of your coded segments according to categories, i.e., the re-contextualized data, you merely need to know how to fill in the screen that sets up your search procedure. For sophisticated searches, however, you must understand the terms and abbreviations on the screen. You won't know what to do unless you read the appropriate section of the manual, - twice. Most of the features described there fall under the heading 'enhancements', which follows this section. Here we will deal only with the simple case of extracting and collating coded text segments. The menu for 'data retrieval' looks a bit complicated at first, but it is easy to get used to it.

```
************************************************************************

introduc.tap [file name]        TAP DATA RETRIEVAL              UNIT

                                Number of Code Sequences in the Pattern:
 ┌───────────────────────┐
 │                       │      For each sequence, type the code(s),
 │     PROCEDURES        │      separated by commas.
 │                       │
 │ P: Pattern Return     │
 │ T: Text Return        │      Sequence 1:
 │ L: Line Mode          │
 │ U: Unit Mode          │      Number of Lines before:
 │ X: eXit to Main Menu  │      Number of Lines after:
 │                       │      Sequence Search Options (OC):
 └───────────────────────┘

 Please Choose One:_

************************************************************************
```

If the researcher is interested only in retrieving text segments, s/he must choose the "Unit Mode", and then "Text Return". After that the cursor jumps to the right-hand side of the screen. For "Number of Code Sequences" one enters "1", and for "Sequence 1" the name of one code or several co-occurring codes (up to four). For "Number of Lines" "0" is entered in both cases; then one passes over the "Sequence Search Options" by pressing the Enter-key. After all this is done, a screen similar to the one on the next page appears.

The screen displays the one segment TAP has found that was coded "Abcd". We know that only one segment was found, because the program tells us so on the top of the screen: "Matches: 1". The "* * * MATCH 1 * * *" is the number of this particular segment; the next segment found would become "* * * MATCH 2 * * *". The researcher may scroll up and down within one segment with the arrow keys, and jump to the next or the preceding segment with the PgUp- and PgDn-keys. A serious shortcoming is the fact that only one search can be set up at a time in one file at a time, and that the results cannot be saved as ASCII files for import into a word processor.

```
*********************************************************************

introduc.tap              TAP DATA RETRIEVAL                UNIT

Matches: 1                PgUp  PgDn   P (Print)   CTRL/K (Quit)

* * * MATCH 1 * * *

Abcd                      $documents are needed for coding.  Of course, the
                          program will print out the text if you prefer to
                          work on paper first.  The text appears as a broad
                          column, about two thirds of the screen width, on
                          the right side, and you can scroll it up and down.
                          The cursor sits in front of the first line when
                          the screen comes up, the is moved up and down the
                          lines with the arrow keys, as one would expect.
                          It can also be moved into the blank left third of
                          the screen (but not to the right into the data
                          text).  As you press the left arrow key the cursor

Option:_
*********************************************************************
```

B Enhancement functions

TAP will count how often each code occurred in one file, or in all files, or in whichever files the user retrieves for that operation. Rather than merely displaying a number, the program will make a table with the code words in the rows (up to 200 different codes), the file names in the columns (up to sixty-four different files), and the frequencies in the cells.

In addition, TAP provides percentages. The percentages are calculated in terms of how often a code occurs in relation to the occurrence of all other codes. If one only had three different codes, for instance (called "Abcd", "Efgh", and "Ijkl"), the count of ten for "Abcd", five for "Efgh", and five for "Ijkl" would yield 50% for "Abcd", 25 % for "Efgh", and also 25 % for "Ijkl". (That's why the use of phony codes as indicators of the end of segments throws off the percentage results.) The researcher can't perform statistical significance tests on these numbers, but they can serve as indicators of relatively greater concern with the matter called Abcd, for instance, or relatively higher awareness of or pre-occupation with an issue or observation.

All the above operations are performed within TAP's "frequencies" module. The program does not stop there, however. In fact, setting up a search becomes so sophisticated (in the "data retrieval" module) that it takes some graphic explanation to get an overall understanding of the basic options available when seeking information about coded segments. Consider the following two configurations:

```
Case 1:    Abcd    Wxyz    Efgh    Stuv    text text text text text
                                           text text text text text
                                           text text text text text
                                           text
```

and:

```
Case 2:    Ijkl                            text text text text text
                                           text text text text text
                                           text text
           Opqr                            text text text text text
                                           text
           Mnop                            text text text text text
                                           text text text text text
                                           text text text text text
                                           text text text
           Klmn                            text text text text text
                                           text text text text text
```

In both cases above we have a certain succession of codes. In Case 1 four codes are attached to one segment. In Case 2 there are four segments which are coded in a certain order. In both cases the order in which the codes follow each other may be important for interpretive purposes. Therefore, TAP lets the researcher explore each. In Case 1 the program becomes very intricate; too much so to describe all the options here. They are explained in the user's manual. Case 1 code arrangements are called 'code sequences'; Case 2 arrangements are called 'code patterns'. Case 1 and Case 2 can be combined: you can have a pattern of sequences. To illustrate, consider the example below:

```
AB  CD              text text text text text text text
                    text text text text text text text

QR ST UV            text text text text text text text
                    text text text text text text text

AB  CD              text text text text text text text
                    text text text text text text text

QR ST UV            text text text text text text text
                    text text text text text text text
```

The 'pattern' consists of two occurrences of the sequences "AB CD" and "QR ST UV".

The occurrences of all these combinations, and of course of all the simple cases, are counted by TAP for each document. The associated text is not extracted for code sequences, but it is extracted for code patterns.

C   Preparatory functions

Preparatory tasks virtually don't exist in TAP. Once a data document is imported, it can be coded right away.

In the practical work with TAP there is, however, one consideration that should be undertaken beforehand. In some cases the researcher might want to obtain the frequency counts of a subset of her/his codes. There could be a group of categories conceptually similar or hierarchically related (one category has several subcategories). In this case, it would be wise to have all codes in the subset share a few letters. The reason is: TAP recognizes these shared letters, which it calls 'keys', in the "frequencies" module. Instead of typing each code separately, one can simply provide the key, and the program will search for and count all codes in which the key is contained.

D   Housekeeping functions

The first task after starting up TAP is always to tell the program which file you want to work with, i.e., which file to retrieve from the data disk. (You must know the exact spelling of the file name and, of course, you must know on which disk the file can be found. TAP does not provide a directory of your files; if you forget what is on your disk, you have to exit TAP and look at the directory from the DOS prompt.) The retrieved file is placed in memory (but not yet on the screen) and does not disappear while you switch around among program modules. Until you specifically ask for another file, the 'current' file remains in memory. Its name is printed on top of the main menu.

When you do ask for another file, TAP will prompt you to save the current file. That is especially important after you have coded the file or modified the coding. You have a chance to give the coded file a new name, and that is a good idea. You might always want to keep a non-coded version of each data file, so that you can code a file in different ways for developing or improving your categories. As you save a file, the program invites you to make a backup copy of it as well.

TAP lets you to make a list of all data files, so the file names don't have to be typed one by one when you want the code frequencies counted. There are two ways of doing it. Either you create a list of file names in your word processor (one file to a line), give it the name extension .TFN, and import it as an ASCII file; or you do this directly within the "frequencies" module (as explained in the user's manual).

Printing your work is easy. The "print" module prints the 'current' data document, coded or uncoded. The results of segment searches are printed directly from within the "data retrieval" module. Frequency counts for code sequences also are printed from within that module, while frequency tables for individual codes are printed from within the "frequencies" module.

Technical Description

TAP was created by Kriss Drass. It was in version 1.0 at the time of this writing (having been a mainframe program for many years before that). An upgrade version is being developed which will remedy the shortcomings described here. TAP operates on IBM PC/XT/AT or 100% compatible microcomputers with DOS version 2.0 or higher. It needs 256K of RAM or less.

The maximum length of a data document is 2500 lines of text (about fifty pages). If there is less than 256K of RAM available at the time of working with TAP, files must be shorter. The maximum number of files to be examined for frequency of code occurrence is sixty-four. There is no maximum number of codes per file, but during one frequency count TAP will look for at most 200 different codes. A code can have up to six characters; upper and lower case characters are distinguished.

Price: $150.00 plus shipping and handling. Distributed by Qualitative Research Management, 73425 Hilltop Road, Desert Hot Springs, CA 92240. Telephone 619/329-7026.

TAP Glossary

code field	a place (marked to look like a small box) in the margin to the left of the data text that holds code words
code menu	a list of codes assigned (variably) to the ten function keys
code pattern	a list of one to five codes or code sequences occurring in a specified order in successive coding units
code sequence	a list of one to four codes attached to one coding unit
coding units	segments of text in data relevant to one topic, as defined by the user
field	see 'code field'
key	a short string of characters within a codeword (that is shared with other code words)
match	an instance of an item found that the program was asked to search for

placement	the place in the order of the four code fields into which a code word has been entered
raw text file	a data document that has never yet been imported (retrieved) by TAP
subsystem	module of the program
text	data segments
unit mark	a symbol (+) that signifies the beginning of a coding unit
units	see 'coding units'

QUALPRO

Introduction

QUALPRO's work screens are simple and straightforward, and the program is very forgiving when you make mistakes. You simply get the chance to try again. Many of its unique characteristics have to do with features that provide working ease and convenience.

Enter text directly into QUALPRO

QUALPRO lets you enter data or other text directly, i.e., you don't have to use a word processor first. Naturally, it doesn't offer the same conveniences as a full-blown word processor, and for long transcriptions you might still want to use your familiar word processor. But the program's writing facility is good enough for typing research notes or other memos. (QUALPRO's editing facility is a 'line editor'.) This means that you don't have to exit the program and get into your word processor whenever you have a fertile analysis idea.

Switch files between QUALPRO and your word processor

Once you learn how to enter the coding information, you can do the coding in your word processor (rather than directly in QUALPRO), and then import the list of codes into QUALPRO as an ASCII file. Conversely, since you can import a coding information file created in QUALPRO into a word processor (you recognize a code file by the extension .COD following your filename), you can switch coding files between QUALPRO and your word processor at will.

Why would you want to switch files? You will want to do this when you need to correct or modify your coding. In QUALPRO, the code entering process is a matter of typing code and line numbers, one line at a time. During the process, once you have pressed the Enter-key you can no longer get back to the previous line. If you need to make a correction, therefore, it's easier to do it in your word processor than to redo the entire coding list in QUALPRO. This might sound cumbersome, but it is actually an advantage: editing is much faster in a word processor. You might even want to create the entire coding information list in your word processor rather than in QUALPRO to begin with. This is especially useful if your word processor has an automatic SAVE feature. If the power gets disrupted, your coding file is still mostly intact. If that happens in QUALPRO while creating a new coding file, all of it is lost.

Help screens

QUALPRO's menus are no mystery: from all menus you can call up a HELP screen that explains every menu option. In almost all operations the Esc-key works to abandon them and return to a menu.

On-screen messages

One more QUALPRO characteristic deserves mention: its on-screen messages. They treat you as a human being, not a fellow computer. There are two kinds: those that tell you what is going on, such as "Please wait while data are being processed", or "File XYZ has been obtained". You are not left wondering what is going on. The other kind are error messages. They don't lead to panic, because they tell you in plain English what is wrong. Example: Rather than being rudely informed: "Error; file not found", you may get the message: "Error trying to access file B:XYZ. The disk is write-protected. Remove the write-protect tab and continue." Now, that's talking!

Underlying Concepts

QUALPRO incorporates three concepts that the user needs to understand: the 'database' notion, the 'heading' notion, and the 'block' notion.

Databases

When working with QUALPRO, you are asked to think of all data from one research project as a 'database'. QUALPRO requires you to give the database a name and, if you use floppy disks, to designate one disk as "Disk 1". This first disk holds the data base name and creates a catalog of all the files that you make part of that data base (when importing or creating a new data file you are always asked to name the database into which to place it). From that point on, you don't need to keep track of the location of your files. Assume that you want to work on document XYZ-5, and you have fifteen data disks. Just insert Disk 1, type the name of the file when prompted, and the computer will tell you on which disk to find it. All you need to do is switch disks. (It's a good idea to label your disks; the program reminds you to do so.) Furthermore, whenever you want to work with all your files, you need not enter their names. The program gives you the option to simply respond y(es) to the question "all files?" When it has finished working with the files on the current disk, it stops, and a message tells you which disk to put in next.

Headings

A 'heading' is information that the program asks you to attach to a data document to explain its nature. Thus you can tell with one glance at a QUALPRO file what the document is about. Rather than letting you enter this information free-form, the program presents you with various 'forms' to fill in, according to the type of data contained in the file. You can choose from the following list of data types:

> Interview
> Observation (narrative field notes)
> Document (a published source)
> Record (a public record)
> Contact Summary (record of a meeting with an informant)
> Diary (kept either by the researcher or a study participant)
> Memo

The information you enter in the heading is brief. On the next page is an example of the prompts you would see on the screen (this one is for interviews).

Once you have entered the information (or have pressed the Enter-key and left the lines blank), your answers are stored as the 'heading'. When the file (or just its 'heading') is called up, everything is neatly printed at the beginning. The heading does not play any role in the coding and searching/assembling process, but it helps in two ways. First, when you code a file on paper, knowing the nature of the data you have in front of you is usually important, and second, since you only have eight characters available to label a file, you might sometimes wonder what a label means. Call up its heading, and you are instantly informed.

```
*************************************************************************

        Please enter the identification number:
        >
        Please enter the interviewer's name:
        >
        Please enter the interviewee's name:
        >
        Please enter the language of the Interview:
        >
        Please enter the location of the Interview:
        >
        Please enter the date of the Interview:
        >
        Please enter the time of the Interview:
        >
        Brief Comment:
        >

*************************************************************************
```

The heading file is saved as an ASCII file. This means that you can create it in your word processor and import it into QUALPRO, and vice versa. You need to know what form it takes as an ASCII file when typing it on your word processor, i.e., what information goes on each line. The QUALPRO manual tells you.

If you don't want a heading on a file, simply press the Enter-key in response to each prompt, which leaves all lines blank and advances you to the next menu choice.

Blocks

A block is a way of subdividing data text. Blocks are (automatically) numbered in consecutive order. If your data come in natural chunks, such as free-flow answers to a sequence of questions, you might want to use this feature. Whenever a text segment is extracted, the block number is printed out with it, and if, for example, you have set it up so that block 12 refers to question 12, you have valuable context information that saves you from going back to the original text.

Blocks are easily marked in the original data file by inserting a line with nothing but one period on it. Their use is optional.

Program Structure

QUALPRO has only four menus. Two menus get you started, and the remaining major structural division is between operations performed on a single file and operations performed on multiple files. Each type of operation has its own menu. The menus are related to each other as shown below.

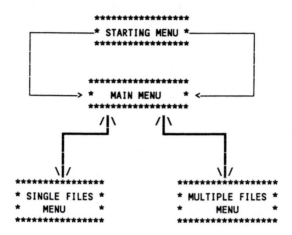

The complete program architecture looks quite complicated, but since you merely choose from the four basic menus, without worrying about the internal structure behind them, it is not confusing to work with the program. The drawing on the next page shows you from which place (program function) you can go to which other one. If you like maps, read the full-scale QUALPRO map by finding the star-bordered boxes first. They designate the menus. Then find the double-line connections that link the basic functions. After that you may want to explore the rest of the map, or simply take in its Gestalt.

(If you decide to study the map, you might find yourself puzzling over a few terms. "List files" simply means that all file names in the currently selected database are shown. "Files" lets you choose a file and have its text shown on the screen or printed on paper. "Headings" shows the heading of a particular file only. The "coding lists" are lists of code words with their associated line numbers.)

The headings describe the files they are attached to, as explained earlier. Creating headings is automatically a part of creating or importing a new file, which is why there is no special module for constructing them.

Code lists cannot be edited; there is no module for modifying the coding of segments. Instead, the code lists can be manipulated in your word processor (explained below).

QUALPRO architecture:

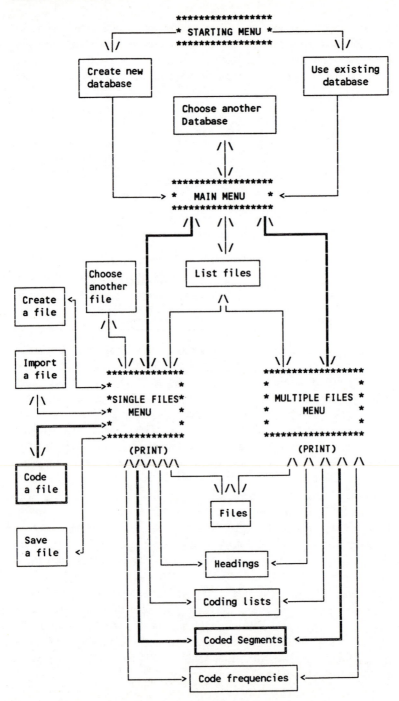

How QUALPRO Works

If you have read the chapter on the basic functions of text analysis programs, you may recall that their two main functions are coding and searching/assembling. Let's see how QUALPRO does them:

A   The main functions

a   Coding ("Code a file" module)

QUALPRO numbers the lines of files automatically when they are either created in the program or imported from a word processor, and saved. The numbers then serve as 'hooks' for the program to hang the codes on. The actual coding task must be performed on a paper printout of the line-numbered file. To make such a printout, you must be in the "single file" menu (you get there by entering the correct database name and file name in response to prompts from the two first menus), and select the "file" choice, which will give you the various printing options. Choose the one "to the printer" and the resulting printout looks somewhat like the one below.

```
-------------------------------------------------------------------------
                          Database:  INFO
-------------------------------------------------------------------------
File name: INTRODUC                   Record  Number: 1
Author: Tesch
Language:                             Location:
Date: 1-1-1989                        Time:
Brief Comment: Example

                              * 1 *
  1   1. Enter text directly into QUALPRO                            1

                              * 2 *
  3   QUALPRO lets you enter data or other text directly,           3
  4   i.e., you don't have to use a word processor first.           4
  5   Naturally, it doesn't offer the same conveniences             5
  6   as a full-blown word processor, but it is certainly           6
  7   good enough to write research notes or other memos.           7
  8   (QUALPRO's editing facility is a line editor.)                8
  9   This way you don't have to exit the program and get           9
 10   into your word processor if you have a fertile idea          10
 11   while in the middle of working with QUALPRO.                  11

                              * 3 *
 13   2. Switch files between QUALPRO and your word                13
 14   processor                                                    14
                              * 4 *
 16   Once you know how the program wants you to enter             16
  . . . etc.
-------------------------------------------------------------------------
```

The first section is the 'heading'; I typed my name and other information only where it made sense to me, leaving the other items blank. The numbers between the asterisks are the block numbers, which the program inserted upon my request at every blank line in the original, i.e., at every new paragraph.

It is a good idea to format the text in the word processor, as I have done, with a wide margin on the left or right side so that the code names can be entered there (or use 14 inch paper if your printer has a wide carriage). Now the task is to mark the beginnings and ends of segments and add the associated code names on the printout. Codes can overlap or segments can be nested within others in whatever manner you wish. Below is an example of a way in which coding on the printout can be done.

```
------------------------------------------------------------------
                          * 2 *
3    QUALPRO lets you enter data or other text directly,    Abcd ⌐  3
4    i.e., you don't have to use a word processor first.          | 4
5    Naturally, it doesn't offer the same conveniences           | 5
6    as a full-blown word processor, but it is certainly         | 6
7    good enough to write research notes or other memos.  ─────┘  7
8    (QUALPRO's editing facility is a line editor.)                8
9    This way you don't have to exit the program and get          9
10   into your word processor if you have a fertile idea         10
11   while in the middle of working with QUALPRO.                 11
                          * 3 *
13   2. Switch files between QUALPRO and your word               13
14   processor                                                   14
                          * 4 *
16   Once you know how the program wants you to enter    Efgh ⌐  16
17   the coding information, you can do the coding in           | 17
18   your word processor (rather than directly in              | 18
19   QUALPRO), and then import the list as an ASCII            | 19
20   file. Since you, conversely, can import a coding   Ijkl ┬ 20
21   information file created in QUALPRO into a word           ‖ 21
22   processor (you recognize it by the extension .COD         ‖ 22
23   following your filename), you have the freedom to  ──────┘‖ 23
24   switch coding files around at will.                 ──────┘ 24
                          * 5 *
26   Why would you want to switch files around?  You            26
27   will want to do this when you need to correct or           27
28   modify your coding.  In QUALPRO entering codes     Abcd ⌐  28
29   happens line by line.  You can't edit a line of          | 29
30   code information after having hit the Enter-key.         | 30
31   If you need to make a correction, therefore, it's        | 31
32   easier to do it in your word processor than to redo      | 32
33   the entire coding list.  Though this might sound   Ijkl ┬ 33
34   cumbersome, it really is an advantage: editing is        ‖ 34
35   much faster in a word processor.  Furthermore, many      ‖ 35
36   word processors now have an automatic SAVE feature. ─────┘‖ 36
37   When the power gets disrupted, your coding file is        | 37
38   still mostly intact.  If that happens in QUALPRO          | 38
39   while creating a new coding file, all is lost.     ──────┘ 39
------------------------------------------------------------------
```

The above shows one particular way of arranging the coding on paper. It doesn't matter how you do your coding, as long as you know what you mean by it. Once you have coded a file on paper, either tentatively or permanently, the rest is clerical work. You again go to the "single file" menu and select "code". The program responds with simple directions about how to enter the coding information. The directions look like this:

```
*************************************************************************
      The Format: Name of Code, From Line Number, To Line Number

      To end coding a block type a period (.) on a line by itself.
      To end coding all blocks enter two periods (..) on a line.
      Please enter codes for block 1, lines 1 to xxx.

*************************************************************************
```

According to these instructions, you type your code names, and then the line numbers where the associated segment starts and ends. Here is an example of what such a list of coding information looks like:

```
*************************************************************************
      >Abcd,3,7    [meaning code Abcd goes from line 3 to line 7]
      >Efgh,16,23
      >Ijkl,20,24
      >Abcd,28,39
      >Ijkl,33,36
      >..

*************************************************************************
```

As mentioned earlier, you can also create this list in your word processor. (Just remember: one coded segment to a line, and no spaces anywhere.) Then you convert the word processing file into ASCII, giving it the name of the corresponding data file with the extension .COD, and you are ready to use it in QUALPRO. That's all there is to it.

The coding list is easily modified if you change your mind about segments or code names; but not on the same screen. When you type the list in QUALPRO, you can't go back anymore once you have pressed the Enter-key to advance to the next line. You must finish the entire list first. Then import it into your word processor to edit it. You can correct code names or lines numbers, add and delete lines, or throw out the whole list and create a new one. You can even keep various different coding systems by making lists with different names. The 'no corrections' problem is eliminated if you create the code list in your word processor, so you might want to choose that option from the beginning.

Any time you want to add new codes to an existing list, you make exactly the same menu choices as if you were coding the file for the first time, then type the new lines. The program recognizes that a .COD file for this file already exists, and will add the new codes to the existing ones.

b   Searching/assembling coded segments ("Coded-segments" module)

Searching/assembling is even easier than coding. Under normal circumstances, you would want to search all or most of your files. Therefore, you go to the "multiple files" menu and select "codes". You are then asked whether you want to search all of your files (in the database) and for all codes. If you do not, you can enter the names of the files and/or codes you are interested in. The computer then tells you it is "collecting data", and shows you the results in the following format:

```
**********************************************************************
Codes in file INTRODUC

**********************************************************************
File INTRODUC    Code Abcd found in lines 28 to  39

                    Block 5 (lines 26 - 39)
 28  modify your coding.  In QUALPRO entering codes              28
 29  happens line by line.  You can't edit a line of             29
 30  code information after having hit the Enter-key.            30
 31  If you need to make a correction, therefore, it's           31
 32  easier to do it in your word processor than to redo         32
 33  the entire coding list.  Though this might sound            33
 34  cumbersome, it really is an advantage: editing is           34
 35  much faster in a word processor.  Furthermore, many         35
 36  word processors now have an automatic SAVE feature.         36
 37  When the power gets disrupted, your coding file is          37
 38  still mostly intact.  If that happens in QUALPRO            38
 39  while creating a new coding file, all is lost.              39

All the codes in lines 28 - 39 are:
Abcd Ijkl
**********************************************************************
```

Between the first two lines of asterisks QUALPRO prints the name of the file in which it searched. Between the next two asterisk lines, it prints one of the segments it found. On top it repeats the file name and tells you the code for which it searched, followed by the line numbers that contain the segment. Next, you find out from which 'block' in the document the segment was taken. Then comes the segment itself, including the line numbers. Lastly, QUALPRO gives you a list of all codes associated with this particular segment, the 'search code' being first.

Another example of segment retrieval is provided on the next page.

```
****************************************************************************
File INTRODUC    Code Efgh found in lines 16 to  23

                        Block 4 (lines 16 - 24)
16  Once you know how the program wants you to enter          16
17  the coding information, you can do the coding in           17
18  your word processor (rather than directly in              18
19  QUALPRO), and then import the list as an ASCII             19
20  file. Since you, conversely, can import a coding           20
21  information file created in QUALPRO into a word            21
22  processor (you recognize it by the extension .COD          22
23  following your filename), you have the freedom to          23

All the codes in lines 16 - 23 are:
Efgh Ijkl
****************************************************************************
```

The segments appear in the sequence in which they were entered in the first file you coded if you specified "all codes", or in the sequence in which you entered the codes when prompted to specify the search codes. They are not in alphabetical order. The occurrences in the first file you saved are printed first, then the next, etc. If you want the printouts in a particular order, or if you want them for particular files or codes only, type in the names in that order, rather than responding "Y(es)" to the prompts "All files?" and "All codes?".

In an actual research study the computer would be directed to print out all the segments it finds as one print job, rather than presenting them individually, as we have done here. The resulting printouts become the basis for data interpretation according to the categories of your organizing system.

Note that at the bottom of each segment's printout the computer lists the co-occurring codes, if there are any. If the researcher is interested in potential relationships among categories (codes), this helps direct her/his hunches.

B   Enhancement functions

QUALPRO provides one additional function to help you with your analysis: it will count how often each code appeared in a single file, in all of them, or in whatever portion of them you identify. It is as easy as choosing the "code frequencies" option from the appropriate menu. A code frequency count looks like this:

```
****************************************************************************
   Code Frequency for file INTRODUC

      Code Abcd has been used 2 times.
      Code Efgh has been used 1 time.
      Code Ijkl has been used 1 time.
****************************************************************************
```

When the code frequencies in "all" files are counted, they are displayed one file after the other. In order to get a total for each code *across* files, one has to use a special small program on the QUALPRO disk. This means, one must leave QUALPRO and call up the special program. The manual provides instructions. It is quite easy. The user types in only five entries: the program name (freq), the name of the file in which the codes are to be counted, a file name under which to save the output, a disk specification, and a command to type the frequencies right on the screen. The codes are automatically listed in alphabetical order.

The entire process looks like the reproduction below (one interaction per line, with the computer messages in bold type).

****

A:\> freq   [this is the way to load the special program]

FREQ version 1.1 Written by Eric Pepke 1 Oct 1987

Please enter the name of the input file: b:INTRODUC

Please enter the name of the output file: b:FREQUENC

3 code frequencies listed.   [this is the first output, meaning that the program found three different code names in the file]

A:\> b: [we now have to type the name of the drive or the disk that contains the data]

B:\> type FREQUENC

Code >Abcd has been used 4 times.
Code >Efgh has been used 3 times.   ⎤ [total for each code]
Code >Ijkl has been used 3 times.   ⎦

****

C Preparatory functions

Aside from converting word processing documents into ASCII, there is not much preparation needed before you start working with QUALPRO. Make sure the margins are set such that no text line is longer than sixty-nine characters. The only other requirement is that you place two periods on a line by themselves at the end of your file. That is the 'end-of-file' signal for QUALPRO. If you want to, you can subdivide your documents into 'blocks' (a single period on a line by itself). If you don't, the entire document is considered "Block 1", which you can ignore.

QUALPRO automatically numbers the file lines.

As described above, however, each file must be made part of a database. This is done by responding to prompts whenever a new file is created in the program or imported from a word processor. You are also asked to attach a 'heading' to each file. The prompts are unavoidable, but you can opt to leave the lines blank and do without a 'heading'.

D   *Housekeeping functions*

You are not lost when you forget a file name. One advantage of the 'database' notion is that all files belonging to your current data base are catalogued, not just those on your current disk. When you choose "catalog of files" from any menu, you get the list on the screen.

Calling up files from the disk is straightforwardly done with menu choices. Printing is an option provided every time you make a selection from the "single file" or "multiple files" menus. The program reminds you to save your most recent work any time making the next menu choice puts you in danger of losing it. You are not told, however, whether a file with the same name already has been coded; the program always adds new codings to the already existing ones.

Technical Description

QUALPRO was created by Bernard Blackman. At the time of this writing, it was in version 3.3. The program operates on IBM PC/XT/AT or 100% compatible microcomputers with DOS version 2.0 or higher. It needs at least 128K of RAM.

The length of a data document is limited only by disk size, which means it is practically unlimited when using a hard disk. The maximum number of files is 1000. The maximum number of codes per file is 1000. A code can have up to fifteen characters.

Price: $125.00 plus shipping and handling. Distributed by Qualitative Research Management, 73425 Hilltop Road, Desert Hot Springs, CA 92240. Telephone 619/329-7026.

QUALPRO Glossary

block
: a subdivision of a data document, to be created by you if you wish to subdivide a data document into sections according to topics or other criteria

catalog
: a list of files in a database

code summary	a list of codes and line numbers, exactly in the way you entered them
contact summary	a written record of any meeting with a 'contact' person who serves as an informant and thus provides you with data
database	a set of data files that you consider as belonging together and assign to that set. Each database must have a unique name
document	a published work (articles, books, etc.) that you are using as data for your project
existing file	a file that was already saved within QUALPRO
field note	(as used in messages on the screen means) any type of data
global frequencies	the frequency counts for all codes in the files of one data base
global summaries	an alphabetized list of code names in one file or in multiple files
heading	a formalized set of identification items that explain the nature of a data document
identification #	a number that you might want to give to any of your data documents for organizing purposes
record	any piece of data that doesn't fall into the other data categories QUALPRO lists
stripping a file	getting rid of special non-standard characters, a process that happens when converting word processing files into ASCII
type text	enter text directly into QUALPRO

The Ethnograph

Introduction

The Ethnograph is an elaborate program with many screens and menus. That may sound intimidating, but the program is not confusing to work with. It is well structured, and each screen presents all the information needed to perform the tasks at hand, or go on to the next screen. Getting acquainted with The Ethnograph is much like getting acquainted with a powerful word processor. It doesn't take much time or effort to begin working with it, just some familiarity with its basic structure and terminology. Only with experience, however, will the researcher become fully aware of the program's potential.

More than other programs, The Ethnograph requires prior planning to take advantage of its power. The program's capability to search selectively, and to embed context information in the original data are powerful advantages for some research projects. For both, the researcher has to prepare the data before or at the time of entry into the program. I will describe both features in greater detail in the enhancement and preparatory functions sections of this chapter. In a selective search, the researcher can instruct the program to compile coded segments from files with specific characteristics, such as interviews with women only, or field notes from before a certain date, and so on. Characteristics can be combined in a single search to create a very fine comb with which to sift data. Comparing the results of selective searches may provide important clues as to the differences among subgroups of respondents or locations, and thus constitute a first step in theory-building.

If done skillfully, embedding context information eliminates the need to the return to the original data when extracted segments are interpreted. One type of context information can be used to identify speakers in a conversation or group interview. Later, the program can count the number of times a particular speaker has spoken. Alternatively, the same context information could be used, for example, to describe non-verbal interaction during an interview, with the same option of obtaining the frequency of each type of interaction. Another type of context information can be used to indicate any kind of conceptual or situational circumstances that pertain to a passage in the raw data and that the researcher considers important for the correct interpretation of segments extracted from that passage.

The one attribute that determines most distinctly the program's character or 'feel' is its frequent interaction with the user. You have to be extremely hasty to leave an error uncorrected in The Ethnograph. At every turn, the user is asked whether the choice just made is the one s/he really had in mind, or whether the entries (of file names or code names) are typed correctly. If not, the user always gets the chance to redo things. The coding procedure can even be set to present automatically the most recent entries for review after every fourth entry (called the 'novice mode'). The program practically begs the user to make sure no typo in a code name goes undetected, since a misspelled code results in losing its associated segment. It's a mother hen program.

One of the greatest benefits from this program's care for the user comes from its automatic saving of new work. Normally, one would expect a file to be saved once the user is done working with it. The Ethnograph goes further; it saves every code entry immediately. You never can lose more than a few seconds' worth of hard labor should a blackout surprise you in the middle of coding thirty pages of field notes.

The user's manual displays the same attitude. It is far more elaborate than others, taking the user by the hand and walking her/him through the program keystroke by keystroke. (There is also a 'quick look around' section, for the impatient.) In addition, it explains a lot about coding and qualitative analysis in general. For the novice qualitative researcher it almost substitutes for the senior researcher's guidance in matters of data preparation.

The Ethnograph is aesthetically pleasant - if you have a color monitor. The screen outlays are well proportioned, and the colors emphasize the information that is most relevant for the user's next action.

Underlying Concepts

The Ethnograph is designed around the concept of de-contextualizing and re-contextualizing (see the chapter on the mechanics of interpretational analysis). Data are segmented, coded, and collated according to coding categories. Although the program can accommodate many types of studies (including some types of discourse analysis), it is geared especially toward depth-exploration of data. The user must make a paper printout of the original data with line numbers (inserted by the program), and manually do original data with line numbers (inserted by the program), and manually do 'code-mapping'. Code mapping is the way The Ethnograph User's Manual describes segmenting and hand-coding of data. Performing the coding manually invites more intensive dwelling on the data than screen coding does. Data are expected to be viewed from many angles; and the organizing system is expected to evolve gradually. Modifying the existing coding is so taken for granted that The Ethnograph even has a special function for it.

Program Structure

The program begins with The Ethnograph procedure menu that works like a hub. It lists the various procedures the program performs. Each procedure is a separate program module, so the user always must return to the procedure menu to begin another procedure.

The map below shows the program's basic structure.

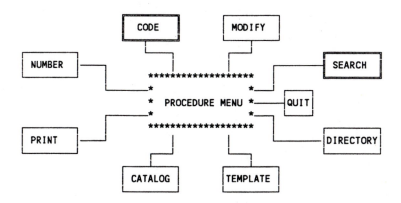

Each module (procedure) begins with an Opening Menu that provides the user with a list of functions that can be performed in that module. As the user makes choices, The Ethnograph guides her/him along with a succession of further menus. Thus the graph above should have additional branches sprouting from each module. If you found the full-scale map of QUALPRO (page 242) a bit confusing, a complete map of The Ethnograph would be totally overwhelming. Even a map of just one module can become formidable, as the drawing on the next page demonstrates.

The diagram shows the coding module. In this case, the file to be coded already has some codes attached to it. The Ethnograph presents a message, informing the user of this fact. The user then has various choices (see the "file already coded" box below). In this case s/he has decided to continue the coding process on the file.

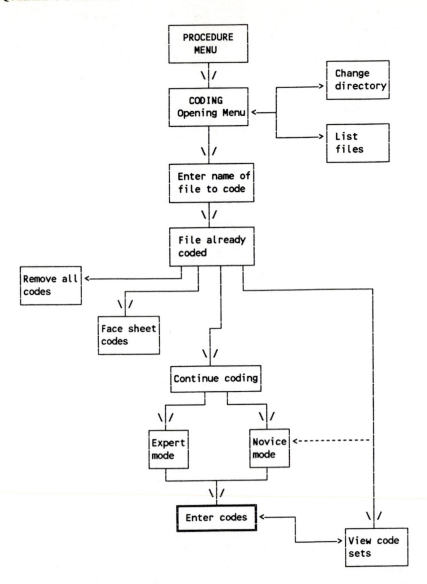

Even though the drawing is elaborate, it does not show every option. If the user had chosen "face sheet codes", for instance, an entire branch with options would sprout from there. The "view code sets" box at the bottom right also offers several choices, including the one to return to the opening menu. (We will return to the connection between "view code sets" and the "novice mode" later.)

How The Ethnograph Works

A   The main functions

a   Coding

Let's first take a look at The Ethnograph's Procedure Menu:

****

```
ETHNOGRAPH PROCEDURE MENU

N - NUMBER    Data Files
C - CODE      A Data File
P - PRINT     Numbered/Coded Files
S - SEARCH    For Coded Segments
M - MODIFY    Coding Schemes
L - LIST      Code Words
G - CATALOG   Data Files
T - TEMPLATES for Facesheets
D - DIRECTORY Change Data File Directory
Q - QUIT
```

****

Notice the "N"-choice. A data document cannot be coded until The Ethnograph 'numbers' it, which means that the program attaches consecutive numbers to every line of the document. The Ethnograph uses these line numbers to connect codes with text segments. (All it 'knows' about the segments is the lines on which they start and end.) Once a data file is numbered, The Ethnograph provides a data printout that has the following format:

```
----------------------------------------------------------------------
A. INTRODUCTION                         1

The Ethnograph is an elaborate program  3
with many different screens and menus.   4
Although that sounds as if it could      5
become confusing, it doesn't, since      6
the program is well structured and       7
presents on each screen all the          8
information the user needs to navigate    9
around in it, and out of it.  Getting   10
acquainted with The Ethnograph is much  11
like getting acquainted with a          12
powerful word processor.  It doesn't    13
take all that much to begin working     14
etc.
----------------------------------------------------------------------
```

The wide right margin is available for 'code mapping'. Code mapping is done by drawing a square bracket along the right hand side of the text for each segment, with the code name(s) next to it. A code map may look like this:

```
A. INTRODUCTION                           1

The Ethnograph is an elaborate program    3 ⌐ ABCD
with many different screens and menus.    4 |
Although that sounds as if it could       5 |
become confusing, it doesn't, since       6 |
the program is well structured and        7 |
presents on each screen all the           8 |
information the user needs to navigate    9 |
around in it, and out of it.  Getting    10 ⌐
acquainted with The Ethnograph is much   11
like getting acquainted with a           12
powerful word processor.  It doesn't     13
take all that much to begin working      14
with it; just some familiarity with      15
its basic structure and terminology.     16
Only with experience, however, will      17
the researcher become fully aware of     18
the program's potential.                 19

More than other programs, The            21 ⌐ EFGH
Ethnograph requires prior planning to    22 |
take advantage of its power.  Two of     23 ⌐ IJKL
the features that can be used to the     24 |
research project's advantage are the     25 |
capability to search selectively         26 |
through certain files only, and to       27 |
embed context information in the         28 |
original data.  Both features will be    29 ⌐
described in more detail below in the    30
sections on enhancement functions and    31
preparatory functions, respectively.     32 ⌐
In a selective search, the program can   33 ⌐ ABCD
be instructed to compile coded           34 |
segments from files with specific        35 |
characteristics, such as interviews      36 |
with women only, not men, or field       37 |
notes from before a certain date, not    38 |
after, and so on.  Characteristics can   39 ⌐ IJKL
be combined (in a single search) to      40 |
create a very fine comb with which to    41 |
sift through the data.  Comparing the    42 ⌐
results of selective searches may        43 |
provide important clues as to the        44 |
differences among subgroups of           45 |
respondents or locations.                46 ⌐
```

Once the document is mapped, the user chooses the coding procedure from the program's start-up menu, the "Procedure Menu" (see above). S/he enters the name of the file to be coded, then indicates whether "text codes" or "face sheet values" are to be entered. Face sheet values are the ones that enable the user to conduct selective searches later on (described below in the section on enhancements). The normal coding of data segments is "text coding". When the user chooses text coding, s/he is presented with the following form on the screen:

```
************************************************************************
                            ENTER CODE WORDS
                UP-Prev Field  DN-Next Field . F1-Del  F2-Ins
    PREVIOUS START LINE: 0                     END = Go to next Code Set

 ┌──────────────────────────────────────────────────────────────────┐
 │ START LINE   CODE WORD   STOP   CODE WORD   STOP   CODE WORD  STOP │
 │ _____   _____   ____   _____   ____   _____  ____  │
 │  _            1-                 5-                 9-              │
 │               2-                 6-                10-             │
 │               3-                 7-                11-             │
 │               4-                 8-                12-             │
 └──────────────────────────────────────────────────────────────────┘

************************************************************************
```

This blank form is meant for codes that begin on the same line. The user enters the line number where the code mapping bracket begins in the first column ('start line'), and the cursor then jumps to the numeral 1. The first code is typed here, as well as the line number at which the bracket ends. As you see, twelve code names can be entered for the same start line number. They may belong either to the same segment (in which case all would have the same stop line number, as well), or they can belong to different, overlapping segments, each with its own stop line number.

Once the form is filled out (most commonly with just one or two code words), pressing the End-key safely stores the entries and brings up a new blank form. Note that just above the box in the screen a line says: "PREVIOUS START LINE: 0". This handy feature enables the researcher to interrupt a coding session at any time, and return to it whenever convenient. The program keeps track of the place at which the session was interrupted, and lets the user continue from there. However, the researcher's work does not have to be confined to coding beyond that point only; any start line number can be entered as long as it is greater than the very first line number with which the coding for this particular data document began. In other words, to insert new codes into an already coded document, you would proceed as if you were continuing the coding process.

When the researcher is finished coding a document, s/he can ask The Ethnograph to print it out on the screen or on paper. The code-mapped document above would now look like the one on the next page:

Note that the code words are not listed in the right margin next to the square brackets. Instead, they are inserted in a blank line, extending into the left margin a bit and preceded by a symbol. The reason for this odd arrangement is: theoretically, there could be twelve brackets in the right hand margin, and the program must reserve space for them in case a user decides to take advantage of that option. Consequently, space must be found elsewhere for the code names. The symbol preceding each code tells which bracket it is associated with. In simple cases like this one you probably could have figured out the association even without the symbol. However, if there were ten codes in one line, and ten brackets in the right margin, you would be thankful that these symbols enable you to sort things out.

****

```
        A. INTRODUCTION                    1

   #-ABCD
        The Ethnograph is an elaborate program    3  -#
        with many different screens and menus.    4   |
        Although that sounds as if it could       5   |
        become confusing, it doesn't, since       6   |
        the program is well structured and        7   |
        presents on each screen all the           8   |
        information the user needs to navigate    9   |
        around in it, and out of it.  Getting    10  -#
        acquainted with The Ethnograph is much   11
        like getting acquainted with a           12
        powerful word processor.  It doesn't     13
        take all that much to begin working      14
        with it; just some familiarity with      15
        its basic structure and terminology.     16
        Only with experience, however, will      17
        the researcher become fully aware of     18
        the program's potential.                 19

   #-EFGH
        More than other programs, The            21  -#
        Ethnograph requires prior planning to    22   |
   $-IJKL
        take advantage of its power.  Two of     23   |-$
        the features that can be used to the     24   | |
        research project's advantage are the     25   | |
        capability to search selectively         26   | |
        through certain files only, and to       27   | |
        embed context information in the         28   | |
        original data.  Both features will be    29  -# |
        described in more detail below in the    30     |
        sections on enhancement functions and    31     |
        preparatory functions, respectively.     32    -$
```

(continued on next page)

```
#-ABCD
      In a selective search, the program can    33 -#
      be instructed to compile coded            34  |
      segments from files with specific         35  |
      characteristics, such as interviews       36  |
      with women only, not men, or field        37  |
      notes from before a certain date, not     38  |
$-IJKL
      after, and so on.  Characteristics can    39  |-$
      be combined (in a single search) to       40  | |
      create a very fine comb with which to     41  | |
      sift through the data.  Comparing the     42  |-$
      results of selective searches may         43  |
      provide important clues as to the         44  |
      differences among subgroups of            45  |
      respondents or locations.                 46 -#
```

****

The researcher could use a printout like the one above to check her/his coding. However, The Ethnograph provides a special feature within the coding module that lets you automatically **review and correct your coding** work at regular intervals (this happens when you choose the "novice mode" for coding), or whenever you want to do so (when you choose the "expert mode"). You don't see all codes and their associated line numbers at once, but a table with four 'code sets' at a time:

****
SUMMARY TABLE: Check that CODES, START and STOP lines are correct

SET#	STRT	CODE ----- STOP	CODE ----- STOP	CODE ----- STOP	CODE ----- STOP
1	3	#ABCD 10			
2	21	#EFGH 29			
3	23	$IJKL 32			
4	33	#ABCD 50			

ARE THE VALUES IN THE TABLE CORRECT? (y/n):
****

In this table only one code appears per start line number (because we entered only one code name in each case), but there is room for twelve of them. Note that each 'code set' has been assigned a number. A code set is the set of all code words beginning at the same start line, irrespective of their stop lines. (Disregard, for the moment,the strange symbols in front of each code word.) If you discover a misspelling or an incorrect line number, you respond with "N" to the prompt on the bottom of the screen, then tell the computer the number of the code set with which you wish to work, and you are presented with the following options:

****

```
┌─────────────────────────────────┐
│        CODE EDIT MENU           │
│                                 │
│   1 - Change  START LINE        │
│   2 - Change  CODE WORD         │
│   3 - Change  STOP LINE         │
│   4 - Delete  CODE SET          │
│   5 - Delete  CODE WORD         │
│   6 - Add     CODE WORD         │
│   0 - No Changes                │
└─────────────────────────────────┘

         Select Option:
```

****

This menu can be activated at any time during the coding process, or after coding has been completed. Later, you might want to **modify your coding** of the document in individual cases. The original coding module is used for that purpose. If, however, you have changed your entire coding system (let's say you have broadened a coding category, have coded newly accumulated documents accordingly, and now wish to replace two old codes with one new one in the previously coded files), there is a special program module available to deal with just these cases. You would choose "M", for "MODIFY Coding Schemes", from the Procedure Menu, and would be presented with the following options:

****

```
┌───────────────────────────────────────────────┐
│             OPENING MENU                       │
│                                                │
│  S - SELECTIVE  Change/Delete (Single File)    │
│  G - GLOBAL     Change/Delete (Multiple File)  │
│  D - DIRECTORY  List Files or Change Directory │
│  R - RETURN     to Procedure Menu              │
└───────────────────────────────────────────────┘

       Select Option:
```

****

This module is used when the user wants to make the same change in more than one place. The difference between 'selective' and 'global' is between making the same change in a number of places (all of which can be indicated on the same entry screen) and making that change wherever a specified code word occurs, across all data documents.

b   Searching/assembling coded segments

When the researcher is ready to look at the segments that have been coded into categories, s/he chooses the "S" module from the Procedure Menu (standing for "SEARCH For Coded Segments"). The program asks:

```
************************************************************************
 ---------------------------------------------------------------
|                        SEARCH OPTIONS                         |
|                                                               |
|    Locate segments by  |  Use Face Sheet  |  Send output to   |
|    <S>ingle or         |  Values          |  <S>creen or      |
|    <M>ultiple codes?   |  in Search?      |  <P>rinter?       |
|                                                               |
|    (s/m):              |  (y/n):          |  (s/p):           |
 ---------------------------------------------------------------
************************************************************************
```

This screen is quite self-explanatory, especially if you remember that "face sheet values" refers to the information attached to each file that permits the selective search through files that meet particular criteria. The next step is entering the names of the files that are to be included in the search, and the names of the codes to search for. The results can be printed out on paper, all in a row, or individually on the screen. One retrieved segment would look like this:

```
************************************************************************
ETHNOGR

SC: ABCD

#-ABCD
        :  The Ethnograph is an elaborate program    3 -#
        :  with many different screens and menus.     4  #
        :  Although that sounds as if it could        5  #
        :  become confusing, it doesn't, since        6  #
        :  the program is well structured and         7  #
        :  presents on each screen all the            8  #
        :  information the user needs to navigate     9  #
        :  around in it, and out of it.  Getting     10 -#
-----------------------------------------------------------------------
************************************************************************
```

The first word, "ETHNOGR", is the name of the file from which the segment was extracted. "SC" stands for 'sort code', meaning that "ABCD" was the code we instructed The Ethnograph to search for. The same code is repeated a bit further down, where we are told which symbol it is associated with. Note how the square bracket is simulated in the right margin.

The above is the simplest case: One segment was retrieved that is coded in only one way. There are no additional codes or overlaps. If there were, a segment would appear on the screen (and printout) in the following form:

```
*****************************************************************************
ETHNOGR

E: #-EFGH

SC: IJKL

$-IJKL
        :    take advantage of its power.  Two of     23  |  -$
        :    the features that can be used to the      24  |   $
        :    research project's advantage are the      25  |   $
        :    capability to search selectively          26  |   $
        :    through certain files only, and to        27  |   $
        :    embed context information in the          28  |   $
        :    original data.  Both features will be     29  -#  $
        :    described in more detail below in the     30      $
        :    sections on enhancement functions and     31      $
        :    preparatory functions, respectively.      32     -$
        ---------------------------------------------------------------------
*****************************************************************************
```

This time an additional entry appears at the top of the segment: "E: #-EFGH". "E" stands for 'external', which means that the segment associated with the code "EFGH" started (or ended, as the case may be) outside the retrieved segment. The symbol "#" precedes it, which appears at line 29 in the right hand margin. The "EFGH"-segment began somewhere outside this excerpt, and ends on line 29. (If there were a co-occurring code *within* the segment, it would be indicated in a similar way.)

The results screens in The Ethnograph can become quite cluttered with information about co-occurring and external codes and context reminders (see the section on preparatory functions below for context reminders). However, once the user has worked with the program for a while and become familiar with the way it displays its results, the important items begin to catch one's eyes. It helps to use colored highlighters on printouts to emphasize the particular items one is most interested in.

B   *Enhancement functions*

a   *Multiple code searches*

The Ethnograph specifically searches for co-occurrences of codes and prints out the text of any segment coded with two or more codes simultaneously. An example will explain the notion of co-occurring codes.

In the screen reproduction above a segment was retrieved that was coded "IJKL", but partly also "EFGH". Let's assume that the researcher has reasons to believe there might be a connection between categories "IJKL" and "EFGH". S/he, therefore, enters the "code"-module and chooses "M"ultiple codes. A whole new side of The Ethnograph appears: its screens ask the user to design a search request using Boolean operators (see the chapter on text retrievers for an explanation of Boolean operators).

The simplest case is our example above: all segments shall be found that are coded with one code word AND another code word as well. The Ethnograph now retrieves all instances of the co-occurrence of these two code words and prints them out in a form similar to the one for single code words. The user has a choice between seeing a display with only those lines on which the overlap occurs, regardless of how far each coded segments goes on beyond the actual overlap (the 'small picture'), and seeing the full extent of each coded segment (the 'big picture') beyond the overlap itself. In the screen reproduction only lines 23-29 are coded with both codes. Lines 23-29 would, therefore, be the only those retrieved in a 'small picture' view. Code "EFGH" begins somewhere before (actually, on line 21), and code "IJKL" continues to line 32. A 'big picture' would show lines 21 through 32.

b   *Selective searches*

When The Ethnograph (and most other text analysis programs) searches for coded segments, the segments are retrieved one file at a time, in the order in which the file names were entered. Thus, if in studies with relatively large samples half of the interviewees were women and half were men, and the researcher would like to find out whether the two groups tended to respond differently with regard to a specific topic, s/he would have to enter the file names in gender order. Then s/he could cut the printout where files with a different gender begin, and compare the segments in the first part with those in the second part. If s/he wanted to subdivide the data further, the process would soon become cumbersome. Therefore, in The Ethnograph the researcher can attach brief pieces of information to each data document about the nature of that document. For field notes this information could be site names or observation dates, for interviews it could be socio-demographic data such as age, gender, income, or anything else on the basis of which the researcher might later wish to compare subgroups within the sample.

The Ethnograph calls these pieces of information 'face sheet variables'. They are not inserted into the data text itself, but are attached to the data file much like the codes (but without line numbers). Each data file must have the same set of variables, i.e., if gender were one of the variables, each file must have a gender 'value' attached to it. The Ethnograph, therefore, provides a form that can be used for the entire set of data files, a 'template'. A template is nothing more than a list of the 'variables', chosen and named by the researcher. Variables do not have to be binary, such as male/female. They can take on any value. (Templates accommodate up to forty such variables.) The only further condition is that 'text' variables are distinguished from 'numeric' variables (since the program has to be told which ones will require some elementary arithmetic, such as "everything greater than 35").

Attaching face sheet values is a separate operation that is carried out within the program's coding module. However, The Ethnograph, not surprisingly, will refuse to accept face sheet values unless a template has been designed that tells it what the variables are. The user selects "T" from the Procedure Menu for "TEMPLATES for Facesheets", and is guided through the template-making process from there. Later, when the researcher asks the program to retrieve coded segments, s/he will always get the option to use the face sheet values in her/his search.

c Frequencies

The Ethnograph counts the frequency of the occurrence of each code word for individual data documents (not across documents). It creates lists that can be sorted either alphabetically or in order of decreasing frequency. These lists may be reviewed on the screen or printed out.

If the 'speaker identifier' feature is used (described in the next section below), the same counting procedures can be applied to 'speakers'. Both functions are performed within the 'LIST Code Words" module, accessible from the Procedure Menu.

C Preparatory functions

Numbering the lines of a data document is required for all further work with The Ethnograph, but it is not handled automatically. The process involves merely choosing "N" from the Procedure Menu, entering of a file name, and waiting a few seconds while the program busily runs a line number count. When it is done, a message informs the user of the completed task, and s/he can begin the coding process.

Before a data document is imported from a word processor into The Ethnograph, however, a number of steps can be taken that will support later interpretation of the re-contextualized data. The Ethnograph, more than any other text analysis program, provides for the attachment of information about the original context that is printed out with segments when they are extracted. There are two types of context information: 'speaker/section identifiers' and 'contextual comments'.

Speaker/section identifiers, as the name suggests, can be used to indicate who is speaking, or what a section of field notes is about. They are merely abbreviations that are inserted into the original data text. So that The Ethnograph can identify them as context indicators, they are made to protrude into the left margin in the data document. On the next page is an example of the section identifier "Planning" inserted (at line number 21):

Any segment that is extracted from below the identifier will be preceded by the word "Planning", and the researcher will know that the segment came from a section that had to do with planning. (The colon tells the program where to end the identifier.) The identifier is valid until the program encounters a new identifier further down in the text. Of course, the researcher is not confined to 'speaker' or 'section' information, but can use these identifiers in any way that is helpful to her/his research, or not use them at all.

```
*****************************************************************************
Planning: More than other programs, The    21
   Ethnograph requires prior planning to    22
   take advantage of its power.  Two of     23
   the features that can be used to the     24
   research project's advantage are the     25
   capability to search selectively         26
   through certain files only, and to       27
   embed context information in the         28
   original data.  Both features will be    29
   described in more detail below in the    30
   sections on enhancement functions and    31
   preparatory functions, respectively.     32
*****************************************************************************
```

Contextual comments are meant to be broader units of context information. They refer to larger portions of text, and can be up to thirty-five characters long. Again, the use is up to the researcher. In the sample below, the word "Introduction" is used as a contextual comment:

```
*****************************************************************************
+INTRODUCTION                                1

   The Ethnograph is an elaborate program    3
   with many different screens and menus.    4
   Although that sounds as if it could       5
   become confusing, it doesn't, since       6
   the program is well structured and        7
   presents on each screen all the           8
   information the user needs to navigate    9
   around in it, and out of it.  Getting    10
   acquainted with The Ethnograph is much   11
   like getting acquainted with a           12
   powerful word processor.  It doesn't     13
```

(continued on next page)

```
    take all that much to begin working        14
    with it; just some familiarity with        15
    its basic structure and terminology.       16
    Only with experience, however, will        17
    the researcher become fully aware of       18
    the program's potential.                   19

Planning: More than other programs, The       21
    Ethnograph requires prior planning to      22
    take advantage of its power.  Two of       23
    the features that can be used to the       24
    research project's advantage are the       25
    capability to search selectively           26
    through certain files only, and to         27
    etc.
*************************************************************************
```

Just as the speaker/section identifier, the contextual comment juts out into the left margin. It is distinguished from an identifier by a plus symbol. This symbol tells The Ethnograph that it must list this information in addition to the speaker/section identifier when extracting a segment. Let's assume lines 23 to 29 constitute a segment for analysis, and are coded into the category "FEATURES". When The Ethnograph is asked to find segments coded with "FEATURES", it will print its results in the following way:

```
*************************************************************************
ETHNOGR   PLANNING          +INTRODUCTION
SC: FEATURES

#-FEATURES
    :    take advantage of its power.  Two of     23 -#
    :    the features that can be used to the     24  #
    :    research project's advantage are the     25  #
    :    capability to search selectively         26  #
    :    through certain files only, and to       27  #
    :    embed context information in the         28  #
    :    original data.  Both features will be    29 -#
----------------------------------------------------------------------
*************************************************************************
```

Note that in addition to the file name ("ETHNOGR"), the section identifier and the contextual comment are listed above the segment. They are meant to provide sufficient information about the segment's original context to prevent improper interpretation. Of course, the researcher could always return to the intact data document to review the original context. This is merely one more of the features that make the researcher's work less time-consuming.

Context information like speaker/section identifiers and contextual comments must be inserted into a data document before it is imported into The Ethnograph, since the program itself does not provide word processing functions. They can be used or disregarded. In some studies they might not be needed, while in others they could make all the difference. The decision is up to the researcher.

D   Housekeeping functions

In a polished program like The Ethnograph all housekeeping functions are performed smoothly. There is hardly anything the user must know or remember about housekeeping (except that files must be line-numbered), since there will always be prompts to be responded to. All saving is done automatically, so nothing can get lost. The program is very forgiving when the user makes mistakes or forgets a file's location or the proper spelling of its name. From the Procedure Menu, and also from inside each procedure module, the user can ask to see the list of files on the active disk or subdirectory, and can change the disk drive or subdirectory in search of a file.

To make life easier for the researcher, a list of file names called a 'catalog' can be compiled and stored. The user is asked to give a name to the catalog, and whenever s/he wishes to work with all her/his data, s/he enters the catalog name; the program will then automatically supply the file names.

Just about anything the researcher might want to look at can be printed on paper. All the user needs to do is respond to the prompts that ask whether the material shall be sent (printed) to the screen, the printer, or a disk. The latter constitutes The Ethnograph's ASCII conversion that makes it possible to import Ethnograph output files into a word processor or other program.

Technical Description

The Ethnograph was created by John Seidel. At the time of this writing, it was in version 3.0. It operates on IBM personal computers and IBM-compatibles with DOS version 2.0 or higher. The RAM requirement is 256K. Version 4.0 is scheduled for release in 1990. Among the new features are the 'code book' which allows the user to keep track of all code words used, 'combined files' (the user can create new data files from parts of existing files), the ability to create cross-tabulations of code word frequencies across files, the ability to search for words in the text, and the ability to find coded segments within a specified distance from each other.

A data document may have up to 9999 lines. There is no limit on the number of code words per file. A code may have up to ten characters. Multiple file procedures can be carried out on up to eighty files.

Price: $150.00 plus shipping and handling. Distributed by Qualitative Research Management, 73425 Hilltop Road, Desert Hot Springs, CA 92240. Telephone 619/329-7026.

The Ethnograph Glossary

batch edit options	options within the Modify Coding Schemes module that determine whether and how the changes to be made are reported and verified
big picture	an option when printing out segments that were simultaneously coded with two or more codes; prints out all lines of all segments involved
catalog	a list of file names
code mapping	manual segmenting of text and attaching of codes to the segments
code set	all coding beginning at the same start line
contextual comment	context information inserted into the original data document, can be up to thirty-five characters long
expert mode	used when entering codes with their start numbers and stop numbers; does not provide automatic reviews of code sets entered
external code	the name of a code that overlaps with the sort code, but begins or ends outside the retrieved segment
face sheet values	the information entered for face sheet variables in individual files
face sheets	a set of information items that characterize an individual file in comparison with other files, such as socio-demographic data
global change/delete	the changing or deleting of a code word in all files listed by the user
modifying coding scheme	making changes or deletions of codes in more than one place at once
nested segments	smaller segments within larger ones
novice mode	used when entering codes with their start numbers and stop numbers; provides automatic reviews of code sets after every four entries
numeric variables	face sheet variables that are expressed in numbers (such as age or date)
overlapping segments	segments whose start or stop lines overlap each other

selective change/delete   used in the Modify Coding Schemes module to make several changes at once, but only at specific places

small picture   an option when printing out segments that were simultaneously coded with two or more codes; prints out only those lines common to all segments irrespective of the further extent of each segment

sort code   the code specified in a search for coded segments

speaker/section identifier   context information inserted into the original data document to indicate the author of the succeeding text or the name of the particular section of the document; can be up to ten characters long

template   a format for attaching the same kinds of face sheet variables to all files

text variables   face sheet variables that are not expressed in numbers (such as gender or ethnicity)

text information   data text

text codes   codes that assign text segments to the categories of the coding systems

variable   used in connection with face sheets; an information item that is assigned a value according to the characteristics of each file

TEXTBASE ALPHA

Introduction

TEXTBASE ALPHA was originally developed for interviews, but it can handle any kind of qualitative data. It takes advantage of the structure of data to make coding easier. The program's enhancements are oriented mainly toward numeric manipulations (including a count of all words used in the data documents), which does not distract from the fact that the program performs the main functions of de-contextualization and re-contextualization elegantly. The coding is performed directly on the screen. Unlike other text analysis programs, TEXTBASE ALPHA enables the user to specify the exact beginnings and ends of text segments, rather than just the lines on which a segment starts and stops. Consequently, when retrieved, coded segments are not surrounded by parts of irrelevant sentences.

For structured data from interviews or questionnaires, TEXTBASE ALPHA provides electronic coding of each question (or whatever analysis unit the researcher specifies). This is called "pre-structured" coding, since the researcher must format the data document according to its inherent structure before it can be used by TEXTBASE ALPHA. Once a document is coded with this automatic feature, it can be further coded with the "unstructured" coding function. In "unstructured" coding, codes are inserted in the document on the screen at any place the researcher wishes. (It does not work the other way around; freely coded documents can not be electronically coded at some later time.) Neither coding is permanent. Codes can be added and deleted easily at any time.

Anticipating fairly large numbers of interviews or questionnaires, TEXTBASE ALPHA is able to conduct selective searches. This means it will search through data documents with specific characteristics, as instructed. These characteristics are usually socio-demographic variables, as for instance the gender or age of interviewees or respondents. However, the researcher may employ any kind of identifier to have the computer assemble subgroups of her/his data files, in order to compare these groups.

TEXTBASE ALPHA lets the user work mainly with menus, just like all other MS-DOS text analysis programs; its special twist is that all menu choices are function keys. F1 is always the 'Help'-key that explains the menu choices. It is available from menus and from some working screens, i.e., screens in which the user enters file names, code names, or other instructions for the computer. The Esc-key usually lets the user return to the most recent menu, or terminate the program altogether. Coding work is saved automatically. During a working session, a list of file names is either supplied automatically, or available upon request.

The program comes in color, and makes some use of windows (boxes with instructions, prompts, or other information) that occupy different places on the screen and that may even overlap each other. Unless the researcher wants to use pre-structured coding, the program requires little prior planning or preparation. TEXTBASE ALPHA is consistent, and the user can become familiar with it fairly quickly. The program was developed in Denmark; an English-language screen version of it and an English user's manual are available.

Underlying Concepts

The main concept on which TEXTBASE ALPHA is founded is the data base, i.e., a collection of data rather than individual files. This collection is the 'textbase', and the program assumes that most operations shall be performed on all data documents (once each is segmented and coded), or on a selection of documents according to socio-demographic data. The individual document names that constitute the 'textbase' are listed in a special file (the "selection file"), which also holds each document's socio-demographic variables or other characteristics according to which data documents can be grouped. Creating such a selection file is one of the first tasks the researcher should undertake when beginning to work with TEXTBASE ALPHA (retrieval of coded segments is not possible without it). Later, the name of this file serves as the input to the program whenever a list of all file names is needed.

Another concept incorporated in TEXTBASE ALPHA is the notion of parallel files: the original data file (data document) and the corresponding code file, called 'catalog file'. The catalog file is created by TEXTBASE ALPHA as the researcher codes a data file. It makes a list of the code names and the associated segment boundaries. This file is used together with the original data file when coded segments are searched for and assembled according to the researcher's organizing system. The catalog file is automatically updated every time the researcher adds codes to the data text. Since the file can be viewed and manipulated on the screen, certain changes in coding can also be made directly in the file.

The information contained in the catalog file is the basis on which numeric operations are carried out (see the section on enhancements, below).

Program Structure

The structure of the program is mirrored in its opening menu. A map of it looks somewhat like this:

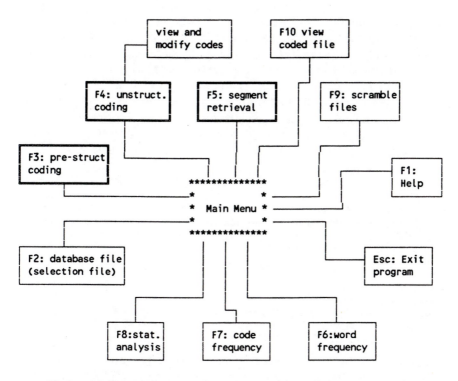

The modules on the bottom of the map have to do mostly with numerical operations, which will be explained in the 'enhancements' section below. An unusual 'enhancement' is the ability to 'scramble' a file, i.e., make it inaccessible for all but the user who knows the 'key'. This is a useful function when data reside on a large hard disk that is shared with unauthorized persons.

How TEXTBASE ALPHA Works

A   The main functions

a   Coding

TEXTBASE ALPHA has two distinct ways of coding. One is for data that have internal structure, and the other for narrative texts of any kind. The second can be used to augment the first; once a structured questionnaire or interview is coded according to its questions, it can be further segmented and coded according to smaller or overarching analysis units.

Pre-structured coding:
Pre-structured coding is done electronically. It works by locating words at a specific location in the data text and using these words as codes. The location of the word is taken as the beginning of the segment to be coded. A segment's boundaries run from one located word to the next, where the new segment begins. The words are not spelled out for the computer, as they are in a search. Instead, they are located through formatting. There is only one formatting requirement for automatic coding: Any word that begins at the first character position of a line becomes a code word. Let's look at an illustration:

Note in the following text the words that jut out into the left margin:

```
*****************************************************************************
Paragraph1 - TEXTBASE ALPHA was originally developed for interviews, but it
    can handle any kind of qualitative data.  Its 'enhancements' are oriented
    mainly toward numeric manipulations (including a count of all words used in
    the data documents), which does not distract from the fact that the program
    performs the main functions of de-contextualization and re-contextualization
    elegantly.  The coding is done directly on the screen.  Unlike other text
    analysis programs, TEXTBASE ALPHA enables the user to specify the exact
    beginnings and ends of text segments, rather than merely the lines on which
    a segment starts and stops. Consequently, when retrieved, coded segments are
    not surrounded by parts of irrelevant sentences.

Paragraph2 - For structured data from interviews or questionnaires, TEXTBASE
    ALPHA provides electronic coding of each question (or whatever analysis unit
    the researcher specifies). This automatic coding is called "pre-structured"
    coding, since the researcher must format the data document according to its
    inherent structure before it can be used by TEXTBASE ALPHA.  Once a document
    is coded with this automatic feature, it can be further coded with the
    "unstructured" coding function.  In "unstructured" coding codes are inserted
    in the document on the screen at any place the researcher wishes.  (It does
    not work the other way around; freely coded documents can not be electroni-
    cally coded at some later time.) Neither coding is not permanent.  Codes can
    be added and deleted easily at any time.
```

(continued on next page)

Paragraph3 - Anticipating fairly large numbers of interviews or question-
naires, TEXTBASE ALPHA is able to conduct selective searches. This means it
will search through data documents with specific characteristics, as
instructed. These characteristics are usually socio-demographic variables,
as for instance the gender or age of interviewees or respondents. However,
the researcher may employ any kind of identifier to have the computer
assemble subgroups of her/his data files, in order to compare these groups.

****

The word "paragraph" was inserted at the beginning of each paragraph, followed by a number. (Note that the number is not separated from the word. To the computer this means that the number is part of the word, and each word is different from the others, since it ends with a different number.) In automatic coding, the computer registers every word that begins at position 1. Therefore, the regular text lines may not begin there, but must be indented.

To electronically code a file, you would choose F3 from the main menu, provide the name of the file that is formatted as the text above, and the program would respond almost immediately with a list of the code names it has identified and noted ("Paragraph1", "Paragraph2", "Paragraph3") and a count of the total (three in this case). The text has been partitioned, correspondingly, into three segments, each one exactly a paragraph long. Invisible to you (unless you check the disk directory), the program has simultaneously created a file that has the same name as the original text file, but with the extension .KAT. This is the associated catalog file. This text is now ready to be searched. Pre-structured coding does work fast.

If the data are interview or questionnaire transcriptions, the researcher could make the question numbers begin at position 1 while indenting all the rest, and the entire transcription would be coded automatically according to the questions.

Unstructured coding:

For unstructured coding, the data text is called up to the screen. The F4 choice from the main menu brings up a blank screen with a 'bottom bar', a long thin box at the bottom of the screen. This bar is characteristic for TEXTBASE ALPHA's coding; it contains the changing information about the coding status. At the beginning, you are prompted to enter the name of the file in the bar. As soon as this is done, the text of the file you specified fills the screen, the cursor moves freely around it, and scrolls the text up and down. The screen looks like the reproduction on the next page.

Coding on that screen requires three moves:

1. The bottom bar lists the file name and registers the cursor location in terms of line number and position (the same way most word

processors do). Place the cursor in the text where you want the segment to begin and press the Ins-key.

2. The cursor jumps to the bottom bar, where you are prompted for the name of the code. Type the name (up to twenty characters) and press the Enter-key when done.

3. The cursor is back in the text. Place it where you want the segment to end, and press the Ins-key. Immediately, the bottom bar registers this segment boundary in terms of the cursor line and position.

```
*************************************************************************
Paragraph1 - TEXTBASE ALPHA was originally developed for interviews, but it can
  handle any kind of qualitative data.  It takes advantage of the structure of
  data to make coding easier.  The program's enhancements are oriented mainly
  toward numeric manipulations (including a count of all words used in the data
  documents), which does not distract from the fact that the program performs
  the  main  functions  of  de-contextualization  and  re-contextualization
  elegantly.  The coding is performed directly on the screen.  Unlike other
  text analysis programs, TEXTBASE ALPHA enables the user to specify the exact
  beginnings and ends of text segments, rather than just the lines on which a
  segment starts and stops. Consequently, when retrieved, coded segments are
  not surrounded by parts of irrelevant sentences.

Paragraph2 - For structured data from interviews or questionnaires, TEXTBASE
  ALPHA provides electronic coding of each question (or whatever analysis unit
  the researcher specifies). This is called "pre-structured" coding, since the
  researcher must format the data document according to its inherent structure
  before they can be used by TEXTBASE ALPHA.  Once a document is coded with
  this automatic feature, it can be further coded with the "unstructured"
  coding function. In "unstructured" coding codes are inserted in the document
  on the screen at any place the researcher wishes.  (It does not work the
  other way around;  freely coded documents can not be electronically coded at
  some later time.)  Neither coding is not permanent.  Codes can be added and
  deleted easily at any time.

Paragraph3 - Anticipating fairly large numbers of interviews or questionnaires,
  TEXTBASE ALPHA is able to conduct selective searches.

 ┌──────────────────────────────────────────────────────────────────────┐
 │Text:Alpha      section:              F1: Help      Cursor position:│
 │Type code name:                                        1   1        │
 └──────────────────────────────────────────────────────────────────────┘

*************************************************************************
```

When the coding of one segment has been completed, the bottom bar changes to reflect the information that was entered. The text on the screen remains the same; the new bottom bar is reproduced on the next page.

```
****************************************************************************
┌──────────────────────────────────────────────────────────────────────┐
│Text:Alpha      section: Paragraph1          F1: Help      Cursor position:│
│Code name:Efgh   8.14 ->   13. 8                              13   8    │
└──────────────────────────────────────────────────────────────────────┘
****************************************************************************
```

Let's first look at the bottom line in the bar: The 'code name' ("Efgh") is followed by the location indicators for the beginning of the segment ("8.14"), and an arrow that points toward the location indicator for the end of the segment ("13. 8"). In the top line the file name is listed ("Alpha"). The next entry, "section: Paragraph1" indicates that the "8.14 -> 13. 8" segment is within another segment, coded "Paragraph1".

The current cursor location is indicated in the right hand corner of the bar: line 13, 8th position (in this case, it is still at the place where the segment ends.) Unlike word processors, which change to line 1 whenever a new page begins, TEXTBASE ALPHA ignores pages and instead numbers the lines consecutively throughout the entire data document. Therefore, no ambiguities can arise about segment boundaries.

In the text on the coding screen nothing changes as you indicate segment boundaries and enter code names; you cannot see any boundary marks or codes. However, the bottom bar always lists whatever codes are attached to the text as the cursor passes through coded segments. When there are several code names, the file name is omitted from the bottom bar to make room for the extra code names.

While the researcher cannot see the coding as s/he works with the text, TEXTBASE ALPHA provides the option to interrupt the coding and print out the coded text, using two keystrokes. The Esc-key takes the user out of the coding module and back to the main menu. From there, F10 is selected, the program prompts for the file name, and then immediately prints a version of the data file that indicates the segment boundaries with square brackets, looking somewhat like the reproduction on the next page.

The code names are inserted between the lines of text. Square brackets show the boundaries of the segments. In addition, the precise information on the segment boundaries is indicated in the form of numbers on the right side of the text, opposite the code names. "1: 1 -> 17:39", for instance, means: the segment runs from line 1, character position one, to line seventeen, character position thirty-nine.

Another way of viewing one's coding is to look at the code list that TEXTBASE ALPHA creates. This list is used for error-correction and modifying of codes; the process is described in the next section.

```
***********************************************************************
          ┌  example                                    1: 1 ->    17:39
       ┌  │  level                                       1: 1 ->     3:34
     ┌ │  │  1          This is an example of a coded file made by
     │ │  │  2          Alpha.  You may have coded sections inside each
     └ │  │  3          other or overlapping each other.
       │  │  format                                      4: 1 ->    17:39
       ┌  │  4          But if you use all 80 characters for the lines,
       │  │  5          you may get in trouble because the brackets
       │  │  6          need some of the character positions.
       │  │  7          The are two solutions to that problem:
   ┌   │  │  solution_1                                  8: 1 ->     8:37
   └   │  │  8          1.  You can use shorter lines
       │  │  solution_2                                  9: 1 ->    17:39
   ┌   │  │  9          2.  When you print the list use condensed
   │   │  │  10             printing, and of course TEXTBASE ALPHA
   │   │  │  11             prepares the list for printing in this mode
   │   │  │  12             (17 cpi).  But printers are different, so the
   │   │  │  13             selected solution, which works on IBM
   │   │  │  14             compatible printers, may not work on your
   │   │  │  15             printer.  If this happens to be the case, try
   │   │  │  16             using your word processor to prepare a list
   └   └  └  17             printed in condensed mode.
***********************************************************************
```

   TEXTBASE ALPHA provides several ways to make coding more efficient. First, whenever the Ins-key is pressed for the beginning of the next segment, the previously entered code name appears in the bottom bar, ready to be re-used. Pressing the Enter-key would install it. If the user wants a different code, the old one disappears as typing starts. Secondly, the same segment boundaries can be re-used with another code word by pressing the F4-key and typing a new code word. Another feature is useful for browsing through the data and looking for one particular topic, coding it wherever it is encountered. In this case, the appropriate code word is placed into the bottom bar (by pressing F5 and typing it) at the beginning of the process. Then, the cursor can be moved around in the text. Whenever the topic is encountered, the Ins-key is pressed at the beginning and end locations of the relevant segments, and the segments will be coded with the code word in the bottom bar. (Pressing the Del-key returns the user to ordinary coding.) Lastly, TEXTBASE ALPHA will search for words and phrases in the data text that the researcher considers relevant (F3-key). The cursor jumps to the place where the search phrase is found, and the researcher can decide whether or not to code the surrounding text. The search can be repeated by pressing the F3-key again.

Modifying of codes:

Codes cannot be changed while in the coding screen. However, pressing F2 when in the coding screen calls up the code list, which can be edited. Here is an example of such a list:

```
****************************************************************************

        1     1:  1   -->    16:  0    Paragraph1
        2     8:  3   -->    35: 30    Abcd
        3     8: 14   -->    13:  8    Efgh
        4    13: 10   -->    24: 31    Ijkl
        5    17:  1   -->    27:  0    Paragraph2
        6    28:  1   -->    40:  0    Paragraph3
        7    28:  1   -->    39: 18    Efgh
        8    31:  2   -->    39: 18    Abcd

****************************************************************************
```

This list contains only eight code sets (but could hold up to 500). The first column provides a running count. It is followed by the beginning and end locations, and the code name. The list may also be displayed in alphabetical order. Furthermore, the computer can be asked to search for a specific code, if the list gets too long to find the code name manually.

In this list the cursor can be moved up and down the numbers on the left, and various function keys allow the researcher to change the name of the code word (associated with the number indicated by the cursor), or to delete the entire code set. The boundary location numbers, however, cannot be changed. The code set would have to be deleted, then re-entered with the correct boundaries in the coding screen.

The program permits the user to check the consistency of her/his coding by pressing the Ins-key when in the code list. The associated text for the segment indicated by the cursor is called up on the screen. Thus one segment after the other (from the same file) can be compared.

b   Searching/assembling coded segments

In TEXTBASE ALPHA searches are conducted with the help of the selection file (the selection is described below in the section on preparatory functions). Unless otherwise specified, the entire selection file (i.e., all files in the data base) is included in the search. The second option is to 'select' files according to socio-demographic or other user-defined variables. To search through an individual file, the file's number is given as the selection criterion (for this option to work, each file must be given a number as it is entered into the selection file). To begin a search, F5 is pressed from the main menu, and the program will prompt for the name of the selection file to be searched:

```
**************************************************************************
┌────────────────────────────────────────────────┐
│ Retrieval of text.                               │
│ Name of selection file:                          │
│                                                  │
│                                                  │
└────────────────────────────────────────────────┘
**************************************************************************
```

The names of the available selection files are listed underneath the box. Since the results will be stored (rather than just held in memory) or printed out, the next prompt asks to supply a name for the output file. Alternatively, the results can be sent to the printer only. Once the program knows where to send the results, a box appears that prompts for the codes to search for. Entries are made one after the other, separated by a space. The box is large enough to hold 126 characters/spaces. If more codes are to be searched for, a list of code names can be prepared in any word processor, converted into ASCII, and saved with a name of the user's choice. Instead of entering code names in the box, the Enter-key will cause the computer to prompt for the name of that file. The rest is automatic.

After code name entering, things begin to become a bit more complicated. TEXTBASE ALPHA assumes that the researcher might want to conduct a selective search, picking out only those data documents that fulfill a certain condition. (More about this in the section on enhancement functions below.) Therefore, the computer asks which files are to be selected. The screen is reproduced below.

```
**************************************************************************
┌──────────────────────────────────────┐        ┌──────────────────┐
│ Retrieval of text                      │        │ Variables:       │
│ Name of selection file:                │        │                  │
│ Project1                               │        │ 1   age          │
└──────────────────────────────────────┘        │ 2   hobby        │
                                                 │                  │
┌──────────────────────────────────────┐        │                  │
│ Use following syntax for criteria:     │        │                  │
│                                        │        │                  │
│ variab.  LR value  LO variab. LR value │        │                  │
│                                        │        │                  │
│ Options        LR            LO        │        │                  │
│ less than      <                       │        │                  │
│ less.equal.    <=      "and"  and      │        │                  │
│ equal to       =       "or"   /        │        │                  │
│ great.equal.   >=                      │        │                  │
│ greater than   >                       │        │                  │
│ different from <>                      │        │                  │
└──────────────────────────────────────┘        └──────────────────┘

┌────────────────────────────────────────────────────────────────┐
│ Selection criteria for textfiles (enter logical relation):       │
│                                                                  │
└────────────────────────────────────────────────────────────────┘
**************************************************************************
```

280

The cursor on the screen sits in the box at the bottom, and the researcher is supposed to enter brief equations, one for each 'variable' to be used in the search (in this case, I had chosen to characterize my data documents with only two variables, age and hobby, see the box on the right). The box on the left (center) appears upon pressing the F1-key (Help), and lists the symbols that must be used in the equations. They won't be explained here; the TEXTBASE ALPHA screen is reproduced merely to give you an idea of what is involved when searching for coded text segments in this program. Actually, there is nothing to it if you simply want to include the entire data base (in the case above it is called "Project1", see upper left box). Whenever you work with the entire data base, you circumvent the entire selection procedure by pressing the Enter-key without entering anything at all, and the search begins.

Once the Enter-key is pressed, the program shows that it is busily working by flashing segments on the screen. If you have specified that the output is to go to the printer, your printer will be crackling away. If you have provided an output file name, you will notice nothing at all; the procedure simply stops when the search is completed, and you are returned to the main menu. However, your disk now contains a new ASCII file that you can import into your word processor and review there (or you can use the F4-key to view the output on the screen).

Search results from TEXTBASE ALPHA are reproduced below. The two examples were found when looking for the code "Efgh" in the selection file "Project1". At the top of each, TEXTBASE ALPHA lists the name of the individual data file the segment comes from ("Alpha"), then the code name, and then the line numbers where the segment begins and ends. Co-occurring codes are not mentioned. Note that each segment contains only complete sentences; the segment begins at the exact position where the cursor was located when it was coded.

```
*****************************************************************************
Print from Alpha    of Efgh :      8 - 13

            Unlike other text analysis programs, TEXTBASE ALPHA enables the
user to specify the exact beginnings and ends of text segments, rather than
merely the lines on which a segment starts and stops.  Consequently, when
retrieved, coded segments are not surrounded by parts of irrelevant sentences.
-------------------------------------------------------------------------
Print from Alpha    of Efgh :     28 - 39

Paragraph3 - Anticipating fairly large numbers of interviews or question-
naires, TEXTBASE ALPHA is able to carry out selective searches. This means it
will search through data documents with specific characteristics, as in-
structed.  These characteristics are usually socio-demographic variables, as
for instance the gender or age of interviewees or respondents.  However, the
researcher may employ any kind of identifier to have the computer assemble
subgroups of her/his data files, so that these groups can be compared with each
other.
*****************************************************************************
```

B   Enhancement functions

a   Selective searches

As mentioned above, TEXTBASE ALPHA allows the researcher to search through subgroups of files that have certain characteristics in common. The characteristics, of course, are not those of the files as such, but refer to the nature of the data. Each data document can be characterized according to criteria determined by the user. These criteria should be chosen on the basis of potentially important comparisons within the data set. If it is important to compare earlier documents with more recent ones, for example, the creation date of documents should be one of the criteria. These kinds of criteria are called 'selection variables'. They always apply to all documents, i.e., if "date" is a selection variable, then the researcher must provide the date for every document in her/his data base.

The researcher may specify up to fifteen selection variables for the files in the textbase. These variables are stored in the same data base file in which the file names are compiled, where the 'values' for each are permanently associated with each file. When a search for coded segments is initiated, and certain criteria for a variable are specified, the computer will check each individual document's variable values to see whether the values fulfill the condition. Such a condition could be that the document may not be of a date "greater than" the specified date. Only those documents are included in the code search for which this holds true, i.e., for which the value of the date variable is greater than the specified data.

b   Code frequency counts

By choosing F7 from the main menu the user can have each code's occurrence counted either in all files or in selected files. The same selection screen appears as shown above under 'searching/assembling', but can be ignored unless the researcher wants to specify certain criteria. The code name(s) are then entered, and the screen shows flashes of the work being done. When it is finished, the following message appears:

```
*****************************************************************************

 _____     _____
|                                   |    |                                |
|  The list of codes is printed     |    |  Partial list:                 |
|                                   |    |  Type start letters,           |
|  for the file Project1            |    |  or exit with ESC              |
|_____|    |_____|

          There are    12 different codes in the text read.
          The codes have an average occurrence of  1.1
          with a standard deviation of    0.29

*****************************************************************************
```

Meanwhile, the results are stored in ASCII in the output file. They take the following format:

```
**************************************************************************
     Number     count     code

        1         2       Abcd
        2         2       Efgh
        3         1       Ijkl
        4         1       Paragraph1
        5         1       Paragraph2
        6         1       Paragraph3

**************************************************************************
```

The left-hand column provides a running count. The code frequencies are listed in the center column, the code names in the right-hand column. Note that three code names in this case were produced electronically (the ones that refer to paragraphs). If the list is long, the researcher may indicate the letter with which the codes s/he is interested in begins, and the part of the list containing the specified codes is printed on the screen.

c   Code matrix

By pressing F8 from the main menu, TEXTBASE ALPHA offers the option to construct a data matrix which can be used for numeric analysis. The matrix can take the following forms:

a) A table that presents for each selected file its variable values, cross-referenced with the frequency of occurrence of the codes specified by the user, plus the sizes of the associated segments (number of lines).

b) An SPSS 'include file' which gives the same information as mentioned above under a), but for all files. This include file is constructed in such a way that it can be used directly by the statistical program "Statistical Packet for the Social Sciences, PC+". Each data file represents a 'case', and the file variables and the codes are defined as SPSS variables. The file can then be imported into SPSS, where further analysis may be performed using the SPSS procedures.

d   Word occurrence frequency

Similar to a text retrieval program <Text retrievers>, TEXTBASE ALPHA counts and lists all words in a data base (F6 from the main menu). The set-up procedure is similar to the code frequency count. Either the entire data base can be included, or only selected files (according to the value of their variables). A count includes all words; but the user can look at selected words only by specifying their beginning letters. The words will be displayed on the screen with their frequencies.

While the program counts, the text and then the word list flash by on the screen. The results are either stored in an output file (as determined by the user), or sent directly to the printer. The list is arranged alphabetically (numerals first), just like the code frequency list, and the outcome has the following format:

```
****************************************************************************
   File: Alpha

        1        1    1
        2        1    2
        3        5    A
        4        1    ABLE
        5        1    AGE
        6        3    ALL
        7        7    ALPHA
        8        1    ALTHOUGH
        9        1    ALTOGETHER
       10        1    ALWAYS
       11        3    ANALYSIS
       12        7    AND
       13        1    ANTICIPATING
       14        2    ANY
       15        4    ARE
       16        2    AS
       17        1    ASSEMBLE
       18        1    AT
       etc.
****************************************************************************
```

A message informs about the totals:

```
****************************************************************************
      There are   320 different words in the text read.

      The words have an average occurrence of  2.6
      with a standard deviation of   5.56
****************************************************************************
```

The word-list feature makes possible to perform limited linguistic analysis with TEXTBASE ALPHA.

C   Preparatory functions

One of the first decisions the researcher has to make with TEXTBASE ALPHA is whether or not s/he will be using structured coding. If s/he anticipates doing so, the data files have to be formatted accordingly while still in the word processor. All words that will be used as codes must begin at the first position of the text line, while the rest of the regular text must be indented at least one space. Now the data files can be converted into ASCII, imported into TEXTBASE ALPHA, and coded.

Since searches cannot be initiated in TEXTBASE ALPHA until a "selection file" is constructed, the researcher normally would make the creation of the selection file the first task when beginning work on a particular research project. The selection file holds the data base information. Two different types of items are stored in the file: the names of the data documents, and the variable values associated with each document (if the researcher has chosen to attach such variables to the documents).

A special module (F2 from the main menu) facilitates the job. The user is asked to supply a name for the selection file, and then to enter the names of all data files that are to be part of this textbase. Next, variable names must be entered (up to fifteen are permissible), and then the variable values are filled in for every file in the data base.

The same module also provides the facilities for adding files to existing data bases, or for deleting them. Likewise, variables can be added to all data files, or existing ones can be removed. TEXTBASE ALPHA even makes an entire matrix available, with filenames listed vertically, variables names listed horizontally, and the variable values in the cells. The values can be reviewed and edited.

D   Housekeeping functions

TEXTBASE ALPHA saves all coding automatically in a special code list ('catalog') file at the completion of a coding session. The selection file and any editing that has been done, however, must be saved by the user (the program provides a reminder).

Neither the selection file, nor the code list for each file can be printed out directly from the program. However, the selection file and the code lists (the 'catalog files'), are stored as ASCII files and can be printed out directly from DOS, or imported into a word processor and printed out from there. The coded data files can be printed out from within program module F10. For all search results and count results the user has the option to print them out at the time of their creation.

A special feature of TEXTBASE ALPHA is the option to "scramble" data files. This protects them from unauthorized access. Choosing F9 from the main menu lets the user attach a 'key' to the file, which is simply any word chosen by the user and kept secret. Only the insertion of the same key will later allow that data file to be retrieved in readable form.

Technical Description

TEXTBASE ALPHA was created by Bo Sommerlund and Ole Steen Kristensen. It works on an IBM/XT and fully compatible computers and requires 640 K of RAM. DOS version 2.00 or later is required. One database can hold up to 100 data files. There can be up to 500 codes in one data file; the code length may not exceed twenty characters.

Price: $150.00. The English language version of TEXTBASE ALPHA is distributed by Qualitative Research Management, 73425 Hilltop Road, Desert Hot Springs, CA 92240. Telephone 619/329-7026.

TEXTBASE ALPHA Glossary

A comprehensive glossary and a 'how to . . . ' index are provided in the program's user's manual.

HyperQual

Introduction

HyperQual is a program for the Macintosh. Its design is quite unlike the design of the MS-DOS text analysis programs. Some of the main differences are:

1. Data can be entered directly into HyperQual; they are imported from a word processor only if they had been created there previously.

2. HyperQual provides different modes for entering structured and unstructured data, and structured data can be sorted according to their natural structure.

3. Segmenting is done on the screen (although a paper printout of the data can be segmented in preparation for screen work), and segments do not have to be coded at the time they are defined. They can be assembled in a secondary document without codes.

4. The basic coding and assembling can be accomplished in one operation in HyperQual (while in the MS-DOS programs codes are attached to text segments in one step and then remain available for the second step of searching/assembling.)

Since the program is basically an application of the HyperCard software, it cannot be understood without first reviewing some of the concepts and the terminology used in HyperCard.

Underlying Concepts

Cards and stacks

HyperCard can be thought of as a very flexible and interrelated data base. The terminology it uses actually invites comparison with index cards ('cards') and piles of these index cards ('stacks'). This metaphor is somewhat confining, however, since HyperCard cards can contain much more text than would fit on even the largest index card. In fact, each data field on a card can accommodate up to 30,000 characters, about eighteen to twenty double-spaced pages. HyperCard cards are also not separate entities like real cards; they can be linked to other cards in the same stack, or in other stacks. Stacks are given names, and cards are automatically assigned numbers as they are created. These identifications serve to locate individual cards.

Buttons

The feature that links cards is the 'button'. (The metaphor does not refer to a button on a piece of clothing, but the button pressed to turn things on and off.) The user can add a HyperCard buttons to any card. When it is pressed ('clicked' with the 'mouse', in Macintosh language), the button connects to another card or another stack of cards. Connecting to another stack means that the stack is called to the screen by 'opening' it. It is always easy to return to the card with the button by choosing from a pull-down menu the option to go "back".

Backgrounds

Cards can be designed like forms, i.e., they can have an organizing structure or overlay called a 'background'. The individual parts of the structure are called 'fields' (a term used in similar ways in data base managers). HyperQual uses this facility to design 'face' cards. Face cards hold identifying information about the stack, such as the name of the research project whose data are stored in the stack, the date, name of the researcher, etc. They can be used to keep notes that pertain to the entire project, or they can contain the questionnaire or interview schedule employed for the study.

Text searches

HyperCard comes with a text search facility, of which HyperQual takes advantage. Unlike other text analysis programs (except TAP) it lets the user search through the entire data body (one stack at a time) for specific words that may be indicative of material relevant to the study's purpose. When the user activates the search option, s/he is taken to the place where the word is found, and the surrounding text can be highlighted as a segment and transferred to another document in which specific segments are collected. It can be coded at that time, or transferred without a code (there is no automatic coding as in TAP).

Program Structure

HyperQual distinguishes between structured and unstructured text data. They are entered into different types of stacks. If the researcher wishes, s/he may add illustrations and memos to each type of data. These memos and illustrations can be connected to particular cards.

The next page provides a map of the input and output locations for structured and unstructured data.

From the structured data stack, text segments can be transferred to four different output places. One of the four destinations (Data Dump) collates data by structure (for instance, by questions), thus supplying the conceptual context provided by the question. Naturally, this place is not available for unstructured data. In two of the locations, the data segments (called "chunks" in HyperQual) are accepted uncoded ("Selection Dump" and "Bags"), while in the other two the segments appear with their codes (or question references).

From the unstructured data stack, three avenues lead to output places. In the sorted stacks at the very right of the drawing, the data are re-contextualized according to their codes (called "tags" in HyperQual), whereas they are only accumulated for further inspection in the "Selection Dumps" and the "Bags". To these latter two, segments are sent that the researcher deems relevant, but s/he has not yet formulated a category into which to sort them. Therefore, s/he simply plays with collating some "selected" segments in tentative ways to see whether they make sense together. The difference between a "dump" and a "bag" is that only one "dump" is available to the researcher at a time (the contents of which can later be saved and the dump be reused), while up to five "bags" can be worked with at the same time. Also, the segments in the "bags" may be transferred to them with codes attached, thus progressing one step further in the development of an organizing system.

Once segments of data are coded, they can be sorted according to their codes, which results in the creation of new stacks, each of which contains all segments coded the same. Each represents one category of the existing or developing organizing system.

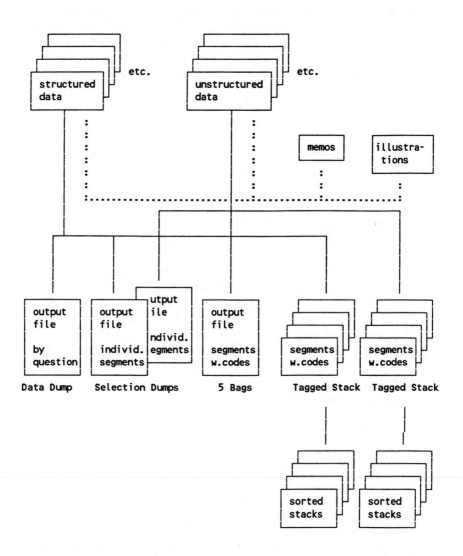

How HyperQual Works

Data entry

As mentioned earlier, as a rule raw data are entered directly into HyperQual (although they can also be imported with the help of the Macintosh's clipboard). If you work with structured data, such as open-ended responses to a structured questionnaire or interview, you would use a stack called the "Xview Stack". If your data are unstructured interviews, field notes, diaries, or any other continuous text, you would work with the "Doc Stack". The two stacks are separate data management modules within the program. They differ from each other in the way data are entered onto their cards. Unstructured data are entered one document per card; structured data typically are entered one response per card. The two processes may be visualized like this:

a   *Unstructured data:*

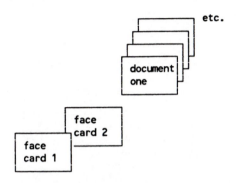

The face cards hold information about the research project, such as its name, date, author or observer name, and any general notes. There is only one set of face cards per project. The number of data cards in the stack, of course, corresponds to the number of data documents. A data card for documents looks somewhat like the reproduction below.

****

Name: ▓▓▓▓▓▓▓▓   Document: ▓▓▓▓▓▓▓▓

Notes: Data:

```
A common misperception is that introducing
a computer into the research process will
rigidify the procedures and perhaps
distance the researcher from the data.
This is equivalent to saying that
introducing scissors will result in the
dissection of the data and the loss of the
researcher's holistic perspective.  Com-
puters, as scissors, are tools.  In them-
selves, they have no influence on the pro-
cess whatsoever.  Their application is
completely dependent on the researcher's
decisions.  If anything, computers are far
more flexible than scissors, or even index
```

****

Cards are like forms. They have 'fields', and the researcher fills in the blanks. The box on the left above is available for notes the researcher might make regarding the text on the right. The text does not actually stop in the middle of the sentence; the card is scrollable. This means that the remainder of the text can be brought up to the screen.

    b Structured data:

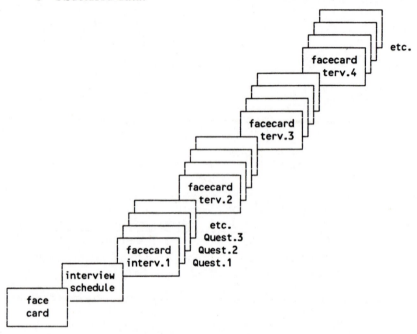

If you compare this drawing with the one for unstructured data in the preceding section, you will notice that this drawing reflects the structure of the data. Each section within the stack holds one interview, and the number of cards in the section corresponds to the number of questions, plus the face card that holds identifying information about the interview.

    A data card for interviews/questionnaires looks much like a data card for documents (shown above), except that it has blank spaces for the number of the interview (a code for the interviewee) and the number of the question.

Segmenting and assembling

In HyperQual it is possible to peruse the data, mark relevant pieces without coding them, and collect these pieces (segments) in another document. This is a valuable maneuver when exploring the data in an open-ended way to find themes. You can browse through either structured or unstructured data. You can identify areas in the data that may pertain to the same topic by making use of HyperCard's search facility that locates words in the text. Once the word is found, the surrounding text can be marked and transferred to an output file. HyperQual calls the process of transferring pieces of text 'dumping', or to be precise, 'selection dumping'. 'Selection' refers to the fact that only selected portions of the data are 'dumped'. HyperQual calls these portions, or segments, data 'chunks'.

Dumping is accomplished with the help of a 'button'. On any given card, any chunk of data can be highlighted with the Macintosh's mouse. The 'button' is a symbol located at the bottom of each data card. If the cursor is placed on it and activated, the highlighted chunk is transferred to an output file, the 'dump'. One after the other, chunks are collected in the 'dump', where the number of the card from which each chunk came is added automatically, as are the name of the stack and the date of the activity. Then the 'select dump' can be printed out with a word processor.

Data chunks don't have to be marked if they are already recognizable as individual segments. Structured data can be 'dumped' automatically according to each questionnaire or interview question (each being on a separate card). In this manner, all responses to each question are collated in the 'data dump'. The 'data dump' is printed out, enabling the researcher to compare all respondents' material across the entire data set to identify commonalities and discrepancies within the responses to the same question.

Coding and assembling

Codes are called 'tags' in HyperQual. Once an organizing system is developed, the researcher will want to code chunks of data and sort them according to categories. HyperQual offers two options, one for coding without further sorting (chunks are collected in 'bags'), and one for coding with subsequent sorting (chunks are collected in stacks).

The difference can be visualized in the way depicted at the beginnings of the next two pages.

As the researcher reads through the data, s/he transfers data chunks, one after the other, into 'bags', which are output text files. Five different 'bags' are available; the researcher determines where each chunk of text is to go. Bags can be emptied and reused (after their content has been saved as a text file or printed out on paper), and the process can be repeated as often as the researcher wishes.

Tagging and bagging:

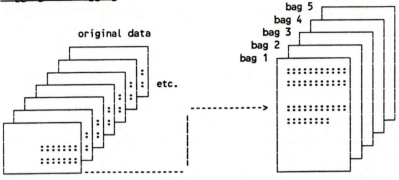

The 'tag' (code) is attached to a chunk as it is sent to a bag. There the tag is inserted at the end of each chunk. Below is an example of a bag holding two chunks of data:

```
-------------------------------------------------------------------------

    Computers, as scissors, are tools.  In themselves, they have no influence
on the process whatsoever.  Their application is completely dependent on the
researcher's decisions.

Tag for above selection = tools
***** Above selection from ***** card id 123

    In the case of computers it is often more important to clarify first what
they don't do, than to describe what they do.  At the current time computers
cannot perform any conceptual functions or even meaning recognition of
language.  They do not think.

Tag for above selection = do-not-do
***** Above selection from ***** card id 456
-------------------------------------------------------------------------
```

Note the card identification numbers at the end of each segment. They facilitate the return to a particular card if the researcher wants to review the context of the segment.

In contrast to "bagging", "tagging and stacking" sends the tagged chunks to cards in a new stack, not to an output text file. Each card receives one segment with its tag(s). Once on the card, the segment can be assigned additional codes, and the cards can be sorted according to any one of the tags.

Tagging and stacking:

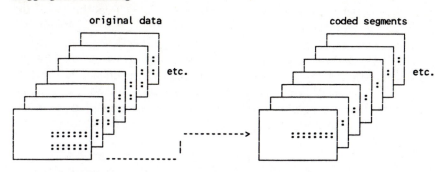

The types of stacks on the right are called "TandS" stacks (for 'tagging and stacking'). Below is an approximate reproduction of a card in such a TandS stack:

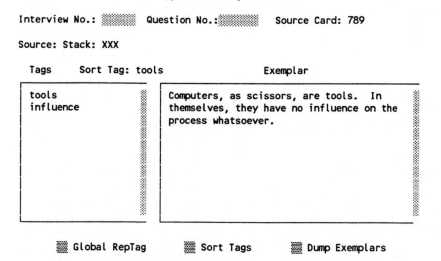

The coded (tagged) data segments are called 'exemplars'. While the top part of the screen provides the source information (where the 'exemplar' came from), the lower part contains two boxes. The one on the left repeats the code that was originally assigned to this segment as it was transferred to the card. The remainder of the box can be used to attach additional codes to the segment. In the right-hand box the text of the segment appears. The "trace" button is used to return directly to the data card that contains the exemplar.

The actual assembling of data chunks with the same tag is accomplished with the sort feature of HyperQual. Note the "Sort Tags" button at the bottom of the card above. When it is activated, the computer prompts for the name of the tag according to which to sort, then asks the user to name the new stack of sorted 'exemplars'. The user may choose to transfer the chunk with only the tag it is sorted by, or with all tag names in the left-hand box. Each new card will look almost identical to the one it came from, except that it is now part of a stack in which all 'exemplars' have the same tag. Again, the "trace" button can be used to backtrack to the source of the exemplar.

When the researcher is ready to look at the content of the entire sorted stack of cards, s/he can make a paper printout, or use the "Dump Exemplars" button to transfer all exemplars in the stack to an output text file, which can be printed out or moved into the word processor. The exemplars can now appear in the final research report as evidence for the researcher's categories.

Tag names can be changed as easily as they can be added. There is even a global replace function available that works for an entire stack. This means a specific tag can be replaced by a specific other one at all places where it appears. This procedure can be repeated for as many stacks as desired.

Multiple codes

Normally, multiple codes are assigned not at the raw data level, but in the "TandS" stack created from the original data stack. The TandS stack, as you may remember, does not hold the full data, but segments, now called 'exemplars'. Ordinarily, the researcher would have sent the exemplars to the stack with a tag attached (although that is not required). The box on the left of each card (see above) accepts additional tags. This means that differently coded text segments cannot have overlapping boundaries, and that a shorter one cannot be nested in a longer segment within one card. Once transferred to where it can be tagged (the TandS stack), the segment is discrete; additional codes can be attached only to a segment exactly as it appears on the card.

The sorting function, originally employed to create homogenous stacks with like-coded text segments, can be used to isolate exemplar cards with the same combination of tags. Technically, there are no limits on sorting an already sorted stack. If you wanted to create a stack, for instance, that holds all exemplars that were coded with "ABC", as well as with "DEF", you would begin with a stack in which multiple tag names are listed in the "tags" box. A first round of sorting creates a new stack consisting only of cards on which "ABC" was found. A second round sorts out from these all cards that contain "DEF". The result is a new stack with only exemplars that were tagged with both "ABC" and "DEF".

This process can be repeated for the simultaneous occurrence of three or more tags. The results, of course, can be printed or transferred to an output file for import into the word processor.

Memos and illustrations

Up to now we have described only the functions that HyperQual and MS-DOS text analysis programs have in common. Two special features of HyperQual deserve mention. They are made possible by HyperCard's ability to link cards to each other, and to 'paint'.

Ideas about the relevance of certain topics, the connections between categories, the emergence of certain discrepancies, etc., usually come to the researcher's mind when working directly with the data. With HyperQual these ideas can be captured as they occur by adding a button to the card that stimulated the idea, and linking it to a card from the "Memos" stack. The stack of memo cards can later be reviewed, and memos can be printed. Of course, any time the researcher looks at a data card with a memo button, that button can be activated, and the associated memo appears.

Some people like to visualize connections or processes graphically. With HyperQual, researchers can create graphs and drawings in HyperCard, then link the illustration to a particular data card or memo card with the aid of a button. It is even possible to link more than one drawing to the same card. Just as with memos, all drawings can be reviewed in their stack (the "Schemas" stack) one after the other, or they can be accessed from the data or memo card to which they are linked.

Technical Description

HyperQual was created by Raymond Padilla. It was available in version 2.0 at the time of this writing. It requires a Macintosh Plus, Macintosh SE, or Macintosh II with at least 1 megabyte of RAM. Only with a very small data set could the program be used with two floppy disks, therefore a hard disk is practically required. The program is dependent on the availability of HyperCard in the system and the user's familiarity with HyperCard operations and terminology. The only limitation pertains to the amount of text on a single card: 30,000 characters, and the amount of storage available in the system. A word processor is needed for printing output text files.

Price: $125.00 plus shipping and handling. Distributed by Qualitative Research Management, 73425 Hilltop Road, Desert Hot Springs, CA 92240. Telephone 619/329-7026.

HyperQual Glossary

background	the way an individual card is designed for entry of information or data, including its buttons
bag	output file for chunks of text and their associated tags
button	a symbol on a card, much like a menu selection, that connects to another card or performs a certain function when activated
chunk	a meaningful portion of text, a segment
distribution disk	original disk that holds the HyperQual program
dump	an output text file containing the content of all data cards with a specific designation (for instance the designation "Question No.1")
exemplar	a chunk of text that has been tagged and sent to the TandS stack
face card	cards at the beginning of a stack or section of a stack designed to hold information about the stack or section
field	a section of a card designated for a specific type of entry
HyperCard	a Macintosh program similar to a combined data base and word processor, arranged according to cards and stacks of cards, with multiple linking capabilities
schema	illustration, drawing
selection dump	an output text file that contains selected pieces of text (chunks)
selection	a highlighted chunk of data
source data	raw data
stack	a set of cards with a common stack name
TandS stack	a stack consisting of cards with individual coded exemplars
tag	code
trace	return to the original location of a chunk of text

Conclusion

This book is no longer up-to-date. No book on computers ever is. While I am writing, developments in computer technology and software design continue, many of them still invisible, because they are no more than an idea in someone's mind. Although they were the newest at the time of this writing and not yet reviewed anywhere else, the programs described here are only a beginning. They will undoubtedly change and improve, and new ones will appear. Yet this book is not completely time-bound.

One reason is that this is a book not only about computer programs, but also about one of the most critical aspects of qualitative methodology: the analysis of text data. While some scholars still feel there is a need to assert that qualitative research is not a monolithic enterprise (Fetterman, 1987), has several traditions (Jacob, 1987), or shows great diversity (Atkinson et al., 1988), this state of affairs is taken for granted in this book, and the horizon is much expanded (not one of those authors includes more than seven varieties). Going beyond the definition of the names and outlooks associated with different approaches, the emphasis in this book is on what this methodological diversity means to qualitative researchers.

As has been shown, the diversity in qualitative research types is not paralleled by a one-on-one corresponding diversity in analysis methods. There is diversity, to be sure, but many analysis techniques are shared, and where there are differences, they are not stark but fuzzy, almost fluidly merging into each other more or less on a continuum, with a few branches going off into individual directions. Since the diversity is still great, the opposite poles of the continuum hold distinctly separate methods, but otherwise the commonalities of adjacent entities are greater than their disparities. There are a few commonalities that are almost universal.

By presenting the broad range of qualitative analysis methods and unveiling their commonalities, this book is meant to liberate. It opens the doors for a truly informed choice of methods. It not only encourages the option to go beyond the methodological boundaries of your own 'tradition' and learn from others, but to invent your own strategies. After all, this is how we arrived at so many varieties in the first place. Not one of them is the 'right' one; they simply enrich the qualitative researcher's repertoire. The commonalities tell you what is important in qualitative research; beyond that don't let yourself be confined by established 'labels'. There is a niche for your unique variety as well.

This book is meant to be liberating also by enlarging your assortment of tools available for performing qualitative research, making you more efficient. As you have seen, computers are not alien to 'humanistic' ways of handling data. They merely mimic what qualitative researchers have done for decades as part of their work, and are still doing. That is also the reason why, in spite of rapid software development, not much will change in principle, at least not for some time to come. A revolution in software character will come with a revolution in qualitative analysis methods - and I don't dare to predict which will initiate which, or even whether a revolution is likely to happen at all.

In the meantime, I expect that the software described here will simply become *better*. What is missing in a program today might be incorporated tomorrow. The 'user-interface' (what you see on the screen and the facility with which you can handle the program) will become still more amiable. Text analysis programs are perfect candidates for true hypertext capabilities (HyperQual has but a pale resemblance to true hypertext <How to read this book>), where multi-colored windows would let you see your data and coding system at the same time, while you are connecting pieces of data with each other. As this concept becomes reality, text analysis programmers are surely going to incorporate it.

What, you may ask, about artificial intelligence? Can't we expect from it more than the mechanical jobs that current programs perform? Couldn't an intelligent computer recognize meaningful segments in my data and carve out my analysis units for me? Couldn't it compare topics in these segments and tell me how they relate? Well, we might be getting there, but not very quickly.

One definition of AI is 'software that learns' (Wyland, 1985, p. 93). AI applications have been found so far mostly in so-called expert systems. An expert system simulates the knowledge of an expert in a given field. Rather than just storing data that can be retrieved in individual pieces, an expert system works with rules that enable it to make connections among items as more and more information is provided to it, which 'means that their performance improves with time' (*ibid.*, p. 93). This is what we could have now, but it is difficult to imagine how to use such capabilities for qualitative analysis.

Expert systems don't seem to get us on the right track. There is, however, a development that sounds much more promising: Natural language interfaces. For quite some time programs have existed that have these kinds of interfaces. On the simplest level, the user teaches the program how to understand a limited vocabulary. If you had an address database, for instance, in which one field was named "spouse", you could ask the program: What is the name of X.Y.'s husband? On first try, it would ask you for a definition of "husband". You explain: a husband is a spouse. Now the program immediately retrieves the husband's name. Next time, when you ask for A.B.'s husband, it will know to get you the name of the spouse. Soon it will learn that a "wife" is also a spouse, and so on. You can imagine that the word "when" can become associated with "date" in a bibliographic data base, and "where" with the publisher, etc.

It is a large jump from these humble beginnings to systems that would understand all words in all contexts, but it illustrates the principle. What if a program had 'learned' hundreds of thousands of words and their relationships, something like a network thesaurus or a hypertext thesaurus? The semantic 'domains' in cultures that are studied by language-oriented ethnographers are simple examples of such conceptual connections that form networks. 'Semantic networks are networks of concepts linked to other concepts according to labelled conceptual relations. Each concept occupies a node in a network. Relations include spacial-temporal properties, dispositional properties, and causal properties' (THUNDERSTONE, p. 3). This is a quotation from the description of a text retrieval program that 'utilizes an English language morpheme filter of a type which contains in excess of 250,000 words in associated patterns to accomplish operational analysis and extraction of in-depth information as a subset of a larger body of information' (*ibid.*, p. 1). In other words, the program claims to 'understand text', specifically, to be able to 'interrogate and automatically analyze information for content and meaning' (*ibid.*, p. 1). It is called METAMORPH. I was not able to try out a copy on my computer, since it requires 2 megabytes of disk space and also is somewhat outside the price range of the software described here ($5,000). It seems, however, that the understanding of natural language is not completely out of reach. Eventually, the qualitative researcher might, in fact, be able to count on the computer for more than just cutting and pasting and wild card searches.

But let's look at some closer prospects. QUALOG, AQUAD, and NUDIST permit the exploration of emerging hypotheses about connections among themes and concepts, including the retrieval of confirming and disconfirming instances. NUDIST and ETHNO provide some graphic display of connections that can be represented in inverted tree diagrams. It is easy to imagine that someone will build on existing flowcharting programs to further assist researchers in graphically depicting relationships among categories beyond hierarchies toward networks, and perhaps even three-dimensional models and maps. The maps would be drawn according to information about the data elicited from the researcher or even directly from analysis programs.

The one development, however that would be most welcomed by the qualitative researcher, although just as mundane and mechanical as text organizers, would be natural language recognition and translation into written text. Transcription of field notes and interviews is still the bottleneck in qualitative research; it takes an inordinate amount of time. Systems already exist that recognize individual spoken words, but must get familiar with a particular speaker's voice, and can't follow sequences of words spoken in natural flow. Computer experts expect that in the 1990's machines that take dictation will become available, and eventually will be as affordable and common as word processors are today. In the meantime, at least printed text is already transferrable into computers by scanners, so that researchers who work with existing records need not have them retyped.

This book has shown many ways in which computers, even in their present stage of development, can be useful to the qualitative researcher. It is time to note that they can also constitute a hazard. The most obvious dangers are the following:

1. Although the concept of de-contextualizing and re-contextualizing sounds relatively straight forward, the actual analysis process is, as we have learned in the chapter on different types of analysis, quite complex. If a novice researcher expects the computer to guide her/him through the process, the results could be disastrous. The computer is a servant only, not an expert. The expertise has to reside in the researcher. Without adequate knowledge, some researchers might simply 'muddle through'. Involving the computer in such an adventure is likely to exacerbate judgment errors, especially in terms of clearly separating intellectual and mechanical tasks. Furthermore, as explained in this book, the computer presently facilitates mainly one phase of the process, the handling of data segments. This step is preceded or accompanied by the development of an initial organizing system, and is succeeded by interpretation and the intelligent narrative and sometimes additional graphic presentation of the analysis outcomes. Unless all these are done well, the efficient handling of the mechanical tasks is of no consequence. The computer is not a substitute for competence and clear thinking; in fact, it requires both without compromise.

2. Researchers who have developed facility in the use of computers might be tempted to take advantage of the speed and convenience the computer provides to assign it tasks that are inappropriate. For example, TAP provides a means for 'creating' a coding system by having the computer search for words contained in the data and turn them into codes. This feature could easily be misused, creating an organizing system that contains convenient, but unnecessary categories.

Worse still, a researcher might design the entire analysis process around the functions a computer makes available. Cross-referencing categories, for instance, used to be one of the most difficult procedures in the past. Now it is just as easy as sorting data according to a single code. It is quite imaginable that a researcher would be tempted to artificially upgrade the importance of category relationships in a study that instead requires increased attention to the meaning of individual statements and demands in-depth interpretation. The priorities would be reversed. The analysis would be done a certain way because the computer favors that way. As a result, the computer would be allowed to invade the researcher's conceptual territory or to influence unduly the direction of the process.

3. Researchers who have successfully involved the computer in the analysis of their qualitative data might 'freeze' the process and continue to do it the same way for every project, whether it is appropriate or not. Computer users often develop a curious tenacity in sticking with the program they have become familiar with. Ethnograph users can easily turn into Ethnograph aficionados; users of a certain text data base manager rarely will consider getting a different text manager or a specialized analysis program. They might use the program like the proverbial hammer; every research project that comes across their desk seems in need of treatment by their program. Rather than remaining a servant, the program has become the master. In the process the researcher 'forgets' the creativity that inspires every lively research project. In these cases, the analysis would become rigid, and the computer would live up to its worst reputation.

Not one of the dangers listed above grows out of the nature of the computer itself. It is the attitudes of the people who are using the computer - or not using it - that will determine how this technology is going to affect us.

I am mentioning also those researchers who decline to use it, because their attitudes will affect how widely the computer becomes accepted as a facilitator for qualitative analysis. The less it is accepted, the fewer programmers will find it worth their while to create programs, or even to improve existing ones. Software has become cheap, because big software companies develop multi-purpose programs for large business or general user markets. The cost of the thousands of hours that go into creating a program and its user manual are retrieved through high quantity sales. (The actual production of manual and disk copies represents but a small portion of what it takes to develop a program.) Individual programmers with limited markets and distribution systems spend thousands of hours on their software, as well, but with little hope to ever recover the cost (especially since they are quite aware of the persistent rumor that software piracy runs rampant in the academic world). As long as qualitative researchers are reluctant to use the programs, only a few enthusiasts will continue to provide them. Any expectations about improvements or even breakthroughs in the future are likely to be foiled.

Some researchers resist the computer because they profoundly disagree with Robert Merton, who twenty years ago concluded that 'codification [of methods of qualitative analysis] is devoutly to be desired both for the collection and the analysis of qualitative . . . data' (Merton, 1968, p. 444, footnote 5). By codification he had in mind the establishment of a canon of rules delineated 'with something of the clarity with which quantitative methods have been articulated' (*ibid.*). These researchers argue that it is the very nature of qualitative research NOT to be codified; in effect, that qualitative research (or whatever label they use) would lose its own character and become merely a variation of quantitative research if it were codified. Its essence would be violated if there were a set of rules. Just as in quantitative investigations, one researcher could be replaced by another of the same skill level, and the research project would proceed in exactly the same way and with exactly the same outcomes as if the first person had continued to do it. One of the most persistent themes in qualitative methodology literature is the emphasis on the person of the researcher, and the recognition of each scholar's individuality as a research instrument. Wouldn't the computer streamline the analysis into the very stringencies from which we have finally freed ourselves? Wouldn't one qualitative researcher, using the same program with the same data produce the same findings as the next one? (An outcome that, incidently, would please every scholar who believes in replicability as the basis for reliability.) Most qualitative researchers would find this prospect horrifying.

Qualitative research is to a large degree an art. The question of its validity does not depend on replicable outcomes. It depends on the employment of a data 'reduction' process that leads to a result that others can accept as representing the data. The result of the analysis is, in fact, a representation in the same sense that an artist can, with a few strokes of the pen, create an image of a face that we would recognize if we saw the original in a crowd. The details are lacking, but a good 'reduction' not only selects and emphasizes the essential features, it retains the vividness of the personality in the rendition of the face. In the same way a successful qualitative data reduction, while removing us from the freshness of the original, presents us instead with an image that we can grasp as the 'essence', where we otherwise would have been flooded with detail and left with hardly a perception of the phenomenon at all.

In qualitative research no two scholars produce the same result, even if they are faced with exactly the same task. Their differences in philosophical stances and individual styles will lead them to perceive and present the phenomenon each in her/his own way. There is no one correct way of doing qualitative analysis (which does not give the researcher permission to be a dilettante); there is no one correct way of drawing a face, either. No two artists will produce exactly the same drawing of someone's features. If they are skillful and competent, we will nevertheless recognize the same person in their renditions. 'Pictures' of an experience, social phenomenon, or culture don't have to look exactly alike to be valid, either. If the research is conducted competently, each individual exploration will give us a different perspective on the phenomenon studied. One study alone will not provide the whole picture (just as no single quantitative study does). As qualitative descriptions accumulate, they will make it possible for us to gradually 'recognize' the phenomenon in the sense of a second, fuller knowing. That is the goal of qualitative research.

The artist uses tools such as different brushes or pens to achieve the effect s/he wants. It would be too simplistic to compare computers with these utensils, since computers are much more complex. A program can be more or less useful to you depending on the skill with which it is chosen. However, since computers will never do more than you allow them to do (and especially since presently they are still restricted to helping you organize your data), no matter which analysis software you use, it will not affect your conceptual results more profoundly than your word processor influences the character of your writing. Here as there, good software merely makes your work less cumbersome. Computers will not control you; your power is much greater than theirs.

References

ATKINSON, PAUL; DELAMONT, SARA and HAMMERSLEY, MARTYN (1988) 'Qualitative research traditions: A British response to Jacob', *Review of Educational Research,* 85, 2, p. 250.

FETTERMAN, DAVID M. (1987) 'Qualitative approaches to evaluating education', paper presented at the annual meeting of the American Educational Research Association, Washington, D.C.

JACOB, EVELYN (1987, Spring) 'Qualitative research traditions: A review', *Review of Educational Research,* 57, 1, pp. 1-50.

MERTON, ROBERT K. (1968) *Social Theory and Social Structure,* New York, Free Press.

THUNDERSTONE EXPANSION PGMS INT'L, INC. (informational material), Copyright 1987, 1988, Chesterland, OH.

WYLAND, DAVID (1985, November 11) 'Software that learns', *Computerworld,* pp. 93-104.

Bibliography

AANSTOOS, CHRISTOPHER M. (1987, Winter) 'A comparative survey of human science psychologies', *Methods*, 1, 2, pp. 1-36.

ALLEN, JOBETH; COMBS, JACKIE; HENDRICKS, MILLIE; NASH, PHYLLIS and WILSON, SUSAN (1988) 'Studying change: Teachers who become researchers', *Language Arts*, 65, 4, pp. 379-87.

ALTHEIDE, DAVID L. (1987, Spring) 'Ethnographic content analysis', *Qualitative Sociology*, 10, 1, pp. 65-7.

ATKINSON, PAUL; DELAMONT, SARA and HAMMERSLEY, MARTYN (1988) 'Qualitative research traditions: A British response to Jacob', *Review of Educational Research*, 85, 2, p. 250.

BAILY, KENNETH D. (1987) *Methods of Social Research*, New York, The Free Press.

BAKEMAN, ROGER and GOTTMAN, JOHN M. (1986) *Observing Interaction: An Introduction to Sequential Analysis*, Cambridge, MA, Cambridge University Press.

BARCUS, F. E. (1959) *Communications Content: Analysis of the Research 1900-1958*, University of Illinois, Doctoral dissertation.

BARKER, ROGER G. (1968) *Ecological Psychology: Concepts and Methods for Studying the Environment of Human Behavior*, Stanford, CA, Stanford University Press.

BARRELL, JAMES J. and BARRELL, J. E. (1975) 'A self-directed approach for a science of human experience', *Journal of Phenomenological Psychology*, pp. 63-73.

BARRELL, JAMES J. (1986) *A Science of Human Experience*, Acton, MA, Copley.

BARRITT, LOREN; BEEKMAN, TON; BLEEKER, HANS and MULDERIJ, KAREL (1985) *Researching Education Practice*, Grand Forks, ND, University of North Dakota, Center for Teaching and Learning.

BARZUN, JACQUES and GRAFF, HENRY F. (1977) *The Modern Researcher*, New York, Harcourt Brace Jovanovich, Inc.

BATESON, GREGORY (1978, Summer) 'The pattern which connects', *Co-Evolution Quarterly*, pp. 5-15.

BECKER, HOWARD S.; GEER, BLANCHE; HUGHES, E. and STRAUSS, ANSELM L. (1961) *Boys in White: Student Culture in Medical School*, Chicago, Chicago University Press.

BECKER, HOWARD S. and GEER, BLANCHE (1982) 'Participant observation: The analysis of qualitative field data', in BURGESS, ROBERT G. (Ed.) *Field Research: A Sourcebook and Field Manual*, London, George Allen and Unwin.

BENSON, D. and HUGHES, J. A. (1984) *The Perspective of Ethnomethodology*, London, Longman.

BERELSON, B. (1952) *Content Analysis in Communications Research*, New York, Free Press.

BERG, DAVID N. and SMITH, KENWYN K. (Eds.) (1985) *Exploring Clinical Methods for Social Research*, Beverly Hills, CA, Sage Publications.

BERTEAUX, D. (Ed.) (1981) *Biography and Society: The Life History Approach in the Social Sciences*, London, Sage.

BINSWANGER, L. (1958) 'The case of Ellen West', in MAY, R.; ANGEL, E. and ELLENBERGER, H. F. (Eds.) *Existence*, New York, Basic Books.

BLUMER, HERBERT (1967) 'Society as symbolic interaction', in MANIS, J. and MELTZER, B. (Eds.) *Symbolic Interaction*, Boston, Allyn and Bacon.

BLUMER, HERBERT (1969) *Symbolic Interactionism*, Englewood Cliffs, NJ, Prentice Hall.

BOGDAN, ROBERT C. and TAYLOR, STEVEN J. (1975) *Introduction to Qualitative Research Methods: A Phenomenological Approach to the Social Sciences*, New York, John Wiley and Sons.

BOGDAN, ROBERT C. and BIKLEN, SARI K. (1982) *Qualitative Research for Education: An Introduction to Theory and Methods*, Boston, Allyn and Bacon, Inc.

BRAITHWAITE, R. B. (1953) *Scientific Explanation*, Cambridge, MA, Cambridge University Press.

BRAMELD, THEODORE (1957) *Cultural Foundations of Education*, New York, Harper and Row.

BRAMELD, THEODORE and SULLIVAN, EDWARD B. (1961) 'Anthropology and education', *Review of Educational Research*, 31, pp. 70-9.

BRENT, EDWARD; SCOTT, JAMES and SPENCER, JOHN (1987) 'The use of computers by qualitative researchers', *Qualitative Sociology*, 10, 3, pp. 309-13.

BRUYN, SEVERYN T. (1966) *The Human Perspective in Sociology: The Methodology of Participant Observation*, Englewood Cliffs, NJ, Prentice Hall, Inc.

BULLINGTON, JENNIFER and KARLSON, GUNNAR (1984) 'Introduction to phenomenological psychological research', *Scandinavian Journal of Psychology*, 25, pp. 51-63.

BURGESS, ROBERT G. (Ed.) (1982) *Field Research: A Sourcebook and Field Manual*, London, Allen and Unwin.

BURGESS, ROBERT G. (1984a) *In the Field*, London, Allen Lane.

BURGESS, ROBERT G. (Ed.) (1984b) *The Research Process in Educational Settings: Ten Case Studies*, Lewes, The Falmer Press.

BURGESS, ROBERT G. (1985a) *Field Methods in the Study of Education*, Lewes, The Falmer Press.

BURGESS, ROBERT G. (Ed.) (1985b) *Strategies in Educational Research*, Lewes, The Falmer Press.

CARNEY, T. F. (1972) *Content Analysis: A Technique for Systematic Inference from Communications*, Winnipeg, Manitoba, University of Manitoba Press.

CARR, WILFRED and KEMMIS, STEPHEN (1986) *Becoming Critical: Education, Knowledge and Action Research*, Lewes, The Falmer Press.

COFFEE, PETER C. (1988, August) 'Long dazed journey into bytes', *PC Tech Journal*, pp. 141-46.

COLAIZZI, PAUL F. (1978) 'Psychological research as the phenomenologist views it', in VALLE, RONALD S. and KING, MARK (Eds.) *Existential-Phenomenological Alternatives for Psychology*, New York, Oxford University Press.

COLE, BERNARD C. (1985) *Beyond Word Processing*, New York, McGraw-Hill Book Company.

COREY, STEPHEN M. (1953) *Action Research to Improve School Practices*, New York, Columbia University Press.

CRONBACH, LEE J. (1949) *Essentials of Psychological Testing*, New York, Harper and Row Publishers.

DARROCH, VIVIAN and SILVERS, RONALD J. (1982) *Interpretive Human Studies*, Washington, D.C., University Press of America.

DE BOER, THEO (1983) *Foundations of a Critical Psychology*, Pittsburgh, PA, Duquesne University Press.

DENZIN, NORMAN K. (Ed.) (1970) *Sociological Methods: A Sourcebook*, Chicago, Aldine Atherton.

DENZIN, NORMAN K. (1971) 'The logic of naturalistic inquiry', *Social Forces*, 50, pp. 166-82.

DOBBERT, MARION L. (1982) *Ethnographic Research*, New York, Praeger Publications.

DOUGLAS, BRUCE G. and MOUSTAKAS, CLARK (1985, Summer) 'Heuristic inquiry: The internal search to know', *Journal of Humanistic Psychology*, 25, 3, pp. 39-55.

DOUGLAS, JACK D. (1976) *Investigative Social Research*, Beverly Hills, CA, Sage Publications.

DOUGLAS, JACK D. (1985) *Creative Interviewing*, Beverly Hills, CA, Sage Publications.

DUKES, SHEREE (1984) 'Phenomenological methodology in the human sciences', *Journal of Religion and Health*, 23, 3, pp. 197-203.

EDDY, ELIZABETH M. (1969) *Becoming a Teacher: The Passage to Professional Status*, New York, Teachers College Press.

EISNER, ELLIOT W. (1975) 'The perceptive eye: Toward a reformation of educational evaluation', invited address, annual meeting of the American Educational Research Association, Washington D.C.

EISNER, ELLIOT W. (1976) 'Educational connoisseurship and criticism: Their form and function in educational evaluation', *The Journal of Aesthetic Education*, The University of Illinois Press, pp. 135-50.

EISNER, ELLIOT W. (1981, April) 'On the differences between scientific and artistic approaches to qualitative research', *Educational Researcher*, 10, 4, pp. 5-9.

EISNER, ELLIOT W. (1988) 'Educational connoisseurship and criticism: Their form and function in educational evaluation', in FETTERMAN, DAVID M. (Ed.) *Qualitative Approaches to Evaluation: The Silent Scientific Revolution*, New York, Praeger.

ERICKSON, FREDERICK (1973) 'What makes school ethnography "ethnographic"?' *Anthropology and Education Quarterly*, 4, 2, pp. 10-19.

ERICKSON, FREDERICK (1986) 'Qualitative methods in research on teaching', in WITTROCK, MERLIN C. (Ed.) *Handbook of Research on Teaching*, Third edition, New York, Macmillan Publishing Company.

EVALUATION PRACTICE (1987) 'Reports from TIGs', *Qualitative Methods*, 8, 4, Beverly Hills, CA, Sage Publications.

FARADAY, ANNABEL and PLUMMER, KENNETH (1979) 'Doing life histories', *Sociological Review*, 27, 4, pp. 773-98.

FETTERMAN DAVID M. (1984) *Ethnography in Educational Evaluation*, Beverly Hills, CA, Sage Publications.

FETTERMAN, DAVID M. (1987) 'Qualitative approaches to evaluating education', paper presented at the annual meeting of the American Educational Research Association, Washington, D.C.

FETTERMAN DAVID M. (Ed.) (1988) *Qualitative Approaches to Evaluation: The Silent Scientific Revolution*, New York, Praeger.

FEYERABEND, PAUL K. (1975) *Against Method: Outline of an Anarchistic Theory of Knowledge*, Atlantic Highlands, NJ, Humanities Press.

FILSTEAD, W. J. (Ed.) (1970) *Qualitative Methodology: Firsthand Involvement with the Social World*, Chicago, Rand McNally.

FLORIO-RUANE, SUSAN (1987, Summer) 'Sociolinguistics for educational researchers', *American Educational Research Journal*, 24, 2, pp. 185-97.

GARDNER, HOWARD (1983) *Frames of Mind: The Theory of Multiple Intelligences*, New York, Basic Books, Inc.

GARFINKEL, HAROLD (1967) *Studies in Ethnomethodology*, Englewood Cliffs, NJ, Prentice-Hall.

GEERTZ, CLIFFORD (1973) *The Interpretation of Cultures*, New York, Basic Books.

GEPHART, WILLIAM (1969) 'The eight general research methodologies: A facet analysis of the research process', Center on Evaluation Development and Research: Phi Delta Kappa Occasional Paper.

GIORGI, AMEDEO; FISCHER, WILLIAM F. and VON ECKARTSBERG, ROLF (Eds.) (1971) *Duquesne Studies in Phenomenological Psychology, Vol. 1*, Pittsburgh, PA, Duquesne University Press.

GIORGI, AMEDEO; FISCHER, CONSTANCE and MURRAY, EDWARD (Eds.) (1975) *Duquesne Studies in Phenomenological Psychology, Vol. 2*, Pittsburgh, PA, Duquesne University Press.

GIORGI, AMEDEO; KNOWLES, RICHARD and SMITH, DAVID L. (Eds.) (1979) *Duquesne Studies in Phenomenological Psychology, Vol. 3*, Pittsburgh, PA, Duquesne University Press.

GIORGI, AMEDEO; BARON, A. and MAES, C. (Eds.) (1983) *Duquesne Studies in Phenomenological Psychology, Vol. 4*, Pittsburgh, PA, Duquesne University Press.

GIORGI, AMEDEO (1986, Spring) 'Status of qualitative research in the human sciences; A limited interdisciplinary and international perspective', *Methods*, 1, 1, pp. 29-62.

GLASER, BARNEY G. and STRAUSS, ANSELM L. (1967) *The Discovery of Grounded Theory: Strategies for Qualitative Research*, Chicago, Aldine Publishing Company.

GOETZ, JUDITH P. and LECOMPTE, MARGARET D. (1981) 'Ethnographic research and the problem of data reduction', *Anthropology and Education Quarterly*, 12, pp. 51-70.

GOETZ, JUDITH P. and LECOMPTE, MARGARET D. (1984) *Ethnography and Qualitative Design in Educational Research*, Orlando, FL, Academic Press.

GOODSON, IVOR (1985) 'History, context and qualitative method in the study of curriculum', in BURGESS, ROBERT G. (Ed.) *Strategies of Educational Research: Qualitative Methods*, Lewes, The Falmer Press, pp. 121-52.

GUBA, EGON (1967, April) 'The expanding concept of research', *Theory into Practice*, 6, pp. 57-65.

GUBA, EGON (1978) *Toward a Methodology of Naturalistic Inquiry in Educational Evaluation*, Los Angeles, CA, Center for the Study of Evaluation.

GUBA, EGON and LINCOLN, YVONNA (1981) *Effective Evaluation*, San Francisco, CA, Jossey-Bass Inc.

GUBRIUM, JABER (1988) *Analyzing Field Reality*, Beverly Hills, CA, Sage Publications.

GUMPERZ, J. J. and HYMES, D. (Eds.) (1972) *Directions in Sociolinguistics: The Ethnography of Communication*, New York, Holt, Rinehart and Winston.

HALFPENNY, PETER (1979) 'The analysis of qualitative data', *Sociological Review*, 27, 4, pp. 799-825.

HALFPENNY, PETER (1981, November) 'Teaching ethnographic data analysis in postgraduate courses in sociology', *Journal of the British Sociological Association*, 15, 4, pp. 564-70.

HAMMERSLEY, MARTYN and ATKINSON, PAUL (1983) *Ethnography: Principles in Practice*, New York, Tavistock Publications.

HEIDEGGER, MARTIN (1962) *Being and Time*, New York, Harper and Row. (Originally published in 1927.)

HEISE, DAVID R. (1988, Spring) 'Computer analysis of cultural structures', *Social Science Computer Review*, 6, 1, pp. 183-97.

HEISE, DAVID R. and LEWIS, ELSA M. (1988) *Introduction to ETHNO*, Raleigh, NC, National Collegiate Software Clearinghouse.

HERITAGE, J. (1984) *Recent Developments in Conversation Analysis*, Warwick Working Papers in Sociology, No. 1.

HERON, JOHN (1971) *Experience and Method: An Inquiry into the Concept of Experiential Research*, Human Potential Research Project, University of Surrey, England.

HERON, JOHN (1981) 'Experiential research methodology', in REASON, PETER and ROWAN, JOHN (Eds.) *Human Inquiry: A Sourcebook of New Paradigm Research*, New York, John Wiley and Sons.

HESSE-BIBER, SHARLENE; DUPIUS, PAUL and KINDER, SCOTT (1989) 'HyperResearch: A computer program for the analysis of qualitative data using the Macintosh', paper presented at the annual meeting of the American Sociological Association, San Francisco.

HORVARTH, MICHAEL J.; KASS, CORRINE E. and FERRELL, WILLIAM R. (1980) 'An example of the use of fuzzy set concepts in modeling learning disability', *American Educational Research Journal*, 17, 3, pp. 309-24.

HUBER, GÜNTER L. (1989) *AQUAD: Manual zur computerunterstützten Auswertung qualitativer Daten*, Bericht Nr. 25, Institut für Erziehungswissenschaften I, Universität Tübingen.

HYCNER, RICHARD H. (1985) 'Some guidelines for the phenomenological analysis of interview data', *Human Studies*, 8, pp. 279-303.

JACKSON, PHILIP W. (1968) *Life in the Classroom*, New York, Holt, Rinehart and Winston.

JACOB, EVELYN (1987, Spring) 'Qualitative research traditions: A review', *Review of Educational Research*, 57, 1, pp. 1-50.

JONES, GARETH R. (1983) 'Life history methodology', in MORGAN, G. (Ed.) *Beyond Method*, Beverly Hills, CA, Sage Publications.

KERLINGER, FRED N. (1964) *Foundations of Behavioral Research*, New York, Holt, Rinehart and Winston.

KERLINGER, FRED N. (1979) *Behavioral Research*, New York, Holt, Rinehart and Winston.

KIRK, JEROME and MILLER, MARC L. (1986) *Reliability and Validity in Qualitative Research*, Beverly Hills, CA, Sage Publications.

KRIPPENDORF, KLAUS (1980) *Content Analysis: An Introduction to Its Methodology*, Beverly Hills, CA, Sage Publications.

KUHN, EILEEN and MARTORAN, S. V. (Eds.) (1982, June) 'Qualitative methods for institutional research', San Francisco, CA, Jossey-Bass Inc., *New Directions for Institutional Research Series, Vol. 34.*

KUHN, THOMAS S. (1962) *The Structure of Scientific Revolutions*, Chicago, University of Chicago Press.

LANGEVELD, MARTINUS (1983) 'Reflections on phenomenology and pedagogy', *Phenomenology and Pedagogy*, 1, 1, pp. 5-7.

LAZARSFELD, PAUL F. (1972) *Qualitative Analysis*, Boston, Allyn and Bacon Inc.

LEININGER, M. M. (1985) *Qualitative Research Methods in Nursing*, Orlando, FL, Grane and Stratton.

LINCOLN, YVONNA and GUBA, EGON (1985) *Naturalistic Inquiry*, Beverly Hills, CA, Sage Publications.

LIPSMAN, JEFF (1988) *User's Manual for Concordance Information Retrieval System*, Los Angeles, CA, Dataflight Software.

LOFLAND, JOHN (1967) 'Notes on naturalism', *Kansas Journal of Sociology*, 3, 4, pp. 45-61.

LOFLAND, JOHN (1971) *Analyzing Social Settings*, Belmont, CA, Wadsworth Publishing Company.

LUTZ, FRANK W. and RAMSEY, MARGARET A. (1974) 'The use of anthropological field methods in education', *Educational Researcher*, 3, 10, pp. 5-9.

MALINOWSKI, BRONISLAW (1922) *The Argonauts of the Western Pacific*, London, Routledge and Kegan Paul.

MARTON, FERENCE (1981) 'Phenomenography - Describing conceptions of the world around us', *Instructional Science*, 10, pp. 177-200.

MARTON, FERENCE (1986, Fall) 'Phenomenography - A research approach to investigating different understandings of reality', *Journal of Thought*, 21, 3, pp. 28-48.

MASLOW, ABRAHAM (1966) *The Psychology of Science*, New York, Harper and Row.

MASSARIK, FRED (1986) 'Forschung in der humanistischen Psychologie; ein Gespräch (geführt mit Gerhard Fatzer)', *Jahrbuch der Zeitschrift für humanistische Psychologie, Forschung I*, pp. 9-22.

MAXWELL, A. E. (1975) *Analyzing Qualitative Data*, New York, Halsted Press.

MEHAN, HUGH and WOOD, HOUSTON (1975) *The Reality of Ethnomethodology*, New York, John Wiley and Sons.

MELTZER, B. N.; PETRAS, J. W. and REYNOLDS, L. T. (1975) *Symbolic Interactionism: Genesis, Varieties and Criticism*, London, Routledge and Kegan Paul.

MERTON, ROBERT K. (1968) *Social Theory and Social Structure*, New York, Free Press.

MILES, MATTHEW B. and HUBERMAN, A. MICHAEL (1984) *Qualitative Data Analysis: A Sourcebook of New Methods*, Beverly Hills, CA, Sage Publications.

MILLS, C. WRIGHT (1959) *The Sociological Imagination*, New York, Oxford University Press.

MONTESSORI, MARIA (1913) *Pedagogical Anthropology*, (trans. by Frederic Taber Cooper), New York, Stokes.

MORGAN, GARETH (Ed.) (1983) *Beyond Method: Strategies for Social Research*, Beverly Hills, CA, Sage Publications.

MOUSTAKAS, CLARK (1981) 'Heuristic research', in REASON, PETER and ROWAN, JOHN (Eds.) *Human Inquiry: A Sourcebook of New Paradigm Research*, New York, John Wiley and Sons, pp. 207-17.

MULKAY, MICHAEL (1985) 'Agreement and disagreement in conversations and letters', *Text*, 5, 3, pp. 201-27.

MURDOCK, G. P. (1971) *Outline of Cultural Materials*, New Haven, CT, Human Relations Area Files.

NELSON, THEODOR H. (1974) *Dream Machines (The Flip Side of Computer Lib)*, South Bend, IN, Theodor Nelson.

PACKER, MARTIN J. (1985) 'Hermeneutic inquiry in the study of human conduct', *American Psychologist*, 40, 10, pp. 1081-93.

PARKER, JAMES T. and TAYLOR, PAUL G. (1980) *The Delphi Survey*, Belmont, CA, Fearon Pitman Publishers, Inc.

PARLETT, MALCOLM and HAMILTON, DAVID (1972) 'Evaluation as illumination: A new approach to the study of innovatory programs', Occasional paper, Edinburgh: Centre for Research in the Educational Sciences, University of Edinburgh.

PATTON, MICHAEL Q. (1975) *Alternative Evaluation Research Paradigm*, Grand Forks, ND, Study Group on Evaluation, University of North Dakota.

PATTON, MICHAEL Q. (1980) *Qualitative Evaluation Methods*, Beverly Hills, CA, Sage Publications.

PLUMMER, K. (1983) *Documents of Life: An Introduction to the Problems and Literature of a Humanistic Method*, London, Allyn and Unwin.

POLANYI, MICHAEL (1958) *Personal Knowledge*, Chicago, IL, The University of Chicago Press.

POLKINGHORNE, DONALD E. (1982, Summer) 'What makes research humanistic?' *Journal of Humanistic Psychology*, 22, 3, pp. 47-54.

POLKINGHORNE, DONALD E. (1983) *Methodology for the Human Sciences*, Albany, State University of New York Press.

PRICE, DON D. and BARRELL, JAMES J. (1980) 'An experiential approach with quantitative methods: A research paradigm', *Journal of Humanistic Psychology*, 20, pp. 75-95.

PSATHAS, GEORGE (Ed.) (1973) *Phenomenological Sociology: Issues and Applications*, New York, John Wiley and Sons.

RATHJE, W. L. (1984) 'The garbage decade', *American Behavioral Scientist*, 28, 1, pp. 9-29.

REASON, PETER and ROWAN, JOHN (1981) *Human Inquiry: A Sourcebook of New Paradigm Research*, Chichester, NY, John Wiley and Sons.

RENNIE, DAVID L.; PHILLIPS, JEFFREY R. and QUARTARO, GEORGIA (1987)'Grounded Theory: A Promising Approach to Conceptualizing Psychology', Unpublished manuscript, York University.

REYNOLDS, DAVID (1988) 'British school improvement research: the contribution of qualitative studies', *International Journal of Qualitative Studies in Education*, 1, 2, pp. 143-54.

RICHARDS, THOMAS J. (1987) *User Manual for NUDIST: A Text Analysis Program for the Social Sciences*, Replee P/L, Melbourne, Australia.

RICOEUR, PAUL (1971) 'The model of the text: Meaningful action considered as text', *Social Research*, 38, pp. 529-62.

RIST, RAY C. (1975) 'Ethnographic techniques and the study of an urban school', *Urban Education*, 10, pp. 86-108.

RIST, RAY C. (1980) 'Blitzkrieg ethnography: On the transformation of a method into a movement', *Educational Researcher*, 9, 2, pp. 8-10.

ROCK, P. (1979) *The Making of Symbolic Interactionism*, London, Macmillan.

ROGERS, MARY F. (1983) *Sociology, Ethnomethodology, and Experience*, Cambridge, MA, Cambridge University Press.

ROSCH, ELEANOR (1978) 'Principles of categorization', in ROSCH, E. and LLOYD, B. B. (Eds.) *Cognition and Categorization*, Hillsdale, NJ, Lawrence Erlbaum Associates.

ROSENGREN, KARL E. (Ed.) (1981) *Advances in Content Analysis*, Beverly Hills, CA, Sage Publications.

ROWAN, JOHN and REASON, PETER (1981) 'On making sense', in REASON, PETER and ROWAN, JOHN (Eds.) *Human Inquiry: A Sourcebook of New Paradigm Research*, Chichester, NY, John Wiley and Sons.

SCHATZMAN, LEONARD and STRAUSS, ANSELM L. (1973) *Field Research*, Englewood Cliffs, NJ, Prentice Hall.

SEIDEL, JOHN (1988) *THE ETHNOGRAPH: A User's Guide*, Littleton, CO, Qualis Research Associates.

SHARROCK, W. and ANDERSON, B. (1986) *The Ethnomethodologists*, New York, Tavistock Publications.

SHELLY, ANNE (1984) 'Using logic programming to facilitate qualitative data analysis', paper presented at the annual meeting of the American Educational Research Association, New Orleans.

SHELLY, ANNE and SIBERT, ERNEST (1985) *The QUALOG User's Manual*, Syracuse, NY, Syracuse University, School of Computer and Information Science.

SINDELL, P. (1969) 'Anthropological approaches to the study of education', *Review of Educational Research*, 39, pp. 593-607.

SMITH, JOHN K. and HESHUSIUS, LOUS (1986, January) 'Closing down the conversation: The end of the qualitative-quantitative debate among educational inquirers', *Educational Researcher*, 15, pp. 4-12.

SMITH, LOUIS (Ed.) (1974) *Anthropological Perspectives on Evaluation*, AERA Monograph Series in Evaluation, Chicago, Rand McNally.

SPINDLER, GEORGE (Ed.) (1955) *Education and Anthropology*, Palo Alto, CA, Stanford University Press.

SPINDLER, GEORGE (1955) 'Education in a transforming American culture', *Harvard Educational Review* 25, 145-56.

SPRADLEY, JAMES P. (1979) *The Ethnographic Interview*, New York, Holt, Rinehart and Winston.

SPRADLEY, JAMES P. (1980) *Participant Observation*, New York, Holt, Rinehart and Winston.

STAKE, ROBERT E. (1975) 'Program evaluation, particularly responsive evaluation', Occasional Paper #5, The Evaluation Center, Western Michigan University.

STAKE, ROBERT E. (1978) 'The case study method in a social inquiry', *Educational Researcher*, 7, 2, pp. 5-8.

STONE, PHILLIP J.; DUNPHY, DEXTER C.; SMITH, MARSHALL S. and OGILVIE, DANIEL M. (1966) *The General Inquirer: A Computer Approach to Content Analysis*, Cambridge, MA, The M.I.T. Press.

STRASSER, STEPHAN (1963) *Phenomenology and the Human Sciences*, Pittsburgh, PA, Duquesne University Press.

STRASSER, STEPHAN (1969) *The Idea of Dialogal Phenomenology*, Pittsburgh, PA, Duquesne University Press.

STRAUSS, ANSELM L. (1987) *Qualitative Analysis for Social Scientists*, Cambridge, MA, Cambridge University Press.

STUBBS, MICHAEL (1983) *Discourse Analysis: The Sociolinguistic Analysis of Natural Language*, Chicago, The University of Chicago Press.

SUCHMAN, E. A. (1967) *Evaluative Research: Principles and Practice in Public Service and Social Action Programs*, New York, Russell Sage Foundation.

SURANSKY, VALERIE (1980, May) 'Phenomenology: An alternative research paradigm and a force for social change, *Journal of the British Society for Phenomenology*, Vol. 11, 2, pp. 163-79.

TAYLOR, STEVEN J. and BOGDAN, ROBERT (1984) *Introduction to Qualitative Research Methods*, New York, John Wiley and Sons.

TESCH, RENATA (1976) *The Humanistic Approach to Educational Research*, Santa Barbara, CA, The Fielding Institute.

TESCH, RENATA (1987) 'Emerging themes: The researcher's experience', *Phenomenology + Pedagogy*, 5, 3, pp. 230-41.

TESCH, RENATA (1988) 'The contribution of a qualitative method: Phenomenological research', paper presented at the annual meeting of the American Educational Research Association, New Orleans.

THOMAS, WILLIAM I. and ZNANIECKI, FLORIAN (1918) *The Polish Peasant in Europe and America*, Boston, Richard G. Badger.

THORNDIKE, EDWARD LEE (1927) *The Measurement of Intelligence*, New York, Bureau of Publications, Teachers College, Columbia University.

THORNDIKE, ROBERT L. (Ed.) (1951) *Educational Measurement*, Washington, D.C., American Council on Education.

THUNDERSTONE EXPANSION PGMS INT'L, INC. (informational material), Copyright 1987, 1988, Chesterland, OH.

TORBERT, WILLIAM R. (1983) 'Initiating collaborative inquiry', in MORGAN, GARETH (Ed.) *Beyond Method*, Beverly Hills, CA, Sage Publications.

TURNER, BARRY A. (1981) 'Some practical aspects of qualitative data analysis: One way of organizing the cognitive process associated with the generation of grounded theory', *Quality and Quantity*, 15, pp. 225-47.

TYLER, STEVEN A. (Ed.) (1969) *Cognitive Anthropology: Readings*, New York, Holt, Rinehart, and Winston.

URMSTON PHILIPS, SUSAN (1984) 'The social organization of questions and answers in courtroom discourse: A study of changes of plea in an Arizona court', *Text*, 4, 1-3, pp. 225-48.

VALLE, RONALD S. and KING, MARK (Eds.) (1978) *Existential-Phenomenological Alternatives for Psychology*, New York, Oxford University Press.

VAN DIJK, TEUN A. (Ed.) (1985) *Handbook of Discourse Analysis, Vol. 4*, London, Academic Press.

VAN KAAM, ADRIAN L. (1959, May) 'Phenomenological analysis: Exemplified by a study of the experience of really feeling understood', *Journal of Individual Psychology*, pp. 66-72.

VAN KAAM, ADRIAN L. (1966) *Existential Foundations of Psychology*, Pittsburgh, Duquesne University Press.

VAN MAANEN, JOHN (Ed.) (1979) *Qualitative Methodology*, Beverly Hills, CA, Sage Publications.

VAN MANEN, MAX (1984) Practicing phenomenological writing, *Phenomenology + Pedagogy*, 2, 1, pp. 36-69.

VON ECKARTSBERG, ROLF (1977) *Psychological Research Methods at Duquesne*, unpublished monograph, Duquesne University.

VON ECKARTSBERG, ROLF (1978) 'Person perception revisited', in VALLE, RONALD S. and KING, MARK (Eds.) *Existential-Phenomenological Alternatives for Psychology*, New York, Oxford University Press.

WALKER, R. (1974) 'Classroom research: A view from SAFARI', in *Innovation, Evaluation Research and the Problem of Control,* Norwich, University of East Anglia.

WALKER, R. (1983) 'The use of case studies in applied research and evaluation', in HARTNET, A. (Ed.) *The Social Sciences and Educational Studies,* London, Heineman, pp. 190-204.

WALLACE, ANTHONY F. (1962) 'Culture and cognition', *Science,* 135, pp. 351-57.

WATSON, LAWRENCE, C. (1976, Spring) 'Understanding a life history as a subjective document', *Ethos,* 4, 1, pp. 95-131.

WEBB, S. and WEBB, B. P. (1932) *Methods of Social Study,* London, Longman's.

WEBB, EUGENE J.; CAMPBELL, DONALD T.; SCHWARTZ, RICHARD D. and SECHREST, LEE (1966) *Unobtrusive Measures: Nonreactive Research in the Social Sciences,* Chicago, Rand McNally Publishing Company.

WEBER, R. PHILIP (1985) *Basic Content Analysis,* Beverly Hills, CA, Sage Publications.

WERNER, OSWALD and SCHOEPFLE, G. MARK (1987) *Systematic Fieldwork, Vol. 1,* Beverly Hills, CA, Sage Publications.

WERNER, OSWALD and SCHOEPFLE, G. MARK (1987) *Systematic Fieldwork, Vol. 2,* Beverly Hills, CA, Sage Publications.

WERTZ, FREDERICK J. (1985) 'Methods and findings in a phenomenological psychological study of a complex life-event: Being criminally victimized', in GIORGI, AMEDEO (Ed.) *Phenomenology and Psychological Research,* Pittsburgh, PA, Duquesne University Press.

WERTZ, FREDERICK J. (1987, Winter) 'Meaning and research methodology: Psychoanalysis as a human science', *Methods,* 1, 2, pp. 91-135.

WIGGINS, JERRY S. (1982) 'Circumplex models of interpersonal behavior in clinical psychology', in KENDALL, PHILLIP C. and BUTCHER, JAMES N. (Eds.) *Handbook of Research Methods in Clinical Psychology,* New York, John Wiley and Sons.

WILLEMS, EDWIN P. and RAUSH, HAROLD L. (1969) *Naturalistic Viewpoints in Psychological Research,* New York, Holt, Rinehart, and Winston.

WILLIAMS, R. (1976) 'Symbolic interactionism: The fusion of theory and research?', in THORNS, D. C. (Ed.) *New Directions in Sociology,* Newton Abbott, David and Charles.

WILSON, STEPHEN (1977) 'The use of ethnographic techniques in educational research', *Review of Educational Research,* 47, 1, pp. 245-65.

WOLCOTT, HARRY (Ed.) (1975, Summer) Special issue on 'Ethnography of Schools', *Human Organization.*

WYLAND, DAVID (1985, November 11) 'Software that learns', *Computerworld,* pp. 93-104.

Author Index

319

Subject Index

directories
for electronic files, 151, 161,
162, 183, 225, 233, 253-255,
260, 275
discourse analysis, 23, 27, 28, 31,
32, 58, 61, 75, 77, 79, 80, 97,
98, 103, 252
document case study, 72

ecological psychology, 38, 39, 41,
58, 64, 85, 88, 98
education
see research in education
educational connoisseurship
and criticism, 48, 50, 52, 58, 70,
73, 74
educational research
see research in education
electronic coding
in TAP, 229
in Textbase Alpha, 271, 274,
275, 289
emancipatory action research, 38,
39, 49, 50, 63, 66, 89
empirical phenomenology, 40
enhancements in analysis
programs, 150, 151, 155, 158,
162, 206, 220, 230, 257, 271,
274, 282
ETHNO, 31, 81, 108, 110, 111,
211-226, 301
ethnographic content analysis, 26,
30, 58, 64, 73, 85, 88, 98, 99
ethnographic research
see ethnography
ethnography, 3, 14-19, 24-28, 31,
43, 45-47, 50, 52, 57, 58, 61-63,
66, 67, 72, 74, 77, 79-82, 89,
90, 97, 98, 100, 103, 104, 182
ethnography
of communication, 47, 50, 58,
61, 62, 79, 80, 97, 98, 100, 103
ethnology, 89

ethnomethodology, 3, 15, 17, 22,
23, 27, 28, 30, 31, 58, 61, 62,
72, 79, 82, 83, 95, 98, 100, 101
ethnoscience, 25, 27, 29, 58, 61,
62, 72, 79, 81, 82, 97, 98, 103,
182
evaluation, 15, 18, 19, 43-45, 47,
48, 50-53, 58, 63, 65, 66, 72,
74, 75, 89, 90, 91, 99, 100, 101,
106
see also qualitative/illumina-
tive evaluation
evaluative research
see evaluation
event structure analysis, 27, 29,
64, 85, 88, 94, 97, 98, 103
existential-phenomenological psychology, 33, 34, 36, 40, 42, 73,
100, 101
experiential research, 36, 39, 40,
42, 70

facecard
in HyperQual, 292
face sheets
in The Ethnograph, 254, 255,
257, 261, 263, 264, 268
file names, 155, 183, 185, 193,
219, 233, 243, 246, 248, 249,
264, 266, 275, 277, 281
frameworks
in ETHNO, 212, 213, 215-220
frequencies of codes, 110, 151,
158
in The Ethnograph, 264,
267
in Qualpro, 247, 248, 250
in TAP 224-227, 231, 233,
234
in Textbase Alpha, 282, 283
frequencies of words, 79, 80, 182,
185, 188-190, 192
in Textbase Alpha, 284